Praise for JOURNEYS NORTH

"FEW THINGS ARE more innately human, rooted deeply in our shared history, than storytelling and traversing land masses on foot. In *Journeys North*, master storyteller Barney Scout Mann invites us to gather around his campfire as he weaves the narratives of ordinary people hiking thousands of miles across desert and mountains. The unfolding of their stories against the backdrop of nature at her most sublime, and her most fierce, reveals their primal humanness in powerful relief. Their interactions, with nature and with each other, prove that we are more connected and wildly capable than we believe."

—HEATHER "ANISH" ANDERSON, adventurer and author of *Thirst*

"BARNEY SCOUT MANN has painted an exciting and profoundly moving portrait of a long trail and the quirky humans moved to walk it. A fantastic book!"

—ASPEN MATIS, author of *Girl in the Woods*

"THE PACIFIC CREST Trail is more than a simple footpath. Its wild scenery offers life-changing experiences and a welcoming, supportive community. Scout's unique tale and the stories of the people he met along the way speak to the power of true friendship and the transformative potential of America's great outdoors."

—MARK LARABEE, associate director of communications
and marketing for the Pacific Crest Trail Association

"BEAUTIFULLY CRAFTED AND brutally honest, this narrative does justice to the essence of what a thru-hike entails, from the exuberant first steps to the pure grit and determination of finishing fever pitted against nature's forces, visiting the highs, lows, and pain along the way. This is not a how-to primer, but instead a peek inside the dreams, demons, and aspirations that motivate and drive hikers onward, becoming 'trail family' along the way. While this is a snapshot of a handful of hikers in a single year, it is a timeless and true tale."

—DONNA SAUFLEY, trail angel and owner of Hiker Heaven

"THE LONG TRAILS teach us the importance of wilderness, value of freedom, and a realization of what's important in life. It's about those we meet too, and this is where *Journeys North* triumphs. The building of new friendships, and nurturing of the existing ones is a delight to read. A truly worthwhile memoir."

—KEITH "FOZZIE" FOSKETT, long-distance hiker
and author of *The Last Englishman*

"*JOURNEYS NORTH* TAKES us along on a challenging and rich hike of the Pacific Crest Trail. The year is 2007, when Barney 'Scout' Mann and his wife, Sandy 'Frodo' Mann, set out to thru-hike from the Mexican border to just over the Canadian border. Scout's imagery transported me, but most engrossing of all may be the relationships that formed as Scout and Frodo worked their way north while walking their 20-to-30-mile days, with four other hikers—Blazer, Dalton, Tony, and Nadine—and an extended family with dozens more. A rich tale of adventure, freedom, accomplishment, fears and tears—you need to read this book!"

—SUSAN "BACKPACK45" ALCORN, author of
We're in the Mountains Not Over the Hill

"BARNEY SCOUT MANN speaks of the 'capacity for surprise' on the Pacific Crest Trail. For this stunning book, however, hone your capacity for shock—primal intimacy with the lives of Blazer, Dalton, Nadine and Pacha, Tony, many others as well as Scout and Frodo, and the Pacific Crest Trail itself. When someone asks, why thru-hike a long trail, Mann says 'You have to really, really want to do it.' Read *Journeys North* as if your life depended on it."

—GAIL D. STOREY, author of *I Promise Not to Suffer*

"HIKING THE PACIFIC Crest Trail is an experience unlike any other due to the landscape, the community, and the internal transformation that takes place on a 2663-mile trail. In *Journeys North*, Barney Scout Mann weaves together all three components in a captivating narrative."

—JENNIFER PHARR DAVIS, author, speaker, adventurer

"MANN EASILY CAPTURES the nature of the thru-hiker community . . . *Journeys North* put me back on the trail and kept me up reading all night."

—KAREN BERGER, Triple Crown hiker and
author of *Great Hiking Trails of the World*

"*JOURNEYS NORTH* IS a masterclass in story telling. Barney Scout Mann invites readers into his trail family to experience a journey in goosebump-inducing detail. This book hits at the core of what makes a thru-hike such a profoundly beautiful experience—the people you meet along the way."

—ZACH DAVIS, editor in chief of *The Trek*

"HERE'S THE NEXT best thing to being on the Pacific Crest Trail yourself!"

—RICHARD LOUV, author of *Our Wild Calling*
and *Last Child in the Woods*

JOURNEYS NORTH

The Pacific Crest Trail

BARNEY SCOUT MANN

MOUNTAINEERS
BOOKS

MOUNTAINEERS BOOKS is dedicated to the exploration, preservation, and enjoyment of outdoor and wilderness areas.

1001 SW Klickitat Way, Suite 201, Seattle, WA 98134

800-553-4453, www.mountaineersbooks.org

Printed in Canada

Distributed in the United Kingdom by Cordee, www.cordee.co.uk

23 22 21 20   2 3 4 5 6

Copyeditor: Laura Lancaster
Design and layout: Melissa McFeeters
Cartographer: Martha Bostwick
All photographs by the author unless credited otherwise
Cover illustration: *Thousand Island Lake, Banner Peak, Sierra Nevada* by Obi Kaufmann
Inside covers: *A few of the thousands of hikers who have slept at Frodo's and the author's San Diego house the night before starting the Pacific Crest Trail. The inside front cover features the PCT symbol on the Southern Terminus Monument at the Mexican border. And the inside back cover is the PCT symbol on the Northern Terminus Monument at the Canadian border.*

Library of Congress Cataloging-in-Publication Data is on file for this title at https://lccn.loc.gov/2020004774.

Mountaineers Books titles may be purchased for corporate, educational, or other promotional sales, and our authors are available for a wide range of events. For information on special discounts or booking an author, contact our customer service at 800-553-4453 or mbooks@mountaineersbooks.org.

♻ Printed on 100% recycled and FSC-certified materials

MIX
Paper from
responsible sources
FSC
www.fsc.org   **FSC® C016245**

ISBN (paperback): 978-1-68051-321-9
ISBN (ebook): 978-1-68051-322-6

An independent nonprofit publisher since 1960

To my parents, Don and Micky Mann,
there for my first step.

To my wife, Sandy "Frodo" Mann,
there every step of the way.

Pacific Crest Trail

CANADA

Bellingham •   Manning Park ■
   Ross Lake
Rainy Pass
   Glacier Peak
Seattle •   Stevens Pass

WASHINGTON

Snoqualmie Pass
Mount Rainier ∧   Goat Rocks
   Mount Adams

IDAHO

Portland •   *Columbia River*
Bridge of the Gods   Mount Hood
   Mount Jefferson
The Three Sisters   • Bend
Willamette Pass

OREGON

Crater Lake
Ashland •
Seiad Valley ■
Etna •   ∧ Mount Shasta
   Old Station
Lassen Peak ∧
halfway point ■
Sierra City ■
   Lake Tahoe

NEVADA

Echo Lake
San Francisco •
   Tuolumne Meadows
   • Mammoth Lakes

CALIFORNIA

Muir Pass   Mount Whitney
   Kennedy Meadows
Tehachapi Mountains   Walker Pass
   Mojave Desert
Agua Dulce •   McDonald's ■
   Big Bear City •
Los Angeles •   ∧ Mount San Jacinto
   Warner Springs Resort ■
San Diego •   Campo ■

MEXICO

Pacific Ocean

0   100 Kilometers
0   100 Miles

Contents

AUTHOR'S NOTE   9

INTRODUCTION: FRODO'S BIRTHDAY   11

SAND

Campo to Agua Dulce, 454 miles

1. Will We?. 15
2. First Steps. 19
3. Midnight 24
4. "Where's Dr. Mann?" 30
5. Outhouse Dinner 35
6. Harvard or Me 40
7. "Blazer, I Need You" 43
8. General Delivery. 53
9. Canada? No Way! 60
10. The Question. 65
11. I Quit 70
12. Nutella 76
13. Donovan's Final Service 80
14. Who Smells the Worst? 85
15. Tony's Promise 92
16. Naked Bucket Brigade 94
17. Hiker Heaven. 102

DIRT

Agua Dulce to Walker Pass, 203 miles

18. Hikertown 111
19. Tehachapi 116
20. Trail Magic 121
21. Night at Walker Pass 127

GRANITE

Walker Pass to Lake Tahoe, 442 miles

22. Kennedy Meadows 133

23. Shower Buddies 143

24. Sacrifice 147

25. Getting Naked 150

26. No Good Choices 158

LAVA

Lake Tahoe to Bridge of the Gods, 1051 miles

27. Watermelon 171

28. Halfway .177

29. Under Lock and Key 188

30. Not-a-Moose 200

31. The Cave 212

32. Superheroes 225

33. Tazul 236

SNOW

Bridge of the Gods to Canada, 500 miles

34. Shattered 243

35. Lost 253

36. Before the Storm 265

37. The Knife's Edge 271

38. Cutthroat Pass 277

39. Harts Pass 284

40. Trail's End 291

EPILOGUE   307

THE FUTURE OF THE TRAIL   313

ACKNOWLEDGMENTS   315

Author's Note

WELCOME TO A world where Amanda is Blazer, my wife, Sandy, is Frodo, Paul is Bounty Hunter, and Tim is Figaro. On the Pacific Crest Trail no one knows me as Barney; they only know me as Scout. Names like these are a long-trail tradition. But you don't pick your trail name—your fellow hikers do. There's a story, often embarrassing, behind each one. *Journeys North* follows six thru-hikers and, just as if you were on the trail, people are referred to by their trail name once they have one.

More than a village, it feels like a whole town helped create this book. To all of you: thanks.

Introduction
Frodo's Birthday

BLAZER COULDN'T FEEL her toes. In the predawn gloom, the twenty-five-year-old stomped a path over a foot of fresh snow, but the effort barely blunted the cold. This was the second blizzard in three days as the Gulf of Alaska hurled once-in-a-generation storms at Washington's Cascade Range. After five months hiking the Pacific Crest Trail, Blazer was wearing her fifth pair of running shoes, and the studded soles were ground flat—much like her muscles, sinews, and joints. She'd come over 2600 miles—only 40 left to reach Canada. She'd sworn days before, "I'll crawl if I have to."

Right behind her, Frodo and I brushed fat snowflakes from our bent shoulders and packs. A dim light penetrated the pine and spruce thicket. "Happy birthday, Frodo," Blazer piped up. We jerked as if poked. In the thirty years we'd been married, I'd never forgotten Frodo's birthday. But this time, focused on the cold, on not getting lost, and on surviving, we both had.

"What do you want for your birthday?" Blazer asked.

Frodo, her breath visible, didn't hesitate: "I want to finish the day alive."

TWO MORE STORMS swept in over the next three days, smothering the Pacific Crest Trail in thigh-high drifts. On Thursday night Seattle KING 5

TV News reported: "Three Pacific Crest Trail hikers are missing." Chatter lit up the internet within minutes. "Goodness, it's so cold now." "May the Lord protect them." Past midnight, one of sixty soon-to-be-rescuers wrote: "I am headed out to Stevens Pass to work the search."

BUT THEY WEREN'T searching for us. They were searching for Nadine.

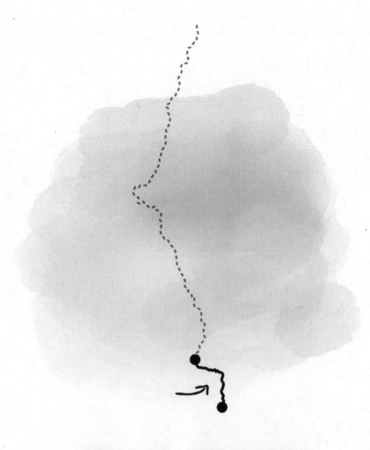

SAND

Campo to Agua Dulce

454 miles

1

Will We?

SANDY STRODE INTO the Lake Morena campground at 10:00 a.m., her tanned, freckled cheeks flush from the desert heat. Ten miles this morning meant she was right on time. Twenty dusty miles behind her was the start of the Pacific Crest Trail at the Mexican border.

My wife is a five-foot-two timepiece. I can set my watch by her, just as her high school biology students did for years. Taking four steps to my three, Sandy is fond of saying that we fox-trot and waltz up any trail, marking 4/4 and 3/4 time. This discordant dance had carried us far.

As the child of an engineer and a home economics major, she has planning and punctuality in her genes. With the same fervor that she applied to earning her PhD, Sandy had worked up a 149-day itinerary for our hike of the PCT. All 2650 miles, day upon day, mileages, major climbs and descents, water sources and notes—hundreds of hours of work—were reduced to an eye-squinting, double-sided chart smaller than a Hallmark card. By day 149, we both will have ascended over 85 vertical miles, ranging from the PCT low point of 170 feet at the Columbia River to the trail high point, 13,180-foot Forester Pass in the High Sierra. We'll have traversed the full length of three states—California, Oregon, and Washington—as well as twenty-six national forests, seven national parks, five state parks, and three national monuments. My copy was tucked into my chest pocket.

"It's a tool," she'd insisted. I hoped she wasn't going to wield it like a bat.

Sandy's first entry, Campo, was a two-store San Diego County back-water of 2500 souls, elevation 2800 feet. Campo boosters pointed to its railroad museum and youth detention center, but hikers knew it as the southern terminus of the Pacific Crest Trail. For several weeks each spring, hikers set out from this small town, socks gathering desert-grass burrs, eyes darting to lizards and jackrabbits, and feet poised to jump at the buzz of a rattlesnake.

I stretched out my lanky arms for a hug when I saw Sandy approach, nuzzling my nose and gray mustache into her short-cropped brown hair, but her pack made it impossible to wrap my arms around her. After all these years, you'd think I'd take hugging her for granted—never. I trea-sure every hug, touch, and time I make her laugh.

A hundred campsites thrummed around us. Hastily addressed boxes of cast-off gear were piled high in the temporary post office set up in the bed of a pickup truck. A six-sided pavilion designed to hold two hundred was packed beyond capacity for talks about water, bears, stream cross-ings, and snow. This was the annual end-of-April PCT Kickoff weekend at Lake Morena, the largest long-distance-hiker gathering west of the Mississippi. Of the six hundred at the gathering—present and past hik-ers, dreamers who'd never set foot on the trail, gear vendors, trail main-tenance volunteers, Forest Service personnel, and trail association staff—about 160 were like Sandy and me, this year's hope-filled thru-hikers. Planning to take on the PCT in one go, many of us were thinking the same thing: *Will I make it?*

Not only were my wife and I the rare thru-hiking couple, but we also already knew thirty-five of our fellow thru-hikers. Over the past several weeks, they'd arrived as strangers at our San Diego home from the East Coast, New Zealand, Britain, Australia—all over. After hosting them for a day or more and driving them the 60 miles east to start the trail, we'd become fast friends. I'd sworn each one to secrecy when I showed them the velvet pouch, with its glint of gold inside: a custom ring I'd had made for Sandy. "It's a surprise. Don't tell."

WHETHER THEY HIKE the 2650-mile Pacific Crest Trail, the 2180-mile Appalachian Trail, or the 3100-mile Continental Divide Trail, nearly every thru-hiker ends up with a trail name. It's emblematic of the separate reality of a long trail, and most hikers wear theirs like a badge. If Sandy had picked one herself, she'd be Intrepid or Dauntless. But trail names are bestowed, not chosen, often for something unique, smart, or just plain dumb that a hiker does. Few of the hikers we met in those early days had a trail name of their own, but it didn't take long for them to acquire one.

Mark had a shock of wavy brown hair and intense brown eyes, incongruous with his bantam-weightlifter's build. He was the first chair cellist for the Honolulu Symphony Orchestra. Early on, sitting with others during a trail break, he mused, "Wouldn't it be awful if you ended up with a trail name like . . . Cuddles?" The name stuck.

Lauren was a cross-country runner, fresh out of college. Every day on the trail, she had a moment when she felt, *This is the best day of my life.* Worried about hitching rides into small trail towns to pick up supplies, she concocted a plan with Coyote, a Canadian hiker closing in on sixty. He would lie down on the side of the road and pretend to be ill while she frantically waved down the first vehicle to approach, asking for help for her "grandfather." "You're Gazelle," Coyote offered up, "because you're speedy, agile, and thin of leg."

At six foot four, Max had a shaved head and a long, purple hiking skirt. On his thirteenth day on the PCT, he lost the trail at low-lying San Gorgonio Pass. After the 7000-vertical-foot switchback descent from Mount San Jacinto's ponderosa pines to swirling sand and cacti, he reached Interstate 10. Knowing the trail had to be on the other side, he ran across all eight lanes of the busy artery between Los Angeles and Palm Springs. "Freeway" became his own legend.

Sandy loved the concept of trail names, but she got huffy about gender-confusing ones. "How can Cucumber Boy be a girl? How can Hot Sister be a guy?" Don't talk to her about Girl Scout. She had avidly read Girl Scout's online journal for weeks before discovering "she" was a "he."

Nine months ago, the idea of commissioning a custom ring for Sandy had popped into my head. Cast from platinum and gold, it would commemorate our planned PCT thru-hike and our thirtieth wedding anniversary. Front and center would be the round-edged PCT trail emblem, a single tree set against a mountain silhouette. A recessed channel would have four trail icons in bas-relief—the southern border monument, then California's Mount Shasta and Oregon's Mount Hood, and last, the northern monument. I gave her the ring in Campo, weeks before our anniversary, to mark the start of our hike. Both of us had cried.

Maybe I should have known. *The Lord of the Rings* movies were still popular, and I had given her "the one ring" at the start of a quest to far places with great unknowns. Within hours of arriving at Kickoff, some of the hikers we had hosted surrounded Sandy in what felt like a coronation. "We know your trail name!" they cried. The shouts echoed over her. "You are Frodo."

"Noooo," she protested, "Frodo's a GUY."

To this day she's Frodo.

MY PARENTS NAMED me Bernard, but everyone has always called me Barney. To my trail community I am simply Scout.

2

First Steps

I FIRST SET foot on the Pacific Crest Trail when I was thirteen. My parents never camped, much less backpacked, but they dutifully dropped me off once a week at Troop 19 meetings in Culver City. Bent under a thirty-five-pound load—nearly half my weight—I hiked 50 miles with my troop deep into California's southern Sierra Nevada one summer. I had big ears, newly straightened teeth, and a single-wave haircut straight from *Leave It to Beaver*. At just under five feet, I was the shortest boy on the trek, as well as in almost every class at school.

Our troop was banking on crisp nights, warm days, and views of the Perseids, August's fiery meteors. Instead a tropical storm named Claudia stampeded north; all week my flimsy poncho flapped under leaden, rainy skies.

I was homesick and missed bottled soda. But I'd never felt so free, so accomplished. The Sierra's glistening granite crags and domes were more moving than anything on a museum wall. Every moment held possibility, from the black bear crashing through brush to the rusted trail register at Old Army Pass that hadn't been signed in two years. It didn't matter that I was short—all that mattered was that I could hike.

"WHAT'S THE MOST important thing you've done in your life?"

It was August 2003 and Sandy and I were four hours into our first thru-hike, the 211-mile John Muir Trail. The question came from a lonely teen just out of high school who had attached himself to us near the start. I drew a breath to respond—I certainly had a handful of truthful answers. I could have said: "I've raised three kids" or "I've been married twenty-six years." But that day I answered, "I was scoutmaster of a sixty-five-member Boy Scout troop for five years."

"Scoutmaster," it hung in the air, but felt pretentious. The paperback book we'd torn into sections to read was *To Kill a Mockingbird*—its hero was a nine-year-old girl named Scout.

And so I became Scout.

GROWING UP AN hour from downtown Los Angeles, Sandy chafed at being a girl in the 1960s. While her older brothers played high school basketball, she was the stat girl. When each child finished seventh grade, her Montana-raised parents shipped them to an uncle's ranch for a month. On their visits, her older brothers drove the pickup truck and hay bailer. When it was her turn, Sandy babysat her uncle's kids. But money was lean, so Sandy told her parents that she'd had a good time.

When her older brothers started backpacking with the Scouts, Sandy stewed at home. She thought, *Why won't someone take me backpacking? I'm a good hiker.* Then, in tenth grade, her church's new youth director thought backpacking would be just the thing for their coed youth group. By the end of the next summer, she'd gone on three treks.

THERE WERE SOME 270 of us starting the Pacific Crest Trail in 2007, and already we were spread out. Some had hitched to Kickoff from farther up the trail, and would hitch back on Sunday. Some were 75, 100, or 150 miles ahead and weren't coming back. Others weren't even on trail yet.

Amanda raced barefoot from security to catch her plane in Washington, D.C. Once a three-sport high school athlete and college student body president, at twenty-four she was unemployed and living on her brother's couch. Three days ago she'd sacrificed her most defining feature—she'd shaved her nearly waist-length black curls. On the plane she wrote nineteen pages in her journal. "Am I crazy to think I can do the whole thing? Did I decide one night when I drank too much wine and bought a plane ticket?" She'd only heard of the Pacific Crest Trail four months before. "Holy crap! I gave myself less than 20 days to prepare." But even in her most private writing one topic was off-limits.

Amanda arrived at Kickoff soon after Sandy. She didn't have any trail cred, and envied those who'd already started.

NADINE MISSED KICKOFF, and her first taste of the PCT, like mine, had a bit-tersweet side. In 1998, she'd set out to hike the PCT with a boyfriend and failed. She'd been miserable, cold, hot, hungry, and blistered. The emo-tional toll, trading barbs with her boyfriend, rivaled the physical. Yet, for reasons she didn't fully understand, the memories of that hike were among the best of her life. Now, nine years later, Nadine was back, this time with her dog.

At thirty-three, she had shoulder-length brown curls, a wild expanse of freckles, and flashing green eyes. Her laugh was explosive. She grew up in Roslyn Heights near Queens, New York, far removed from the PCT. Nadine's parents, who emigrated from France and Israel, thought back-packing was frightening. But that wasn't why she hadn't told them about the hike—she hadn't spoken to her parents in over a year.

Nadine was journaling about her hike on a blog named for her dog, Pacha. A fifteen-month-old mix of coyote, wolf, and husky, Pacha was the only dog starting the PCT in 2007.

It took hours to pass the hulking Sierra mountain crest on Nadine's drive south from Davis with two friends. She had been driving her roommate Lori crazy in the run-up to her trek, packing, unpacking, and repacking twenty-eight resupply boxes, twenty of which Lori would mail her over the course of her hike. Together with two hundred pounds of dog food for Pacha, they filled Nadine's "PCT Nightmare Closet."

AT THIRTY-EIGHT, TONY, like Nadine, was one of the rare thru-hikers in his thirties or forties. It's no surprise that the PCT attracts a big gulp of twen-tysomethings, but the next most populous age group is graying, in their fifties and sixties. The trail mixes the youngsters—those not yet locked into life—with those newly freed from careers and kids. Frodo and I nearly fit the latter category: My career was winding down and she was closing in on fifty. We'd launched our kids, our son, Sean, and daughters, Jordie and Nicky, into the world. Each planned to join us at least once on the trek, and Jordie was mailing our resupply boxes.

Age wasn't the only thing that set Tony apart—he'd also already completed a long trail. Two years before, after his fourteen-year marriage disintegrated, Tony had thru-hiked the Appalachian Trail. He had no children, and along with his marriage he'd abandoned his landscaping job. As untethered as a balloon cut adrift, Tony wanted to make choices that were his alone and to have a real adventure, such as thru-hiking an iconic American trail. Now, with a recent buzz cut to go along with his ruddy cheeks and chiseled chin, Tony was ready to tackle another trail, the PCT.

A family wedding in Pennsylvania kept Tony from Kickoff. And while he celebrated with the newlyweds, part of him still didn't believe he was actually going to thru-hike again. He wouldn't believe it until he boarded the plane to San Diego.

One lesson Tony had carried away from his Appalachian Trail trek was that a long trail was no place for dogs. The ones he'd seen were malnourished and clearly hurting. Since finishing his hike he'd thought more than once, *How can you do that to an animal that's so obedient it would literally walk its feet off to stay with you?*

ALAN, A TWENTY-TWO-YEAR-OLD redhead with aquamarine eyes and the beginnings of a beard, hoped to head to grad school after he'd finished the trail. He'd grown up in an outdoor mecca, Boulder, Colorado, but didn't go backpacking till he moved away to college. Smaller and slower than his peers, Alan had excelled in sports because he was tough, ignored pain, and persevered. He believed that is what it meant to be a man. Yet when he packed for college at seventeen, he made room in his duffle for Carmichael—a plush toy cat, his grandparents' gift on the day he was born. When Alan had first heard of the PCT six months earlier, he thought, *That's impossible.* But here he was at Kickoff.

MORE THAN CLASSES on avoiding overuse injuries, practicing Leave No Trace principles, and identifying flora and fauna, more than evenings spent watching hiking videos on a screen clamped onto a Winnebago, one late afternoon event drew everyone at Kickoff: the trail class photos. We, the class of 2007, were first and we felt *People* magazine famous, sitting, kneeling, or standing in ranks five deep.

After the photos, my gut fluttered as it had all day, each time I saw a name badge indicating a past PCT finisher. I felt envy and unbridled anticipation along with fear. But it all just charged Frodo up: "They've had their turn and now it's ours."

Over the last month, three, four, or ten hikers a day had set out one by one. Like thoroughbreds jammed into a starting gate, PCT thru-hikers have a narrow window of time to complete an end-to-end trek. Start before mid-April and snow barricades the way in the Sierra Nevada. Start after early May and risk hitting an impenetrable blanket of snow in Washington's Cascade Range.

As the day ended, my thoughts kept returning to our class photo. We all looked so fresh-faced, with our fists pumping the air. But standing near us in our row was a woman I recognized. Close to our age, she and her husband had set out to hike the PCT a year ago. She'd watched him walk around a bend—the next thing she knew he was dead. Near mile 300, along a steep cliff above Deep Creek, he'd fallen 250 feet. Jordie, our middle child, had made us promise to hold hands on that stretch of trail.

All of us in that photo hid a hard truth in our pockets—more than half of us wouldn't reach Canada.

Who would thrive? Who would become friends for life? Who would we learn to count on? Who would be injured or worse?

3

Midnight

THE MORNING AFTER Kickoff, at precisely 6:00 a.m., Frodo left Lake Morena. Hiking past the last of the campground oaks she wiggled her feet, testing for hot spots. Even though blisters were already forming on her heels and toes, Frodo walked as if her shoes' soles were lined with springs. *I am hiking the Pacific Crest Trail.*

I watched her head out alone.

TWO HOURS LATER, with the temperature eighty-five degrees and soaring, Amanda caught a ride from Kickoff to the southern PCT monument. She stood next to its tight clutch of five fir pillars and signed the trail register: "From Kersey, Pennsylvania, to Manning Park, Canada. April 29, 2007, 8:00 a.m., Amanda." Then she listed a single goal: "To find inner peace."

Amanda's pack weighed nearly fifty pounds, half again that of many others. She felt so out of her element; the farthest she'd hiked before was 10 miles and now she faced a 20-mile day. But as Amanda ran a hand over the peach fuzz already growing on her head, a part of her mirrored Frodo. *Bring it on*, she thought, daring the trail.

On soft feet that would soon callus, coarsen, and chap, she took her first step. "I'm hiking to Canada," she said under her breath.

BORN IN 1982, Amanda was the fourth child in five years brought home to a one-bedroom flat in the north Appalachian country of Pennsylvania. After working long shifts as a machinist at Airco Carbon six days a week, her father drank—even harder than he worked, from Amanda's perspective. He forbade Amanda's mother, Lois, from working. One day, when Amanda was five, Lois towed her gaggle of kids in a Radio Flyer wagon to the corner market. On the way back, Amanda asked, "Why do we pay with stamps?" That was the moment she realized her family was different from others.

Strong and scrappy, Amanda escaped into youth sports. When she ran out on the field, she didn't feel different. In the late 1980s, the family moved into a low-end detached home backed up against a dense hard-wood forest. Soon after, Amanda started a lifelong habit of keeping a journal. She began by filling in the preprinted page with her age: *I'm 8 years old.* Favorite holiday: *Christmas.* Favorite vacation: *Never went on vacation.* Someday I hope to travel to: *California.*

Amanda hid in her bedroom closet when her parents' quarrels escalated into brawls. If she was discovered, she'd bolt through the backyard and into the tangled forest, clutching her teddy bear, Cheerio. Dark forests didn't frighten her. Home did.

The two siblings nearest in age to Amanda were Arwen and Jeremiah, one and three years older, but she was closest to her brother Ian. Thin and studious and nearly five years older, Ian was the one she felt the tightest bond with. Ian felt it, too. He knew that he and Amanda were the ones who'd break free of Kersey and launch themselves to college.

Near the end of seventh grade Amanda came home to find Arwen and Jeremiah in front of the house. Arwen was squatting, holding her knees and rocking back and forth while Jeremiah had a white-knuckle grip on something in his hand. "What's up?" asked Amanda.

Holding it as if it were repulsive, Jeremiah thrust out a tiny cassette tape from their home answering machine. "Listen to this," he said.

In the house, Jeremiah played the tape. A drunk voice rose from the tinny speaker and a string of messages spewed out—their dad cursing. He was leaving this time and wasn't coming back, that was clear. But her mind refused to accept what he said about Ian.

IT WASN'T EVIDENT to Amanda where the actual trail began from the southern border monument of the PCT. At the hub of four deep-rutted roads on top of a small rise, the monument was framed to the south by five strands of ratty barbwire, the old border fence. Behind that was the newer fifty-foot-wide bare track and ten-foot-high steel wall running east and west. Hikers signed the trail register, turned around, and stared north into rolling hills dotted with sage and stray tumbleweeds. Amanda was lucky: four hundred feet downhill she spotted a nearly hidden, gray-painted wooden sign, "Pacific Crest Trail: Lake Morena 19.5 Miles."

She had seen photos of the northern monument at the Canadian border. It was identical to the southern monument, with five pillars of varying heights, but set in the middle of the thirty-foot-wide clear-cut swath marking the United States–Canada border amid densely forested mountains. For an instant, Amanda saw herself standing there.

Planning done, throttle open, Amanda flushed jackrabbits out of the waist-high vegetation as her feet kicked up dust. *Today's going to be a scorcher*, she thought. With Southern California in the middle of a severe drought, one question hung on her and every other hiker's lips: "How much water are you carrying?" The answer meant the difference between relative comfort and a parched thirst. At the extreme—and it happened—it could even mean being airlifted out. The next certain water was 20 miles away at Lake Morena. Most hikers were carrying five or six liters to start with— eleven to thirteen pounds of water. Amanda began with three and a half.

The trail briefly paralleled a dirt road, then passed under a high-power transmission line before entering a stand of ribbonwood, a Dr. Seussian tree with multiple trunks sloughing strips of reddish bark, bent branches, and clumps of tiny leaves. Each of the tree's adaptations suited the dry climate, something Amanda would see over and over along the PCT. Adaptation was a lesson that she and her fellow pilgrims would hearken to, or fail in their journey. The bark strips brushed Amanda's shoulders as she walked by, reminding her of her lost hair.

Castle Rock and its boulder turrets dominated Amanda's first vista as she hiked past eight-foot-tall yuccas, their wrist-thick stalks studded with ivory, bell-like flowers and ringed by a base of bristling rapier leaves. Above her, the sun felt like a heat lamp with the control jammed on high. Outdoor gospel might dictate high-top boots, but Amanda wore low-cut running shoes. The idea to rethink this staple of outdoor attire can be traced to a single ultralight hiking zealot in the '90s. Now, over 90 percent of Amanda's fellow thru-hikers did the same. Half the weight of boots, running shoes dry faster when wet and put hikers' feet deftly in touch with the terrain. The fear that flimsy support would breed a rash of ankle sprains had proved baseless. And in this heat, even her running shoes with their touted breathability were so stifling they felt like sweat-boxes and blister nurseries. In time, another hiker would post a picture of sweat-caked, filthy socks online with the caption: "You know it's time for town when your socks stand by themselves."

Amanda topped a hill and dropped to Highway 94, where a roadside sign said "Mile 1." Below it, a clever hiker had penned in black permanent marker, "Only 2649 to go." This was civilization's edge.

AMANDA WAS TWELVE when her dad abandoned the family, taking their only car. Desperate for work within walking distance, Lois got a job at Rax Fast Food. Amanda wanted her mother to come to her soccer games, but long hours at work prevented her. As the only kid without a ride, Amanda would leave practice early to walk or ride her bike the five miles home. She couldn't stand the embarrassment of the coach offering her a lift.

In the rust of her teens, one shiny spot was Mason's birth. When Amanda was fifteen, her mom got pregnant. For the first three years of Mason's life, Amanda changed his diapers and went grocery shopping. Caring for another life and acting like the parent she wished she had wasn't drudgery. It was an escape and refuge as safe as the forest.

By the time Amanda was in high school, she had a reputation as an aggressive soccer player. Driven and angry—about her home life and more—she defended goals like a Crusader defending the Holy Grail. Her hard work resulted in a college scholarship.

Leaving home, what Amanda most wanted was a clean slate. *I'm not admitting anything about my past.* It felt good to let her new friends think she had the perfect middle-class family, and it was surprisingly easy to pull off. When someone asked her a question she didn't want to answer, she just flipped the question back in return.

After college, Amanda headed straight into a three-year master's program in physical therapy. But only eleven months after she graduated, she announced her plans to hike the Pacific Crest Trail.

TWO MILES INTO her hike, and again at four miles, Amanda crossed shallow tricklets, each an undrinkable mud-laced broth. But the third creek bed was a lush ravine, complete with cottonwoods, cattails, mint, and willows. Already exhausted, Amanda sat down with two young women who were also taking a break. One of them sat on a choice rock at the edge of the puddle, took off her shoes, and nestled her feet in the water. The other read out loud from a trail guide. "There may be poison oak." It has "shiny green leaves each divided into three oval, lobed leaflets." The three looked down and realized poison oak surrounded the rock. That was the fastest Amanda saw anyone move all day.

Soon after, Amanda hit the first climb. It was an 800-foot rise, more curves than switchbacks, and exposed to the sun. *I was so excited to start*, she thought. *Now it's such a grind.* Attaining a shoulder of Hauser Mountain, Amanda could see the trail stretching out toward the horizon along a contoured flank, narrowing to a thin thread. An hour later, that far-off thread was a three-foot span of dirt beneath Amanda's shoes. She thought, *No bike, no car, my feet alone did it!*

One hundred degrees: that's what Amanda's tiny pack thermometer read at 11:30 a.m. With eight miles done, Amanda and the two others holed up under the first shade they'd seen since midmorning. Their impromptu siesta lasted two and a half hours. Every twenty minutes the trio migrated to keep out of the sun. They were already adapting.

TEN DAYS AFTER announcing her decision to hike the PCT, Amanda got a rude shock when her levelheaded friend Heidi doused the grand scheme with ice-water reality: she didn't have enough money. The two had taken a hard look at Amanda's trip expenses, including gear, food, shipping resupply boxes, airfare, and cash for town stops. No amount of fiscal gymnastics—deferring student loans and maxing out two credit cards—came close to bridging the gap. A familiar flush of shame heated

Amanda's cheeks. "You won't make it halfway," Heidi told her. "Two months."

Amanda's mind raced. *I'll hike half*, she thought. *The money will run out and I'll get off the trail.* She felt a measure of relief at the idea of two months instead of five. Straightaway she called Ian, who had first told her about the trail. "Amanda," he said, after her torrent of words subsided, "you're already hiking two months; you really should finish the whole thing." What he said next made her feel odd and surprised. "If it's a matter of money, I'll cover it." Amanda had almost forgotten. *That's what it's like to catch a break.*

AT 2:00 P.M., AMANDA roused herself from the shade and reentered the triple-digit heat, her sweat evaporating as fast as her body generated it. A nubbin compared to what lay ahead on the PCT, the canyon-slashed flanks of Hauser Mountain still knocked her about. Worse, after she made the roller-coaster descent, she saw only open grass in so-called Hauser Creek. Setting down her pack, Amanda felt panicked as she scanned for water. At Kickoff, she'd heard Hauser Creek had a little water and all morning she'd felt secretly smug that the other two were unnecessarily burdened with six liters of water. Now Amanda was out. When she sheepishly asked for some of theirs, she got a second surprise. They were relieved to offload weight before the stiff climb ahead. The trio had hiked 16 miles. Amanda had never hiked that far in a single day.

Sunset was at 7:29 p.m., but the deep canyon shade crept in earlier. As soon as it was relatively cool, Amanda stood up from her break spot beneath a large-leafed sycamore, leaving a body-shaped indentation. Ahead, the clearly visible 1200-foot climb up long switchbacks taunted her. An almost full moon lit the trail by the time she reached the round, undulating top of Morena Butte, and it was after 10:00 p.m. when the trio finally walked into the campground at Lake Morena. They were the last hikers to reach camp that day.

NEAR MIDNIGHT, AMANDA peeked out from her down sleeping bag. Her little thermometer read thirty-five degrees.

4

"Where's Dr. Mann?"

MONDAY, APRIL 30, 2007

IT WAS MIDNIGHT and nearly freezing, but I was warm as toast in my camp at the border, only one hundred yards from the PCT monument. Fifty miles away, Sandy was asleep at our home in San Diego. Twenty trail miles distant, Amanda was already at Lake Morena. *Finally,* I thought, *I start tomorrow.*

I was leaning back in a lawn chair next to one of my best friends, Mitch. In sharp contrast to my beanpole-like shape, Mitch was built like a fire hydrant and still had color in his close-cropped hair and mustache. I had coaxed him into coming to help me hold a vigil, one that would stamp an exclamation point on my separation from normal life.

With our sleeping bags spread out behind us, we stretched our hands over the fire we'd built in an old oil drain pan. Vehicles belonging to both Border Patrol and "Minutemen," self-appointed citizen vigilantes, zoomed around us. Many of the Minutemen had visible guns even though they were supposed to carry only walkie-talkies. Some looked like recent immigrants themselves, which struck me as ironic and surprising. I thought, *When is someone going to ask us for identification?* For all they knew, we were sitting here directing that night's strings of illegal border crossers. At nearly 1:00 a.m., after we'd sat for three hours, a vigilante truck stopped sharply in front of us. The driver rolled down his window, stuck out his wild-haired head, and said in a gruff voice around the glow of a cigarette, "Don't worry. You're safe."

"HEY, SHRIMP!" AS a boy, being the smallest was hard. So was being picked last. There'd be three of us left, standing in gym shorts, and I'd think, *Pick me.* But I never let it show—boys can smell the faintest scent of fear. That's *Lord of the Flies* truth. I danced as fast as I could to make sure I wasn't picked on.

Magazine ads in the '60s poked fun at "98-pound weaklings," the prover-bial butts of jokes. In high school I was a varsity wrestler, in the 98-pound class—for three years. I'd have been a terror at 98 pounds, if I had a killer instinct. By the start of my senior year, I'd reached all of five foot five.

Late that spring, with graduation looming, I was standing in a circle in our school's lunch quad with a group of male friends. We were all wear-ing our creased leather and blue wool letterman jackets for a meeting of Culver City High School's athletic club. As I looked around, I was taken aback. Was it possible? I'd stared up at these guys long enough to have a permanent kink in my neck, but now, at six foot two, I was looking down at all of them. I had to work really hard to keep a smile off my face.

To this day, I remain a very grateful short person living in a tall person's body.

I NUDGED MITCH awake at five. The coals were cold and the near-full moon was drowning in morning's first light. With few words, we packed the lawn chairs, fire pan, and Mitch's sleeping bag into his car. The Minutemen and the Border Patrol were finally asleep. Mitch and I exchanged a hug. If all went as hoped, I wouldn't see him for five months.

When Mitch's car disappeared and the dust settled, I thought about his drive back to San Diego. He'd shower, change into his suit and tie, and go off to work. Meanwhile, I was beginning the journey of a lifetime. As the sun peeked out in the east, I signed the monument register. "I have longed for this moment for an age," I wrote. No one observed me as I took my first step north.

THE AVERAGE PCT thru-hike lasts five months. How do you take the time off? Amanda's life had cratered. Alan deferred graduate school for a year. Nadine was downsized from her job as a vineyard manager, leav-ing her with a fat severance package and a blank calendar. Tony had been working construction ever since he got off the Appalachian Trail, in order to make enough money to hike the PCT.

As for me, I didn't know any other practicing lawyers who'd taken five months off, let alone any managing partner.

"YOU CAN'T DO that. The union won't allow it."

Sandy nearly slammed down the phone. Her rep was supposed to be on her side, but instead had been dismissive and condescending in response to her request for a five-month sabbatical. Except during movies, Sandy rarely shed a tear, but now her eyes were brimming over. She was spitting-nails mad.

After getting her PhD in molecular biology in 1988, Sandy had briefly contemplated working the sixty to seventy hours a week required to stay on the professor track. But with three kids, she stepped away instead, working as a part-time research scientist. When our youngest child, Nicky, was eight, Sandy asked herself, "What do I really want to be when I grow up?"

Eighteen months later, after earning her teaching credential, she found herself at Gompers, an inner-city secondary school where 95 percent of the students lived below the poverty line. If she'd been fresh out of college, Sandy might have crumpled when a six-foot girl jumped up in class and cursed her out. Instead, she met with the girl and her mother, and the young woman ended up a star student. Sandy loved being queen of her own biology classroom.

Three years later, when a position opened up at our neighborhood high school, one of the best in the district, Sandy was surprised at how hard it was to tear herself away from Gompers.

On the eve of our hike, Sandy had been at University City High for seven years. In a school district of twenty-three high schools, she was the most successful Advanced Placement Biology teacher, with sixty to ninety students a year excelling at the national AP Biology exam. She'd told her principal about our trek four years in advance, personally picked out a competent, long-term substitute biology teacher, and prepared eleven weeks of lesson plans, enough to last till the end of the year and the beginning of the next.

Her leave request form was returned "Not Approved." A leave of absence could only be for one semester or one school year, not the end of one school year and the beginning of the next. Her union not only refused to back her up, but stuck the knife in: "The union will fight your request."

As Sandy fumed, I went on the internet and found the union contract. It turned out her leave could be approved by the superintendent. Sandy had worked with him before and she told him, "I'm either returning or I'm not." That was her polite way of saying, "I am going. I'll quit, if I need to." No approval by the union was required. Occasionally it pays to be married to a lawyer.

AS I STRODE away from the monument, I thought of the hikers I knew who'd completed the PCT. How I had envied them. They were hiking giants, and I'd read their online journals avidly, calling out to Sandy when our favorites started posting again after hitting a trailhead. Now it was my turn. I was writing a journal, and others were reading it online. I was hiking the Pacific Crest Trail.

WE HAD ALWAYS planned to start together, and I wanted a fighting chance to catch the hikers who had stayed at our house. But the AP Biology exam was on May 12, and Sandy wouldn't budge. Her students that year would be as ready as in any other year. She had to teach them until the second of May, three days after Kickoff.

It was the perfect setup for a fight, but we reached a compromise instead. I would leave April 30, the morning after Kickoff. She would hike 30 miles during the Kickoff weekend, come back to teach, and then catch me after school on Wednesday at mile 43 in the Laguna Mountains for a late dinner.

FOR ME, THE trail started with my all-night vigil with Mitch. For Amanda it was cutting her hair. Sandy also used her hair as a jumping-off point, cutting it short for the second time in her adult life. *I don't know what I am looking forward to more, starting the hike or getting my hair cut.*

For years she'd wanted to cut her long brown hair, but refrained at my request. Eight days before she started the trail, Sandy tied her ponytail tight and guillotined the long hank with a pair of scissors. Staring at the brown and sun-bleached strands in her hand, she grinned like the Cheshire Cat.

The next day at the end of lunch period, students filtered in through the rear door of her classroom. In the front of the room with her back turned, Sandy heard one of them ask another, "Where's Dr. Mann? Do we have a sub?" Sandy turned around and the student let out a loud shriek.

ONLY FOUR DAYS before heading out, I walked past my name on the door of our eleventh-floor law firm. I turned over the keys and the checkbook to two younger partners. I'd bargained for the time, effectively shoving money across a table. I planned to call once a month to check in.

5

Outhouse Dinner

TONY FLEW TO San Diego the Monday after Kickoff. At the start of the Appalachian Trail he had hoped for adventure, wilderness, and solitude, but for much of the 2180 miles he hiked in a crowd. And, having grown up in southeastern Pennsylvania, he found the terrain all too familiar.

The PCT was different. He'd never walked through a desert and, after the low-lying Appalachians, it fascinated him how much of the PCT was well above 5000 feet. Tony couldn't wait to summit Mount Whitney at 14,500 feet. Also, he'd be starting the trail with fewer than three hundred hikers, not the three thousand that started the Appalachian Trail each year. *This time,* he thought, *I'll find solitude and wilderness.*

Tony was Amish, or would have been Amish if his parents had stuck with the program. Descended from generations of good German stock, his parents broke away from Old Order Amish as adults, leaving Tony to wrestle with that heritage. At school, his classmates told Amish jokes. Tony told them, too, and felt ashamed every time.

But Tony's dad hadn't escaped the plain folks' work ethic. While his friends played on the weekend, Tony worked with his dad at a construction site. His father had a short fuse and expected his son to know how to do any task with little instruction. Even so, Tony was grateful to have a guys' day away from his three sisters and mom. On the way home, he and his dad would get root beer floats, their favorite thing.

Through a lens thirty years thick, Tony can still see the bottle. Pantry shelves lined the basement stairway of the two-story Pennsylvania farmhouse, and the bottle of homemade wine was almost out of reach. He can still feel its smooth contours and recall the clench in his throat as he snuck a swig, not caring if it burned on the way down. He was only six years old, and the act felt grown-up, illicit, and exciting.

Tony was twelve when he had his first beer and fifteen the first time he got drunk. His was a storm-tossed home and he never invited friends over. His father was going through a nasty bankruptcy, his mother developed serious health issues, and one sister was kicked out when she was seventeen—Tony felt caught in an anxious, angry muddle. Then, at sixteen, Tony had his first run-in with the Pennsylvania State Police. He got roaring drunk at a high school soccer game and they were set to take him to jail, but Tony's dad was able to talk the officers down. At home Tony took a swipe at his dad, starting a bare-knuckle fight. The next morning he saw the bruises on his body and the look in his dad's eyes, but didn't remember anything—that was the worst, Tony thought. *Dad could have passed off my being drunk and even taking a swipe at him, but it hurt him deeply that I remember nothing.*

On trail, Tony rarely talked about his youth. But these stories pecked around the edges of his life, like a jay searching for a grub. For Tony it came down to one question and answer: What did he really want? He desperately wanted to fit in.

ALMOST TWENTY-FOUR HOURS after I'd signed the border register, Tony wrote, "Back on a long trail—Life is indeed good! Tony." A Canadian hiker, Ryley, signed in at the same time: "First sunrise of many, a path to happiness, solitude." A big-boned Canadian—a defender on his Vancouver ice hockey team—Ryley had one trail fear he wasn't telling a soul: managing without a toilet in the outdoors.

The light was just softening the edge of the charcoal sky as the pair left the border monument. The stark desert colors were so unlike anything Tony had seen back East. His green pack bulged, but it wasn't because of his lightweight twelve pounds of gear—his "base weight"—it was his six liters of water and six days of food. Altogether, his pack weighed more than forty pounds.

As Tony and Ryley hiked toward Lake Morena, now empty of Kickoff festivities, patchwork clouds began to gather overhead, obscuring the sun. Soon, the sky had darkened as if time had reversed course and they had walked back to dawn. Rain followed shortly after, then hail, and then a thunderstorm pummeled the two hikers. Ryley and Tony scrambled for their pack covers and rain jackets while thinking, *I must be in the wrong place. This is supposed to be desert.*

By afternoon, all trace of the morning's gully-washer had vanished. Full sun and heat were their companions on the exposed switchbacks up Morena Butte. Tony's feet pumped, his hiking legs back under him again. He was well on his way to a 20-mile day.

At Lake Morena, Tony and Ryley joined Gaby, youthful and British-accented, even though he'd grown up in Spain. At a picnic table, the three chowed down on variations of ramen noodles and instant mashed potatoes. Gaby asked Tony, "Would it be cheeky of me if I asked to use your spoon?"

"Sure, go ahead. But where's yours?"

"I forgot to buy one," Gaby answered.

Gaby told them he had flown in to San Diego, gone to an outdoor store, and said, "I want to walk to Canada." Tony gawked when he saw the gear they'd sold him.

Memories of the first day's cloudburst and afternoon broil had already dimmed by the second day, as Tony, Ryley, and Gaby hiked into the mile-high Laguna Mountains. But that night, with the trio camped less than a mile from the crest, high winds and rain squalls came roaring out of a dark sky. Their tents and sleeping bags were put to the test against wind-driven rain and near-freezing temperatures, but Tony slept soundly.

IN JUNE 1987, Tony graduated with eighty of his peers from Pequea Valley High School in Lancaster County. Wanting out of his small town, he applied to and was accepted by American University in Washington, D.C. It was only a two-and-a-half-hour drive from his parents' home, but for Tony it felt light-years away.

Tony managed to keep his drinking under control at first, but by his sophomore year he was failing school and drinking heavily. When a friend back home got married in October of '88, Tony's girlfriend, his high school sweetheart, picked him up on the way to the wedding. It was the first time he would see his high school friends as a group since leaving for the big city, and he wanted to impress them.

At the wedding Tony got drunk and blacked out. When he came to at his parents' house, he couldn't remember how he got there. His blackouts had been getting worse and worse. All he wanted to do was run away.

As Tony stood in his parents' laundry room, clad in a towel and waiting for his soiled clothes to dry, a quote from that semester's French class struck him like a lightning bolt. "Those who refuse to learn from the past are condemned to repeat it." And he knew without a shadow of a doubt what the rest of his life was going to be like if he didn't change. This same moment, this same miserable scene, would repeat over and over. It was clear to him that the choice between drinking or not was the same as living or dying.

Tony started the PCT eighteen years clean and sober.

BY DAY THREE on the PCT, Tony was sitting a quarter mile off trail outside the low-slung Laguna Mountain Store. It served a population of fifty-seven and was the only store for miles, so most PCT hikers made it a mandatory detour. The night's chill was gone, the heat of the day was yet to come, and the temperature was near perfect.

"Would you like some strawberries?" I asked him.

Tony sat up straight, startled. Was someone really offering him food? His mouth gaped when he saw the lush, red fruit. But an odd look crossed his face when he glanced at me.

"You look like a thru-hiker."

Well, I had Tony fooled. My longest hike to date was "only" the 211-mile John Muir Trail. After newbies Ryley and Gaby, Tony was relieved to meet somebody else who had done this before. We chatted a few minutes before parting ways. I might have met my newest lifelong friend, or we might never cross paths again.

By late afternoon, Tony was hiking by himself, crossing the final but-
tresses of the Lagunas. The trees were petering out as the late-day winds
began to build. He was unsure of where to cook dinner. There hadn't been
a landscape feature for miles that offered a windbreak.

Like many thru-hikers, Tony was carrying a homemade alcohol stove
that weighed less than an ounce. Crafted from two cutoff soda-can bot-
toms ringed with sixteen pinholes, it looked more akin to a drink coaster
than a stove. Once lit, an ounce of denatured alcohol would boil two cups
of water in five minutes, and the stove itself would last for 2650 miles. But
the fuel was finicky, requiring the surrounding air to be still. A windbreak
was a must.

Tony was also closely monitoring his water—he had less than a liter left.
It had been 15 miles since he'd filled up at the Laguna Mountain Store.
The next refill possibility was in two miles, at a trailhead parking lot off
Sunrise Highway. The page of the PCT Water Report in Tony's pocket
told him there was a water trough near the parking lot fed by a well. The
water was intended for horse, not human, consumption, but there were
instructions: "Turn the green handle on the ball valve so it lines up with
the pipe, lift the flap over the trough, push down on the float valve, and
get water from the pipe." Cryptic, but promising. He'd also heard the trailhead had a brand-spanking-new pit toilet. *It must have a wind-protected side,*
he thought.

Less than five minutes after he got water, Tony balked when he saw the
outhouse. One of the four sides was wind protected, but a barbwire fence
and shrub thicket barred any access along that wall. Tony stared at the
outhouse door as the shrieking wind peeled away his apprehension about
eating where people defecate.

He entered, propping the door slightly open, set down his pack, and
wedged his back into a corner. Toilet paper rolls sat on a padlocked bar
two feet from his head, but he was blessedly out of the wind. When he lit
the stove, the flame was so faint as to be almost invisible. Tony crouched
over his little stove, struggling to keep warm in every stitch he had. There
in his corner, Tony was happy.

6

Harvard or Me

"FRODO," I ANNOUNCED, "I gave away the strawberries." It was our first morning hiking together, and I had just come back from the Laguna Mountain Store—she hates wasting food so I'd taken the strawberries there as a favor to her. I still found it hard to believe that my wife had accepted the trail name Frodo.

SANDY WAS SEVENTEEN and I was twenty-three when we met at All Nations, the summer camp I directed near mile 372 of the PCT. A sixth-grade outdoor school camp had rented our facilities for two weeks—she was one of their counselors, and made a good impression. When one of my counselors quit a week into the summer season, I called Sandy and asked if she'd like the job. She arrived at camp the next day.

After I left for the University of Oregon School of Law in late August, we wrote each other every other day. At Christmas break, I returned to Los Angeles and we were practically glued together. She was working twenty-five hours a week at Baskin-Robbins, but, even working that hard, she kept a firm grip on one of her school's top three academic spots. With me in the picture, her parents raised the stakes: If she chose to go to the University of Oregon, they wouldn't pay a cent toward college.

Throughout the spring we continued writing. We'd talk after 11:00 p.m. on Friday nights, when the long-distance rates went down. Sandy had started to hear from colleges, including an acceptance from the University of Oregon. Then Harvard replied, offering a great scholarship. In short order, she told me, "I'm going to turn Harvard down." "You at least have to visit," I insisted. We split the cost—Sandy, her parents, and I each picked up a third of the tab for her to visit Boston.

Sandy returned on the last Friday of April. That night, as usual, I had been at the law library till midnight—the first of my final exams was on Monday—before heading home to the old clapboard farmhouse where I rented a room. Sandy told me not to expect her call till 1:00 a.m. since she was working the late shift and cleanup at Baskin-Robbins.

The phone rang and she briefly told me about her trip, asking how I'd been the last few days. Then she said, "Harvard was nice, Barney, but I've decided to go to the University of Oregon."

My mouth was dry. And then the words came out: "Sandy, I want you to be my wife."

Silence. More silence. In the gap, I stammered, "That's fine if you need more time . . ." That was when she roared, "When? Of course, Yes!" There was a pause as we both silently gripped our phones. She thought, *He didn't ask a question. That's awkward; there's nothing for me to answer.* And then, *It's too soon, I'm too young, but what the heck.*

I had a huge grin on my face during the two weeks of finals. Worried about her family, Sandy and I didn't tell anyone until I flew home to Los Angeles. When we told her parents around the dinner table, our news was met with silence and frowns. Minutes passed before someone picked up a utensil and resumed eating.

They were evangelical Presbyterians. I was Jewish. They were Goldwater Republicans. I had a ponytail down my back. But over the next year, including three weeks when I lived in their home while Sandy finished her freshman year of college, their attitude taught me much about acceptance.

On June 19, 1977, after a yearlong engagement, four hundred people attended our wedding in Conejo Valley Park, a mile from her parents' house. I wore bell-bottoms. Sandy sewed her dress and made the four-tier cake. She was still squeezing white frosting borders at 10:00 p.m. the night before. Our families wore smiles as we were married under a chuppah that my brother and I had made.

AT LUNCHTIME ON our first full day together on the PCT, we stopped at a roadside picnic area called Pioneer Mail. It was blustery, but Frodo spread out on the picnic table as if it were a resort recliner. She stuffed her down jacket into one sleeve to use as a pillow, and put her pack under her knees and her hat over her face. She spent an hour resting in that position. Tony passed by Pioneer Mail during our break, but didn't see us, and we didn't see him.

The winds increased that afternoon, turning into a gale by 6:00 p.m. Seven miles after Pioneer Mail, we turned a quarter mile off trail to pick up some water from the Sunrise Trailhead parking lot. While Frodo retrieved water from the pipe draining into the horse trough, I scouted out a place to make dinner.

Gusts of wind beat a loud staccato cadence against the low bushes. At the gravel parking lot's edge, I saw the new outhouse, the only windbreak in sight. *It must have a protected side,* I thought. My heart sank at the sight of the low shrubs and barbwire fence blocking access along the wind-shielded wall. *Should we consider eating inside?* My feet crunched on the gravel as I opened the door.

7

"Blazer, I Need You"

MONDAY, APRIL 30, 2007

TO AVOID THE HEAT, Amanda set out an hour earlier on her second morning with redheaded Alan from Wesleyan College. He'd seen Amanda and her two companions arrive late the night before. The three had joined his group of hikers around a campfire. Watching Amanda with her companions, he thought, *Bossy and intense.* But he hadn't written her off completely and acquiesced when she asked, "Can I head out with you?"

Alan had a Martin backpack guitar strapped to his pack, the instrument's disproportionately long neck dwarfing its shrunken, triangular body. He was still learning to play, but his enthusiasm ran high. Even dog-tired after a twelve-hour day of hiking, he'd limber up his fingers on the frets of the spruce soundboard, which, depending on your ear, gave off a tone dulcimer sweet or softly tinny. The guitar weighed two pounds, two ounces, more than twice as much as his Z-Rest, the sleeping pad he'd brought to cushion his back at night. Ounces for body comfort, pounds for his soul. Unlike Amanda, he carried pages torn from the *Pacific Crest Trail Guidebook* published by Wilderness Press—the three-volume bible of the trail.

Many hikers expected the Southern California section of the PCT to be desert. In fact, National Geographic, in an hour-long special, had branded the whole southern section "700 miles of desert." But Amanda and Alan would soon learn that they were traveling through a string of sky islands: conifer-laced mountain ranges, some running over 100 miles long, split

by valleys with a dozen different variations of desert climates, including
sagebrush scrub, chaparral, and Joshua tree woodland.

The *Pacific Crest Trail Guidebook* divides the PCT's entire 2650-mile length
into sixteen different zones of plants and animals. The driest is creosote
bush scrub, and the highest is alpine fell-field, where it seems every other
plant has the word "alpine" in its name. The first 700 miles has fifteen of
the sixteen zones. No other PCT section rivals that diversity.

Crisp air hit their cheeks as Amanda and Alan hiked through open
chamise chaparral punctuated by oak-shaded nooks. "You romp easily
north," the guidebook read, the only instance of this particular verb in
over one-thousand-plus pages of the three volumes. Even in the pleasant
chill, neither Amanda nor Alan thought "romp" described what it felt like
to labor under packs with full loads of water. If they'd been there later in
the day, with nature's oven set to broil, a different four-letter word would
have come to their lips.

ON THAT SPRING day in seventh grade, when Amanda came home to find
Arwen and Jeremiah looking crushed, she heard many four-letter swear
words in her father's slurred voice. But it was what he said last that really
hurt—so much so that she blocked out her father's exact words. But her
brother Ian remembers.

Ian was seventeen, poised to graduate from Saint Marys Area High
School. He didn't hear the message that afternoon, because his three
younger siblings hadn't dared to tell him—but they'd also been too frightened to erase it. Before Ian left for school the next morning, he noticed
there were messages on the answering machine, so he pushed play. He
heard the slurred voice, foul as a drunk's breath, spewing invective.

"And I married you even though you were pregnant with another man's
child."

Ian understood immediately. *She was pregnant with me!* A shiver went up
his spine. *He's not my father. I'm not related to that dysfunctional man.* Disgusted,
yet awash with relief, Ian erased the messages and left for school.

Amanda and Ian never talked about that day. But she did discuss it with
Arwen and Jeremiah. "He's still our brother," she protested. "It doesn't

matter." Nevertheless, now Amanda knew that her big brother Ian, the one she felt closest to, was not her full-blood brother after all.

AMANDA AND HER new hiking buddy Alan were still close enough to the Mexican border to see frequent evidence of migrants—empty water jugs, worn socks, and torn scraps of carpet used to muffle footsteps. *I've never seen anything like this,* Amanda thought. *What were their lives like? What made them flee their country?* Six miles past Lake Morena, the trail went below Interstate 8, the first underpass of many. High above them, cars—filled with people heading to work, worried about what their boss said yesterday, stressed over emails, the day's headlines, their kids, their spouse—rushed by at breakneck speeds.

Amanda had other concerns. *I better make sound water choices today*, she thought, feeling like a rookie. Anxiously, she asked Alan about his plans for water. He told her that there was water 13 miles after Lake Morena at Cibbets Flat, a campground not far off the PCT. "Do you want to stop there for lunch and fill up?" he asked. "Sure thing," she replied.

Alan lengthened his stride and soon disappeared around a bend, leaving Amanda to climb into the Laguna Mountains, the first sky island, by herself. Even though they were hiking "together," like most hikers that meant leapfrogging, each moving at their own pace. She'd eaten little throughout the day—hiking in the heat often suppresses people's appetites—and Amanda thought she'd done a good job of conserving water. There'd even be a little left when she hit Cibbets Flat.

Trekking poles clicking, Amanda had been in a zone when she realized she wasn't sure how far she'd gone—and she was down to a quarter liter of water. It was the heat of the day, so she decided to wait it out by napping just off trail under a canopy of mixed oaks. At 3:30 p.m. she woke and continued on, hiking into a long canyon. She was starting to get frantic about water. Unlike Alan, Amanda wasn't carrying maps from the guidebook, but only truncated descriptions from three adjunct aids—the *Pacific Crest Trail Data Book*, *Yogi's Pacific Crest Trail Handbook*, and the Water Report. None of these were intended to keep a hiker on trail. That's what happens when you have less than twenty days to prepare.

Amanda had climbed 2100 feet since Lake Morena and was walking in and out of an oak woodland in the Lagunas that was transitioning to mixed pines. At mile 37, she passed the first trailside conifer, a 118-foot-tall Jeffrey pine. She felt even more desperate as the shadows lengthened and she realized she had missed Cibbets Flat. Was Alan ahead of or behind her?

Finally, Amanda heard the sound of running water downhill from the trail. Without hesitation, she plowed down the steep embankment, sliding on scree and loose sand. But the water at the bottom was completely inaccessible. *It's all dagger bushes*, she thought, thwarted by a wall of *Rosa californica*, as thorny and dense as Br'er Rabbit's briar patch. She tried to bull her way through and not get too scratched, but then a shoe slipped and both feet gave way. Awkward and top-heavy from the pack on her back, she somersaulted down and landed in a dagger bush so thick her body was suspended above the ground.

Scratched and bleeding, her sunglasses lost, Amanda hung upside down in a tangle. Every movement opened new bloody scrapes. Finally, wrenching herself free, she fell in the creek with a splash. Soaking wet, bloody, hungry, and tired, she filled up on water at last. After satisfying her thirst, Amanda climbed back to the trail. A few hundred yards later she found a gentle stream flowing nicely beside the PCT.

Amanda never caught Alan that night. Instead, under a full moon, she camped alone for the first time in her life. Around her was spring grass, scattered oaks, and Jeffrey pines set on a rough-shouldered mountain edge, 2000 feet taller than the highest peak in her home state, Pennsylvania. Bedded down with aching shoulders and a dozen still-seeping cuts, Amanda thought, *How can my blisters hurt so much?* But calluses had begun to form, just like a burgeoning sense of power inside of her. *It's so painful.* But in a distant corner of her brain: *This feels glorious. I'm a trail god.* It had been an 18-mile and two-rattlesnake day.

The trail the next morning was cushy pine duff, a relief after loose rock and jarring desert hardpan. Without further incident, Amanda reached the crest of the Laguna Mountains and the junction where hikers could leave the trail to access the Laguna Mountain Store. Eager to catch Alan, and not wanting him to worry about her, Amanda continued on the trail. Alan, meanwhile, was sitting on the store's porch, wallowing in its joys.

IN COLLEGE, ALAN didn't have to foster a backstory about a perfect middle-class family. He'd grown up in a two-story house in an attractive neighborhood in Boulder, Colorado. Even with two siblings, a brother ten years older and a sister seven years older, Alan never had to share a bedroom. Birthdays were looked forward to, not feared, planned precisely by his parents, everything known the day before. *What would it be like to have a surprise party?* was the biggest birthday regret he could muster. Every year, a twelve-foot-tall Christmas tree stood under the ceiling with ease. Alan and his siblings loved to throw ornaments from the banister and see where they'd stick. No home is perfect, but Alan's was one of those that Amanda would have liked to call her own.

Though Alan was never the popular kid, he always had good friends, guys he could be goofy and make elaborate plans with. Even as a kid, Alan kept buddies for the long haul. He was never one for flash-in-the-pan friendships. He wondered who would enter that circle while he was on the PCT.

One of the worst moments in his childhood was in fourth grade, when he took home his first report card with letter grades: straight Bs. He felt stoked on the way home. *Yeah, all Bs, that's great.* When his parents—academics for the National Center of Atmospheric Research—scanned the columns, they made no effort to hide their disappointment. Alan tried to hold back the tears as they told him, "These are mediocre grades. You are more than mediocre."

That moment was a turning point. It helped propel Alan to a top-ranked liberal arts college where he earned a dual degree in physics and math. Then he deferred his grad school acceptance, planning to take a yearlong deep breath before reentering academia. His gap year began with a job doing fieldwork for a lab studying ecology and climate change in the San Jacinto Mountains of Southern California. The PCT ran right through the study area—it was the first time he had heard of the trail. That winter, listening to an older coworker talk on and on about his Appalachian Trail thru-hike in the '80s, Alan started to consider a hike of his own.

But it was a girl who nudged Alan to hike the PCT. Laura, his first love, was going to hike with him partway, and he was looking forward to the time they'd have together. She was as free as anyone he had ever met, and Alan thought he was emulating her ability to get the most out of life by hiking the trail. But when he visited Laura just days before starting, she told him, "No. I'm not going." She wasn't going to hike any part of the trail. Now as he walked the PCT in his wraparound sunglasses, Alan hid the effects of a sucker-punched heart.

Alan had no way of knowing that Amanda's last experience with love had been even worse than his—it had been four years since her last date. Fending off advances was now second nature.

THE TRAIL TREAD on the Laguna crest butted cheek by jowl against a dramatic desert overlook, yet Amanda's view of it was intermittent at best. Between the horizontal rain and microbursts, the 4000-foot plunge into the desert was frequently obscured. Worse, her pack thermometer wouldn't budge above forty degrees. Suddenly, the clouds parted and the sky cleared, a reminder that springtime weather can turn quickly in the mountain ranges of Southern California. As she sat on a rock, snacking on a Snickers bar, Alan strode into view.

"Hey, what happened to your arms?" he asked. Alan was sympathetic as Amanda told him the full story, but he couldn't help himself; picturing Amanda upside down, water still out of reach, he started laughing.

"You're Blazer," he blurted, overcome by the image of her crashing downhill, trailblazing toward water. The name stuck.

As dusk approached, the pair finished the descent from the Laguna Mountains. From a landscape of Jeffrey and ponderosa pines, they dropped into a hardscrabble desert wasteland better suited for the likes of Wile E. Coyote and the Road Runner. Only one man-made feature broke the otherworldly moonscape: Scissors Crossing, the junction of two little-traveled roads. It was there, nearly 80 trail miles north of the Mexican border, that they found their first water cache: fifty one- and two-gallon plastic water jugs stacked on makeshift plywood shelves in rows three deep. In the middle of a 15-, 20-, or 35-mile waterless stretch, a Good Samaritan would see the need and start a water cache. Usually, they would manage to keep it stocked, but the trail adage goes: Never rely on a water cache, take only what you need, and be grateful.

Blazer and Alan attempted to set up camp nearby. There wasn't a designated campsite—there seldom would be—but thru-hikers can generally camp almost anywhere, except on private property. Like most hikers, they observed Leave No Trace principles: camp more than two hundred feet from a water source or the trail, and camp on durable surfaces and on an already-impacted spot.

All day the pair had been at the mercy of the changeable weather, but this was the worst. Knock-about gusts of wind whipped through at 40 to 50 miles per hour, ripping tent flaps from their hands and pulling up stakes. Much like the weather, Alan found his attitude toward Blazer shifting. He'd seen her vulnerable rather than bossy, free-spirited rather than intense. He'd seen her laugh at herself as the butt of a story, and in the teeth of pain. Even as her scabs tore and bled, she'd embraced the name Blazer.

Then they saw two other hikers camped underneath a nearby bridge. Hunched down, Alan plowed his way through the buffeting winds to see if there was room for their tents. He found the other two not only snug but smoking a marijuana pipe. They offered Alan a couple hits.

Alan made his way back to Blazer to let her know they could move. But his tent became tangled when he started trying to pack it up, his mind now fuzzy and his hands feeling like they belonged to a stranger. Finally, leaning into the blasts, Alan started to drag his tent flapping in one fist and his backpack in the other. About halfway to the bridge, he staggered, was knocked down, and then started crawling on all fours.

Alan called into the wind, "Blazer, I need you. I'm not okay right now." Blazer had wrapped up her tent in good order, shoved it into her pack, and was only a few feet behind Alan. Without comment or judgment, Blazer firmly took his hand, helped him with his backpack and tent, and brought him safely under the bridge. Wordlessly, they set up his tent together. From then on, Alan knew he could rely on her.

In her journal that night, Blazer wrote nothing about helping Alan. Instead she wrote: "Blisters! Foot pain! Blah!"

BY NOON THE next day, Blazer had climbed eight miles into the San Felipes. These brawny hills were painted with a palette of sun-bleached browns, and the trail weaved from one dry canyon to the next. It would be another 16 waterless and shadeless miles to Barrel Springs. Alan was ahead. They planned to meet up for lunch and camp together that night.

Blazer's foot woes were getting harder to keep at bay. She'd used every weapon in her blister arsenal—Dr. Scholl's Moleskin, superglue, 2nd Skin, medical tape, duct tape—and aired out her feet every chance she got. Nothing helped.

Then Blazer met Yogi smack in the middle of the San Felipe Hills. Jackie "Yogi" McDonnell was hiking the PCT for the fourth time. Author of the well-known PCT handbook, Yogi could be either talkative or curt. At that moment, she was refilling her water from jugs at the second PCT water cache, Third Gate cache, at mile 91. The water here was hiked in by volunteers who loaded themselves Sherpa-like with five or more one-gallon jugs.

Blazer peppered Yogi with questions. As she took her socks off, Yogi let out a long, empathetic, "Ouch." The torn blisters between Blazer's toes were partly covered by swaths of medical tape and narrow strips of duct tape—a futile attempt to keep them from rubbing. More blisters capped her toes, and inflamed pockets of fluid bulged beneath her nails.

"Your feet have actually swollen," Yogi said. "Girl, you have to get out of those shoes." Blazer's feet had expanded from the many miles she had pounded out over the hot terrain, as happens to many hikers. It was her too-small shoes that were the problem, not inadequate blister remedies.

Ten miles later, after a knee-jarring descent from the San Felipes, Blazer arrived at Barrel Springs. As happy as she was to see Alan there, she was more excited to see an iron pipe trickling water into the aged cement horse trough, a tenuous, precious flow from a spring on the hill above. Blazer and Alan had hiked 24 miles, their longest day yet.

While Alan yanked his gear out in a stream-of-consciousness pack explosion, Blazer laid hers out A to Z as she prepared for the night. She was meticulous and a self-confessed obsessive-compulsive—luckily, no one had suggested OCD for her trail name. Despite their differences, Blazer and Alan found they could goofily chatter on about everything.

Just 10 miles ahead was Warner Springs Resort, an isolated hot springs and golf resort that pulled in tired hikers sure as a siren's call. The aging resort had two mammoth pools—one straight from the hot springs—and condo-style bungalow units available to hikers for eighty dollars. Blazer and Alan planned to split a two-bedroom unit with another pair of hikers for twenty dollars apiece.

After the two walked into Warner Springs the next morning, with Alan running the last hundred yards, they hit the resort's Golf Grill for their first town food in almost a week. Blazer peeled away from Alan when a familiar voice called, "Blazer, come here." It was Yogi beckoning. She marched Blazer straight to the Warner Springs hiker box.

Hiker boxes are a trail institution, where anyone can leave extra clothing, gear, or backpacking food, free for the taking by another hiker. There's one in nearly every trail town, usually in a post office, cheap motel, or handy store. Rooting through the Warner Springs hiker box, Yogi saw what she'd hoped to see, a well-worn pair of men's shoes exactly two sizes larger than Blazer's.

Blazer wore those hand-me-down shoes for the next 70 miles. It was the last time she saw Yogi on the trail, but that good deed saved Blazer's hike.

That night in Warner Springs, Blazer shared a guest room with Alan and two other guys. Except Alan was now Dalton. That day in the pool, two hikers had christened him after the lead character in the movie *Roadhouse*, which they discussed ad nauseam.

For the first time in years, Blazer was sharing a bed with a man. Carefully rolled up in the opposite direction on a luxurious, foot-deep mattress, she didn't miss her thin sleeping pad. Neither Blazer nor Dalton had wanted the other to sleep on the floor, so they each kept to their respective sides. They'd become close, but had not touched.

Blazer was contemplating telling Dalton more about herself. For instance, since starting the trail, she hadn't told anyone she was a trained physical therapist. In the land of the blind, the one-eyed man is king. What did that make her in the land of aches and pains? All around her she had seen hands rubbing at knots in shoulders and massaging aching backs, clenched fists pressed knuckle-deep into a calf or kneading a thigh.

Blazer worried that the moment she told someone she was a physical therapist, all she'd hear would be "Will you look at this?" She could barely keep her own head above water. And if she told Dalton that, would she share the rest of what was bottled up inside her?

Not now, she thought. *I'm not going there. I'll never get any sleep.* She started to drift off. *I can't deal with that. I won't breathe a word to anyone.*

8

General Delivery

ONE DAY BLAZER received a packet of letters from her brother Mason's fifth-grade classmates when she went to pick up her resupply box.

"I'm really wondering, why you decided to take the hike. Aren't most girls your age at home taking care of babies?"

"How did you get your nickname, Blazer? My nickname is Beaner."

"What made you want to go on the Pacific Crest Trail? Was it your annoying brother Mason?"

"Hi, I'm Carly, Mason's best friend. Maybe when I grow up I could do that, but probably not."

"Did you ever fall off a cliff?"

"Do you eat wild live food or do you stop places?"

HOW DID WE, Blazer, Tony, and the rest replenish our food along the trail? In one of two ways, neither of which involved "wild live food." Frodo and I picked up a resupply package of food from a trail-town post office every three to five days. Some hikers, like Tony, purchased food at towns along the way. Each strategy had its trade-offs. Mailing-food-ahead hikers risked wondering three months into their hike, "What the heck was I thinking?" That Top Ramen, those granola bars you thought you'd always love—eventually you can't stand the sight of them. The supply-as-you-go hikers risked having to survive on peanut butter and hot dog buns for days if a small-town convenience store ran low on supplies.

Two Swiss hikers mailed all of their PCT food ahead, including three different breakfasts that they planned to rotate. By the Oregon border, they'd grown to loathe one. They cussed at it in English and a mix of German and French. Other hikers found it highly entertaining to be around on cursed breakfast mornings.

Amanda, even in her three-week frenzied preparation dash, had pored over the advice in *Yogi's Pacific Crest Trail Handbook*. She decided to compromise and sent out eleven boxes from Ian's house before making her mad dash through the Washington, D.C., airport. Nadine had packed a full trail's worth, twenty-eight boxes, but left twenty at home in the "PCT Nightmare Closet" for her friend Lori to mail.

Tony decided to resupply as he hiked, and his mainstay dinners were ramen noodle packets and instant mashed potatoes. But even he planned to mail a few boxes ahead when he got to Oregon and Washington—where there were long stretches without decent stores.

Sandy and I planned twenty-five resupply boxes, leaving our daughter Jordie in charge of the three tables full of food in our garage. She would pack a pre-labeled box with the right combination of dinners, lunches, and breakfasts—and the occasional welcome surprise of Rice Krispies treats or fresh-baked cookies. Of course, we didn't have a mailing address on the PCT, so Jordie sent our food for the next 50 to 100 miles via General Delivery:

> *Barney and Sandy Mann*
> *General Delivery*
> *Idyllwild, CA 92549*
> *(Hold for PCT Hiker—ETA 5/9/07)*

MANY POST OFFICES still accept packages addressed to "General Delivery." Before email or texting, before faxes, before the telephone or the telegraph, the only way to communicate with a person who was traveling was to send a letter or package under their name to General Delivery at the nearest post office. This service survives today as a way to send mail to someone with no physical address. Someone who's homeless, for instance, can get mail this way. The post office will hold their mail until they come in and ask for it.

Homeless. Thru-hiker. Sometimes, in town, with their odd clothes, long beards, and scruffy appearance, it is difficult to tell the difference.

In addition to mailing their resupply boxes, hikers use General Delivery to mail supplies to themselves while on the trail, "bouncing" a box from one post office to another. Tony had used a bounce box on the Appalachian Trail, so he planned to use one on the PCT as well. Then he sent it home after the first 900 miles—it wasn't worth the bother.

Frodo and I used a bounce box, mailing it ahead to a town where we would be in one to two weeks. Beforehand we'd typed out a list of its contents that we tucked inside the box: nail clippers, tweezers, emery boards, disposable razors, travel shaving cream, toothbrush, toothpaste, spare tent stakes, mineral oil, cotton town clothes, cell phone and charger, camera battery charger, camera memory card, sunscreen refills, hand sanitizer, water treatment drops, toilet paper, ziplock bags, an extra pair of reading glasses, eyeglasses repair kit, moleskin, duct tape, swimsuits, small batteries for headlamps, micro-screwdriver, stamps, tampons, medications, aloe, Velcro strips, checks, cash, stamps, pack repair tape, scissors, needles and thread, envelopes, large postal envelopes, packing tape, quarters for laundry, torn-apart books, and Preparation H.

TONY FROZE WHEN he heard movement outside the Sunrise Trailhead outhouse. After not seeing a soul since he'd started hiking that morning, he felt palpable relief as another thru-hiker stepped through the door. His shoulders dropped an inch, relaxing at the thought of someone joining him.

"Scout! Come on in! You're *quite* welcome." Spoken in Tony's sonorous bass, inviting someone into an outhouse for dinner seemed perfectly normal. Tony recognized the look of surprise, then acceptance, and finally gratitude passing across my face. He'd whizzed through the same stages when he'd first poked his nose inside. The room was double the footprint of a two-person backpacking tent. Both of us had come to the same oddball, you-are-not-in-the-city-now decision. Feeling validated, Tony returned his focus to his dinner. He had never felt so grand welcoming someone to such a humble setting.

Frodo, for her part, never asked why we were eating dinner in an outhouse. She accepted my choice with a shrug. We joined Tony, setting up in the next-farthest-from-the-toilet corner. I pulled dinner from our food bag and lit our small alcohol stove as trail talk broke out.

We quickly learned that Tony had hiked the Appalachian Trail, and that he didn't have a trail name for the PCT. But he *did* have a trail name from the Appalachian Trail. If someone in the city had prodded Tony about it, he'd have deflected the question. There wasn't a crowbar big enough to pry out that story. Here, in the Sunrise Trailhead outhouse, Frodo and I merely had to ask.

For the first thousand miles on the AT, he'd hiked with a group of twelve. They got to know one another and spent zero days—where they rested by hiking "zero" miles—together in town. One such stop was the Nantahala Outdoor Center in North Carolina, where Tony had mailed his bounce box. But when he asked for his box, the store employees told him they couldn't find it.

Tony was crestfallen. "That's impossible. You have to go look again." They got the manager involved and, after a long time while Tony and his friends stood around, he returned. "Is this your box?" At Tony's nod, the manager curled his lips and said, "Well, maybe next time you'll remember to put your name on it."

What they'd written on the side of the box, in big letters, was "Unknown." As his friends started laughing, the manager said, "Wouldn't that be a great trail name?" Tony immediately said, "No! It would *not* be a great trail name!" But it stuck. *Unknown.*

As soon as our water boiled, I poured in freeze-dried bits and powder that promised to reconstitute into something warm and edible. From his corner, a wry smile broke across Tony's face as he delivered a bit of hard-gained Appalachian Trail wisdom: "The trail always wins." This, in sum, was his commentary on the three of us eating in an outhouse. But Tony didn't mean "winning" in the sense of an athletic contest. The corollary wasn't "The hiker always loses." Far from it. Looking at Frodo and me in the corner, Tony explained, "I heard an Appalachian Trail guru speak once. He said, 'We stop expecting the trail to be what we want and we start accepting the trail as it is.'"

With dinner done and cleanup minimal, Tony nodded a goodbye and thrust himself back into the wind. Frodo and I cleaned our bowls—supermarket salsa pint containers that also served as our plates and cups. At half an ounce, each weighed less than half of any store-bought camp bowl.

Outside, the wind hadn't let up. Fortunately, in another three miles Tony found Ryley and Gaby sheltering in a high desert crease, out of the wind. More amazing, a scraggly-haired man sat in a camp chair next to a fire crackling in a sawed-off water heater—and he was offering food.

"Hey, Tony, meet Laurence the Spring Guy." Laurence Peabody, his yellowish-gray hair jutting out from under his straw hat in a thick, uncontrolled mane, was a Southern California trail institution. A self-appointed trail watercourse and spring maintainer, he lived off the grid without a phone or electricity, not far from Warner Springs Resort. He was known for popping up anywhere in the first 240 miles of the PCT, setting up a campfire for hikers, and staying the night. Laurence also did trail work and put up signs where he thought they were needed, usually without permit or permission. This "work first, ask later" ethic had gotten Laurence banned from sanctioned trail crews.

The next morning, like the day before, Tony, Gaby, and Ryley headed out at different times. They were in the endgame hills of the Lagunas, amid a loose network of both hiking and jeep trails—Rodriguez Spur Road, Mason Valley Truck Trail, and Chariot Canyon Road.

The PCT dumped out twice onto these "roads"—a lofty title for rutted jeep tracks—before returning to its own path. The trail might follow a road for a short way and then veer off on actual trail tread, or it might stay on the road for a good while. The maps in this area were less than clear. When Tony came to the Mason Valley Truck Trail, he turned left—the wrong way. He walked five miles before Laurence the Spring Guy drove up in his beat-up pickup and said, "You're not on the trail." Then Laurence gave him a ride back.

With his feet again squarely on the Pacific Crest Trail, Tony resolved to catch Ryley and Gaby even though he'd spotted them a five-mile advantage. He navigated the long, gradual downhill that led to Scissors Crossing. It was in desolate country, a mix of dry, nut-brittle brown open space and low shrubs. When he reached the Scissors Crossing water cache, the wind that swirled in dust devils was nothing like the gale that had pummeled Blazer and Dalton just two days earlier.

Tony was single-minded at the water cache: fill up and get moving to catch his friends. But he took a moment to sign his name in the register, and noticed that not long before a woman hiking with a dog had signed in as well. *I'll probably meet them tonight. I really wish she hadn't brought her dog.*

ALMOST NO ONE is neutral about dogs on long trails. Even Yogi's handbook opines on the subject:

> *Dogs don't sit at home and think: "Gee, I think I'd like to walk the 2663-mile Pacific Crest Trail next summer. It will be okay, because I'll take breaks when *I* need rest. I'll walk when *I* want to walk. I'll take a zero day when *I* want to take a zero day. I don't mind extreme heat and cold, because I'm prepared for that both mentally and physically. I run around the park for an hour every Saturday, that's a lot like hiking. I know what I'm getting into."*
> *LEAVE YOUR DOG AT HOME.*

Most national parks ban dogs from the backcountry outright, to protect both the local wildlife and the dogs themselves. Personally, I had no uncertain feelings about dogs on a wilderness trail. Even so, when I saw Nadine with Pacha my first reaction was *Pacha is one of us.* I'd walked up to the front porch of the Laguna Mountain Store and Pacha was right next to a prominent sign: "No Dogs on Porch." Moments later, the store manager poked his head outside and just as quickly disappeared. He returned with a full water dish for Pacha and set it right next to the "No Dogs" sign.

TONY HIKED UP into the San Felipes, where the trail meandered maddeningly as it climbed steadily, fully exposed to a western dipping sun. He felt an equal measure of apprehension, irritation, and hope. Around him was a strung-out cactus garden: jumping cholla, stubby barrel cactus, and the ten-foot spikes of ocotillo stretching toward the sky like impossibly long crab legs. It was the witching hour of the early evening when the jackrabbits dart across the trail, cold-blooded lizards disappear, and rattlesnakes retreat to their dens. It was the hour of bobcat sightings, if hikers are quiet and lucky.

Around a corner at the neck of the next canyon, Tony saw Nadine and her dog. *She's on her own hike,* he thought. *She doesn't deserve to have me dump my negative judgment.* He jammed a big smile on his face and saw Pacha move toward him. *Oh, crap, the dog's not on a leash.*

9

Canada? No Way!

EIGHT MONTHS BEFORE her PCT hike, Amanda had reached an important milestone, one she had planned for years instead of weeks: she graduated from Wheeling Jesuit University, the capstone to three years of graduate school in physical therapy. One hurdle remained before she could begin to practice in earnest—the state licensing exam. Ninety percent of Wheeling graduates passed the state boards on their first try—any bookie would have set her as a heavy favorite.

In her room at Warner Springs, Blazer's first chore had been to care for her hands. She'd known that they were healer's hands since she was eight. Looking down at them, she had wanted to shout, "How dare they tell me I can't use these to help others?"

The next morning, scenery-distorting heat waves were already shimmering above the desert hardpan when Blazer and Dalton hiked out from the resort. It was the eighth day of Blazer's hike, and she thought, *We've come 110 miles!* This was her first experience pulling free from the vortex created by the luxuries of town. It wasn't easy leaving air conditioning, a soft bed, and fresh food, even with a cloudless blue sky overhead. *What will happen*, Blazer thought, *when breaking free from a soft bed means walking out into a freezing rain?*

Like a rotating kaleidoscope, the trail's terrain kept changing. Agua Caliente Creek was shaded by cottonwoods and sycamores while Indian Flats was a desiccated plateau punctuated by rock jumbles and monoliths.

At times, the trail ran into canyons filled with the familiar sight of chaparral, yucca, and beavertail cactus; other times it gave only hints of what was to come: rolling hills foretold mountains, scattered conifers prophesied forests.

One tree Blazer and Dalton passed was a Coulter pine. The tree is known as a widowmaker, with cones the size of large pineapples but double the fruit's dead weight. At the annual Lake Arrowhead Pine Cone Festival (near PCT mile 297), a sixteen-inch-long Coulter cone tipped the scales at four pounds, fifteen ounces. Workers in a grove of Coulter pines are best advised to wear hard hats. Around these trees, hikers are careful to look up before choosing a break spot.

Just as a mariner senses the approach of dry land, the next day Blazer and Dalton felt the approach of their first serious mountain range, the San Jacinto Mountains. Even before they glimpsed a peaked ridge, 11,000-foot Mount San Jacinto—the second most prominent peak in California—stirred the hikers' blood. On the PCT, certain names are spoken in respectful whispers: the Suiattle River, Bear Creek, Forester Pass. Like a chill glacier wind, one such name blew off the slopes of San Jacinto—Fuller Ridge.

The next night they camped with a small group. After watching another hiker laugh and wince as she pulled cactus spines out of her legs, Dalton unstrapped his guitar. Blazer felt a glow as Dalton sang softly, making up riffs about life on the trail.

The pair left their campsite near the crest of 7550-foot Apache Peak the next morning—their third campsite since leaving Warner Springs. Over the next 10 miles, the PCT ricocheted between languid calm and adrenaline rush. One minute, Blazer and Dalton were shuffling across a gentle traverse, the next edging along hard-rock, steep-sided notches and ridges. Shattered rocks and drill holes were strewn about in mute testament to the dynamite blasts that had hacked out the trail. Exposed notches revealed 2000-to-3000-foot drops on both sides. A glance eastward provided a hawk's-eye view of Palm Springs; a turn west overlooked Southern California's vast urban sprawl.

As they hiked, Blazer and Dalton walked in and out of the ghostly remnants of a 1980 fire. Flames had raced in from the east, up Andreas and Murray Canyons, before cresting the summit of Apache Peak. What remained of the manzanita, white firs, Jeffrey pines, and incense cedars was twisted and charred. In blaze-protected swaths, it was as if the fire never occurred, the trail shaded by a conifer potpourri, big bushy evergreens, and mountain mahogany.

Warning lights flashed at Blazer all morning: those hiker-box men's shoes were giving out. The climb into the San Jacintos had transformed them from well-worn to thrashed. Ten miles after their Apache Peak campsite was Saddle Junction, a four-trail intersection that was the San Jacintos' equivalent of a freeway cloverleaf interchange. At 8100 feet, Blazer and Dalton planned to heed the imaginary neon "EXIT" sign and descend 1600 feet in two and a half miles along the Devil's Slide Trail to Idyllwild, a mile-high mountain hamlet of about three thousand souls.

The miles they hiked into Idyllwild were off the PCT, not adding one foot toward their goal to reach Canada, but for now that didn't matter. They needed town food and rest, a hot shower, and the new shoes Blazer's brother Ian had promised to mail to the post office.

Fair-weather flatlanders set Idyllwild humming on the weekends, but Blazer and Dalton walked into town on a relatively quiet Thursday. In town, they saw a seasonal banner hung at the Idyllwild Inn: "Welcome PCT Hikers." Taking advantage of the discount the inn offered to thru-hikers, Blazer, Dalton, and Stomp, a French Canadian, shared one of its widely-spaced, rustic cabins. The discount was a convenience for Dalton and Stomp; for Blazer, conscious of her meager money supply, it was a necessity. While Dalton once again spread out his gear in a mini-explosion, Blazer surveyed their surroundings: the one-room studio had a TV, kitchenette, knotty pine paneling, and only two beds.

Over the past five days, Dalton had started to think, *She's an attractive woman.* Blazer, too, was feeling a pull. But that night, as Stomp slept in the second bed, Blazer and Dalton once again rolled up in opposite directions, like two burritos, in a single twin bed.

Blazer was lucky to be sharing a cabin with these two strong hikers. Dalton and Stomp stepped up to take care of her grocery store and town errands while she soaked her feet in an Epsom salt bath. Covered in tattoos, thirty-three-year-old Stomp had hiked 2500 miles of the PCT the year before until the deep snow of late October in the Cascades put an end to his hike. Now Stomp was back, determined to complete the entire trail.

Blazer peeled layers of tape off her feet and coldly assessed them. *They need a full day of complete rest.* What she wouldn't think about, much less assess, were two festering questions: *What if I see an injury I can do something about? What if I could save someone's hike?* Just as her snug sleeping bag warded off the trail's chill, in the security of the cabin, she warded off these unwanted thoughts.

Measuring the 177 miles she'd hiked thus far, Blazer thought, *It's amazing, but not enough.* When she told Ian that she was going to hike the PCT, he made plans to join her for four weeks. She was supposed to meet Ian and his friend Scott at Kennedy Meadows, the jumping-off point for the Sierra Nevada, on June 9. Kennedy Meadows was at mile 700 on the PCT, over 500 miles ahead of her. Measuring out the days to June 9, Blazer realized she wasn't going to make it.

She called her brother to thank him for mailing the new shoes, and then blurted out, "Ian, I can't make your date. My feet are killing me. I have so many blisters. I don't want to push it. Can you move your plane ticket?" At this, he surprised her. "No, we can't change. Scott's coming with me and he's in medical school. He can't change his time off. Either he goes on without us or we go on without you." Blazer hung up the phone hyperventilating. *I can't make that.* She wanted to shake something, she was so angry. *I really want to hike with Ian.* Her deadline hadn't budged, but something else was slowly changing—her anger was starting to morph into motivation.

After a full zero day, Blazer and Dalton headed back up Devil's Slide Trail. They couldn't resist the recommended side trip up Mount San Jacinto, three miles off the trail. After Mount Whitney, Mount San Jacinto is the most climbed peak accessible from the PCT, but, with so little time to spare, most hikers choose to bypass it anyway.

At the summit, the pair spent three hours sunbathing, eating lunch, playing guitar, enjoying the view, and talking with day hikers about the PCT. One asked, "Where did you start your hike?" Blazer casually replied, "The Mexican border." "No way! You're kidding! Where are you going?"

Dalton jumped in: "Canada." The two loved those questions, and happily basked in the glory for a little while. It drove home for a moment what an amazing journey they were on.

The way Blazer saw the landscape around her had completely changed. Now, when she looked at a faraway feature, even the most distant, she thought, *Two hours.* Or, *A half day.* Sometimes, *Two days.* From Mount San Jacinto, Blazer looked down over 9000 feet at the pinprick-size cars on an almost microscopic freeway in the valley below her. Farther north she spied Mount San Gorgonio and the San Bernardino Mountains, her next sky island. Soon enough she'd walk right next to those peaks. But to get there she needed to drop a knee-jarring 9700 feet, equal to descending the Empire State Building more than nine times—and then climb back up 7500 feet over the following two days. That's what stood between Blazer and the next mountain crest.

Blazer's new shoes felt good as she and Dalton perched on a van-size, tilted rock. Nearby, a wooden sign with deeply carved letters read: "Mt. San Jacinto Peak—El. 10,934." They asked one of the day hikers to take a photo of them. On top of that rock the two were practically draped over each other—Dalton's long hair tied back out of the wind, and Blazer's thickening fuzz a quarter inch long. The two were still town-clean, but that wouldn't last long.

10
The Question

SEPTEMBER 28, 2006

WHEN AMANDA GRADUATED, she was ready to fly. She had landed the perfect job as a traveling physical therapist—three-month assignments, choice locations, free furnished housing, great benefits, and 20 percent higher pay than that of her non-traveling colleagues. But first she had to pass the state licensing exam: three hundred questions, six banks of fifty.

"WHY ARE YOU hiking the Pacific Crest Trail?" If anyone has an answer to that question it is Yogi. She hiked half the trail in 2001, the whole trail in 2002, and, like a homing pigeon, she had returned many times over the next five years to hike a section or to repeat the whole thing. Here's what she has to say on the subject of "why" in her handbook:

> I understand when non-thru-hikers ask me why I hike the trail every year.... But what I DON'T get is when thru-hikers ask me the same question. We'll be somewhere on the trail laughing and cooking dinner. Or taking a break at the top of a pass. Or telling stories on a porch in town. ALWAYS, a thru-hiker will ask me the question.

For the non-hiker Yogi has written a free-verse poem:

> People ask me all the time: WHY do you hike year after year?
> Because the scenery is amazing.
> Because the best people in the world walk long trails.

Because I can't call those people friends unless we have shared experiences.
Because I'm in the BEST shape ever when I'm thru-hiking.
I'm physically fit.
I have legs of steel.
I'm mentally at peace.
I have no stress.
I'm free.
Who wouldn't want to be me?

As the stars in the Sierra sky outnumber those visible in the city below, the firmament of answers dwarfs the number of hikers. Ask a hiker on a given day "Why?"—and the answer that tumbles out is unlikely to match their response from the day before.

For Dalton, one such answer was shorter than a haiku: "It was a girl." But for Blazer there was only one answer and it was an epic poem. She just couldn't say the words.

AMANDA TOOK THE exam on a Thursday. With a pocket full of peppermints, she entered the Prometric Test Center in Cambridge, Ohio, and sat down in a cubicle at a computer. Afterward, Amanda walked to her maroon Subaru, a 250,000-mile automotive dowager, filled with all of her worldly goods. She was essentially homeless and, hip-deep in student loans, nearly penniless. While Amanda drove to the home of a good friend in Greensboro, North Carolina, her permanent address was her family's home in Kersey, Pennsylvania. The exam results would be mailed there, to her mother, Lois. Amanda and Lois set up a code. If Amanda passed, Lois would call to say, "Break out the champagne." And if she didn't pass, "Break out the whiskey."

One evening, three weeks after the test, Amanda was sitting on her friend's front porch. The moment her mother called remains frozen in her memory, like a framed still life. "Whiskey," said Lois.

A score of 600 passed. Amanda's score was 594.

Wholly dependent on friends for a bed and roof over her head, Amanda tried to scrounge work as a substitute teacher while she waited to hear what would become of her job offer. Two weeks later, the traveling physical therapy company called to say she could still work on a temporary license for them in Virginia, but the pay was twelve dollars an hour, not thirty-five, and there would be no travel, no housing, and no benefits.

Amanda could sign up to take the exam again at almost any time, but there was a catch: it could be taken only three times in one year. She told few family and friends that she had failed the first exam. When someone asked, she kept it short. "I didn't pass, but that's okay. I can take it again." She wanted no pity.

A week before Thanksgiving, Amanda took the exam a second time. She took it in Virginia, not far from her workplace. A second time, Lois called: "Pass the whiskey."

Amanda crumbled. She bought a bottle of wine and a pack of cigarettes. In destructive, depressed moments in college, Amanda had bummed cigarettes off a friend, but this was the first time she'd bought her own pack. In the dark, she drank the bottle of wine and smoked cigarette after cigarette. *Who can I turn to? I feel so alone.*

After she failed the second time, Amanda's provisional license should have been revoked, but her company kept her on without asking questions. She knew this was only a temporary fix.

At this juncture, Amanda went home for the Christmas holidays. Ian would be there too, and Amanda acutely felt that she and her closest sibling were drifting apart. Trying to renew the old spark, she threw out, "Ian, would you want to hike the Appalachian Trail with me?"

"Sure, but I think the Pacific Crest Trail is cooler."

"What is that?" blurted Amanda.

Over drinks they decided: "The Pacific Crest Trail, let's do it in 2008."

Amanda's boss was the only one who penetrated her stiff-lipped façade. "You're one of our best physical therapists. You're a new grad. What happened?"

That was when Amanda confessed to developing splitting headaches during the middle of each test. "When I look at a computer screen too long, it hurts the back of my eyes."

"Well, there are glasses for that."

Amanda found a pair to help her cope with the computer glare but they didn't prevent her splitting headaches. Then she learned she could request a written exam and the examiners would even put her in her own room where she could act things out and read the questions out loud.

March 8, 2007. It was the third time and Amanda was a bundle of nerves. If she failed this test, she'd have to wait for next year's test cycle—if she could even face taking the test a fourth time. This was her life's path, one she'd gone so far in debt for that she could barely get groceries. At work, they'd told Amanda she was done after March 31.

After the test, someone asked, "What's your backup plan?" Impulsively Amanda said, "Maybe I'll hike the Pacific Crest Trail."

On March 31, she rolled all her worldly goods back into the Subaru and moved in with Ian in Washington, D.C. Sleeping on his living room couch, she waited for the results.

Amanda couldn't stand the wait. They should have mailed her the results by now. On April 5, she called the Virginia State Board. "This is my third time," she said, "I need to know now." She couldn't crash on her brother's couch forever. "Can you please tell me?" The woman on the phone wasn't allowed to tell Amanda whether she had passed or not, and wasn't about to break the rules. Amanda tried one more plea. "Can you tell me anything?"

The woman said, "All I can tell you is that we're sending you information about taking the exam next year."

Tears streaming, Amanda set down the phone, wiped her face, and slowly walked back into the house. She and Ian had been getting ready to go out for dinner. She looked at him and said, "Bro, I'm shaving my head and I'm hiking the Pacific Crest Trail." That night she bought her plane ticket to San Diego.

WHY DO I thru-hike? My eighty-two-year-old father had a one-word answer.

My cousin Cody called me six months before Sandy and I started our hike. After chatting a while, Cody dropped his voice to a whisper. "Do you know what your dad thinks of your hike?"

I wondered why he was whispering alone in his office at work. "No, Cody, tell me. What does Dad think?"

Still whispering, Cody responded, "He thinks it's *meshugga*."

Meshugga, a Yiddish word with many alternate spellings, roughly means crazy, insane, absurd.

The next day, when Sandy and I were passing through Los Angeles, Mom and Dad took us to lunch. The very same man who told Cody that our hike was crazy had just visited the local library and checked out every book he could find on the Pacific Crest Trail—all five of them. He so wanted to understand my hike.

WHY DO I thru-hike? There's nowhere else I feel so safe and free. A thousand things don't tug at me like in the spiderweb of city life. I am my best self—I'd hike just for that. Once a day, at least, I am dumbstruck by beauty. I pick my nose and scratch where I want. The people I meet are as astonishing as the wildlife. Not to mention the town food—four Michelin stars don't hold a candle to the first meal in a greasy dive after five days on the trail. The Jose Burger at the Paradise Café is almost worth hiking 2650 miles. The cinnamon rolls at the Stehekin bakery are even better. Why do I thru-hike? I could write a book.

11

I Quit

ON HER FIRST PCT hike in 1998, Nadine hurt her knee in the first three weeks, but her boyfriend, Will, wanted her to just tough it out. She needed rest, needed to see if she'd really injured it or not, but he insisted they hike on even when she was limping. When she couldn't match his pace, they started fighting. It didn't stop there; they fought about food and about her being a vegetarian. In 1998, so few people were on the PCT, and they felt as isolated as if they'd washed up on a deserted island.

In 2007, Nadine started her second thru-hike with her dog Pacha. Pacha was the better partner.

Neither Nadine nor her boyfriend thought much of trail names that first time around. They made a game of it, choosing a different trail name every other day. One day it would be Grumpy, and two days later Blister. They thought trail names were juvenile, too much like summer camp.

When the pair got lost in a spring snowstorm, they crashed their way down the north face of San Jacinto Peak without ever reaching the feared razor switchbacks of Fuller Ridge. Both were hypothermic as they navigated crazy snowdrifts and sudden-drop cliffs, unable to see the desert below. *We could have died out there*, Nadine thought when they finally reached the broad valley floor.

But that wasn't why Nadine quit the trail. Nursing her knee, she and Will continued another 500 miles to Kennedy Meadows, putting the entire 700-mile desert section behind them. Faced with high snow in the

Sierra Nevada and tales of fellow hikers who had been turned back, the two of them decided to flip north. Maybe it would be easier, or reinvigorate them, to hike south on the PCT from the Canadian border.

Though the scenery changed, nothing else did. Nadine continued losing weight—dropping over twenty pounds, near 20 percent of her starting weight—and consistently lacked energy. She grew to hate foods she thought she'd go to her grave loving—couscous and her orange-flavored granola—and bickered with Will about snacks and eating meat. The trail was difficult, but it wasn't nearly as difficult as managing emotions as a couple. Communication disintegrated to complaints: "Why aren't we going faster?" "You ate too much of that." "There's not enough for me."

At Stevens Pass in the North Cascades, the couple had trudged 180 trail miles south from the Canadian border. There, the trail crossed four-lane Highway 2, an abrupt artery to civilization. That's where Nadine quit. Watching Will go on, swallowed by a dense weave of mountain hemlock and mixed firs, she tried to compose herself before sticking her thumb out to hitch.

Nadine considered going home to New York. *How can it end like this?*

NINE YEARS LATER, Nadine set out to hike the PCT again. She felt confident; she had ironed out those foot and knee problems with a pair of custom shoe orthotics. *This time the hike is about me. It's not going to be about some guy.*

Now she was thirty-three, not twenty-four. She'd just broken up with a boyfriend when he left for Africa. She'd also just left her three-year stint as a vineyard manager. For the first time in her life, Nadine didn't have to worry about money. Leaving the southern PCT border monument for the second time, she was clear. *Finally, I can be alone with my own thoughts.* When again in her adult life would she feel such absolute freedom? It was strange, as much as Nadine avoided thinking about her youth, the one memory she fondly returned to was about the same thing: freedom.

AN OTHERWISE CAUTIOUS kid, Nadine loved her bike. By age seven, her wavy, auburn-tinted hair would whip out behind her as she pedaled, her smile a mile wide. As long as she didn't go on the main avenue, her parents would let her ride all day around the mile-long loop in her neighborhood. The street names were Harvard, Yale, and Princeton, names that spelled freedom to Nadine.

When she reached her teens, Nadine's wavy locks gave way to a full mop of curls. Her two much-older brothers were long gone, leaving her alone with her parents. In the summer before she started high school, her family took a trip to France. They had a great time, and at the end her parents asked, "Do you like it here?" "Yes," Nadine answered. "Good. You're staying."

It was a coed French boarding school with twenty-eight residents, filled out with a few local kids from the nearby mountain village. Nadine's parents both spoke French, so she could understand it, but her speech and writing were so poor they put her back a year, into eighth grade. Worse, after her parents left, the director of the school cornered Nadine and said, "I don't like Americans. Watch your step."

She might have been the only American, but she wasn't the only student who felt abandoned. Most were the children of diplomats serving abroad. While Nadine was relatively naïve, she still ran wild with her unsupervised classmates. An older girl taught Nadine how to shoplift at a nearby village. But she was horrible at it, and she was the one who got caught.

After one year, Nadine returned to the states and entered Minneola High School on Long Island. To her surprise, she found she was both popular and mysterious, this celebrity who had been to France—everyone wanted to know where she had been for the last year. Returning to the crowded hallways, Nadine felt like everyone knew her name and every school club wanted her to join. But what undercut the pleasure of her newfound status was the reality that when she walked into her own home, her parents made life miserable.

After that year in France, Nadine seemed to do everything right. An honors student, she was voted class president and made the varsity basketball team. Despite that, when she asked her dad once to come to her games, he told her, "You're not playing basketball; you're just out smoking cigarettes and flirting with boys."

By age seventeen, escape and freedom were spelled the same way for Nadine as when she was seven: Harvard. Princeton. But her father was an engineer and times had grown hard—her family didn't have the money for the tuition. Nervous and scared, she took on three jobs during her senior year.

Nadine's dream of going to an Ivy League school evaporated in the face of fiscal reality. Ultimately, she enrolled at the State University of New York at Buffalo with a full scholarship. Away from the strictures of home and high school, she partied for an entire year—doing the bare minimum to still earn straight As. Toward the end of that first year, she realized this wasn't the way forward.

I need to get far away. With the same scholarship and loans, she spent a year abroad at a sister school, the University of Newcastle in Australia. Then she transferred to McGill in Montreal where her French citizenship qualified her for nearly free tuition. Every year, Nadine took on more and more student loans, and every year her parents siphoned off at least a third of the money for themselves. *They're not paying for college, my college pays for them.* Nadine grew more and more estranged from her family.

After three challenging years at McGill, Nadine graduated in 1996 with a degree in medical genetics. At twenty-two, she had never backpacked, and didn't even know the PCT existed. But four months before graduating, Nadine applied to the Alaska and Hawaii divisions of the National Park Service, on a lark. *Whatever, I'll never get this*, she thought, and promptly forgot all about it.

East of campus in Milton Park, Nadine lived in a mansion that had been carved into a dozen apartments. From its size, she believed hers was the old coatroom. Two days before her final McGill exam, she returned home to her cozy apartment and found everything gone. There wasn't a stick of furniture left. The thieves took her stereo, the futon, her clothes—even the kitchen utensils. They had tossed all the grains, pasta, and spices on the floor.

The next night, still badly shaken and feeling violated, she struggled to study for her last exam. In her empty apartment, she got a call from the Denali National Park Superintendent. "We had a ranger cancel on us last minute. You're next on the list. Can you start on Thursday?" Nadine didn't hesitate. The next morning she took her exam and immediately afterward went to Mountain Equipment Co-op. There, she maxed out her credit card on everything the staff recommended—an MSR WhisperLite stove, a North Face Cat's Meow sleeping bag, and a Mountain Hardwear backpack. Not two days after hanging up the phone, Nadine stepped off a plane in Anchorage. When she arrived at Denali National Park, 240 miles north, she thought, *Oh my god, what have I done? I'm in a completely different world.*

The dangers of Denali National Park were legend—grizzlies, moose, wolves, no trails, no bridges over any of the silty, opaque rivers—and the Park Service mandated a strict, comprehensive training regime. No matter how experienced her fellow rangers were, all were trained by the Park Service. In the blink of an eye, Nadine went from looking lost in front of the co-op's shelves of gear to heading out on her first four-day solo patrol. She soon fell in love with backpacking.

In Alaska, Nadine met Will, who told her about the Pacific Crest Trail in late '97. Young and in love, with a passion for hiking, Nadine thought the trail sounded more fun than Anchorage in the winter at minus forty degrees. She quickly agreed to hike the trail with him, starting that spring.

Months later, Nadine stood alone on Highway 2 at Stevens Pass.

BETWEEN HER 1998 hike and setting out in 2007, Nadine would tell friends:

> *That trail breaks you down until you're sniveling in your tent crushed by the thunder and lightning and your aching feet. You worry for miles and miles about some big river crossing ahead. You lose sleep about the snow-covered passes that you know are in your path. But still to this day, I have never felt stronger or more elated.*

In April 2007, thirteen days before starting the trail for the second time, Nadine wrote in her online journal:

> *Preparing for this hike appeals to my obsessive nature. Making sure everything I need can fit into a 2200- cubic-inch backpack is an OCD dream come true. My stove is made out of a soda can and weighs less than an ounce. I've packed and unpacked my twenty-eight resupply boxes a dozen times. Can I really eat mashed potatoes for a week straight? The kicker is, by the end of the first month I'll be tossing all*

this stuff away and eating Doritos and ramen noodles from the local
7-11. All I know is my roommate is a saint for putting up with me.

NADINE'S ROOMMATE LORI did not understand the full extent of her commitment. She wouldn't learn until one night in early October, five months after Nadine started on the trail, when the Davis City police showed up on her doorstep. *I'm a vegetarian and a pacifist*, Lori thought. *What do they want?*

They wanted to know when Lori had last heard from Nadine. Three search and rescue teams—over sixty trained personnel, rescue dogs, and two helicopters—were looking for her in the snow.

12
Nutella

NADINE DROPPED HER pack and sat on it, a habit after six days of hiking. Softer than rock and sharp-pebbled dirt, her kelly-green Granite Gear pack was also cleaner than the alternatives. She and Pacha were closing in on their first twenty-mile day. They were near the midpoint of an eight-mile sidewinding traverse up the flanks of the San Felipe Hills. She should have been glowing, but instead her lips were turned down. Nine years may have passed, but Nadine remembered this exact spot. The shallow canyon mouth was one of dozens that creased the PCT as it contoured up the San Felipe crest. For miles, this flat sand wash was the only space wide enough to pitch a tent.

Unwrapping an energy bar, Nadine pondered her unobstructed view south to Scissors Crossing, the dark mounds of the Cigarette Hills, and two distant roads that threaded the moonscape of Earthquake Valley.

This sand wash was laden with baggage. In 1998, her knee throbbing in the blistering heat, she and Will had argued here. She had wanted to camp, but he wanted to go on. His sharp words rang in her ears as Nadine lingered. Thinking back, she wondered at how fast everything had crashed and burned. Pacha grew restless, and started protectively circling Nadine.

Long nosed and lean, Pacha had just turned fifteen months old. She began every day excited and energized, and didn't complain when Nadine clipped on her dog saddlebag. Her four hiking booties—meant to save

Pacha's paws from the rough trail—were more expensive than Nadine's trail runners.

The sunlight was waning as blustery winds blew waves across Pacha's tawny pelt. With the temperature diving, Nadine pulled her burgundy watch cap snugly over her curls and zipped her olive-green down jacket up to her neck. This day had been quite different from when she hiked this section of trail nine years earlier. Today was chilly. Today her knee was fine. Yet Nadine couldn't shake the conviction that, at age twenty-four on the PCT, something in her had shattered.

Suddenly Pacha tore off down the trail. When Nadine looked up, she saw a hiker with a few days' worth of dark stubble approaching her. Pacha quickly closed the ground between them. *What's this?* Nadine thought. *The universe has just delivered a good-looking guy?* Pacha's bounding rush slowed as the hiker's arms froze, ending the swing and click of hiking poles.

Tony called out, "Hello," his voice piercing the buffeting wind. Pacha neared, her trot slowing to a walk. Still sitting on her backpack, Nadine smiled broadly, her dimpled cheeks spread wide. When she smiled, her eyes scrunched up, framed by gleeful crow's feet. Tony, on the other hand, barely moved his eyes when he smiled. Smiles sat hard on Tony's face. They usually required work, but not this time.

As Pacha approached, Tony glanced up at Nadine. Their eyes locked onto each other's smiles; their thoughts mirrored one another. It felt so natural that within moments Tony asked, "You want to walk together?" Before they met, this eight-mile stretch had seemed a struggle to each of them, but now it felt like a stroll. No matter that Nadine was near a twenty-mile day and Tony near thirty.

In what felt like no time at all they had crossed the San Felipe crest. Together, they descended through the spotty but still stiff wind into the shallow pocket valley where both planned to camp. The sand was so loose that their tent stakes couldn't find purchase, but amid scrub oak and juniper, they found enough rocks to hold the tent guylines taut.

WHEN FRODO AND I saw Tony and Nadine setting up their tents nearby, we moved our stove and food bag over to join them for dinner. It was a far cry from the outhouse supper the night before. All throughout the meal, the two seemed shy with each other.

As soon as we finished using our spoons to scrape our pots clean, Tony pulled out a jar of Nutella—a hazelnut and chocolate spread that's favored as much for its taste as for its high calorie-to-weight ratio. He sat down next to Nadine and asked, "Want to share my Nutella?"

The next day Tony and Nadine hiked together, leapfrogging with Frodo and me, and Gaby and Ryley, for 15 miles. Then, at Barrel Springs, 100 miles north of the Mexican border, the two left the rest of us behind to hike a few more miles after dinner. It was dusk, and they watched the sunset change colors behind the rolling hills. They camped in an open grass plain next to a few oaks. The windless night was deathly quiet and the stars were brilliant crystal points, as the Milky Way quietly washed away with the rise of the bright waning moon.

ON THE TRAIL the moon matters. *Can I night hike tonight? Will I need to shield my eyes to get any sleep? Will I need a headlamp when I get up in the night? Will I cast a shadow at midnight? Tonight, which is the headliner, the Milky Way or the Prince of Tides?* Hikers live by the moon's phases, using it to tell time.

That evening when Tony and Nadine walked out of Barrel Springs, the moon was exactly five days past full. When I completed my nightly rituals, a bit after 9:00 p.m.—the time we all called hiker midnight—I looked up at the Big Dipper. Tracing six lengths from the Dipper's far side through inky blackness, I pointed a finger at the North Star. I did that every night it was clear. There's the North Star—that way to Canada.

NADINE AND TONY cowboy camped, their sleeping bags out on a tarp under the open sky. The two were head-to-head, with their feet pointed in opposite directions. No matter that Tony had hiked the Appalachian Trail, and spent hundreds of nights in the woods: this was only his second night cowboy camping. The Appalachian Trail has over 250 trailside shelters, an average of one every eight miles. The PCT, for its whole length, has a mere handful, and only one, the Ulrich Cabin in Washington, is used regularly by thru-hikers. Tony's second night cowboy camping also happened to be his second night with Nadine. Already he had grown fond of both.

The next morning, with seven miles to Warner Springs, it was hard to tell what had made their steps so light. Was it the fresh flush of a first night alone together, or was it the draw of town food and a soft bed? In gently rolling countryside, three miles from Warner Springs, Tony snapped the de rigueur photo of Nadine and Pacha at Eagle Rock—a thirty-foot-wide spitting image of the national bird with wings outstretched and beak haughtily pointed to the sky. Three miles later, the trio hit Warner Springs Resort—110 miles completed!

There, Nadine blogged on her *Adventures with Pacha* website. After first writing about Tony, Ryley, and Gaby, she continued:

> *I think they let me tag along because they like my dog. Everyone likes Pacha. Yesterday the resort food stand gave her five pounds of ground chuck and bacon. I keep thinking that at some point I'll wake up and realize that the PCT is nothing but grueling hard work. Sometimes it is. Now onward into the San Jacintos where we got lost in a snowstorm last time around.*

13

Donovan's Final Service

SAN JACINTO IS unique among the sky islands punctuating Southern California's deserts. While the others stretch languidly like the backs of arched cats—knobby spines dotted with hunchback peaks—the San Jacintos center around one peak, like the hub of a wheel, with canyons, cliffs, and deep ravines plunging from the summit nearly ten thousand feet to the desert floor. In 1998, Nadine and her boyfriend cartwheeled down one spoke, funneling into a side chute off Fuller Ridge. In early May 2005, during the mountain's worst snowfall in forty years, a different chute sucked down fifty-nine-year-old John Donovan.

Donovan had started the PCT just two weeks prior, on April 19, after retiring from the Virginia Central State Hospital where he had been a social worker for thirty years. In a setting where service to others was the norm, Donovan stood out; many said that his life mission was to help people. He'd take hospital patients on outings no one else would, lifting them one by one into the hospital van to go off to the theater. Donovan had started the PCT with a friend, Lynn, but his feet had swollen so badly by Warner Springs that he was forced to leave the trail.

Now, after hiking alone for 65 miles, Donovan was high in the San Jacintos nearing Saddle Junction in three feet of snow. He'd attached himself loosely to·a mother and son thru-hiking pair, Lookout and Hugemongous, as the trail had become progressively harder to follow.

Donovan repeatedly lost his footing, falling and cursing and then getting up to yell to the pair ahead, "I'm okay!"

Donovan was an obsessive ultralight backpacker. His tent was a single-wall tarp that doubled as his rain gear, and he used socks for gloves. His choices weren't uncommon on the PCT, but he'd reduced his margin for error—the more weight cut, the more wilderness smarts required. Worse, although Donovan had completed the Appalachian Trail, he never paid much attention to maps. The ex-navy man admitted he was navigationally challenged.

A big storm was approaching and, like an army outflanked, Lookout and Hugemongous had changed their plans and were beating a staged retreat—at Saddle Junction they would take the side trail down to Idyllwild. Donovan, however, planned to hike straight through. Lookout took a run at convincing him to change his plans, but soon gave up. They last saw him at 2:00 p.m. Lookout and Hugemongous would wait out the storm in Idyllwild for four days.

IT TOOK TWELVE days before anyone noticed John Donovan was missing. After first looking for him off trail, the authorities got serious about finding him. Thirty searchers, dogs, and a helicopter spread out from Fuller Ridge, casting a wide net over the San Jacintos.

Four months later, while Lookout, Hugemongous, and others were completing their thru-hikes, Riverside Mountain Rescue Unit posted: "We want everyone to know that we don't consider the search over. Several team members have made it a personal goal to find John. We will not quit searching until John is found."

A YEAR LATER, two inexperienced day hikers, twenty-eight-year-old Brandon Day and twenty-four-year-old Gina Allen, took the Palm Springs tram up into the San Jacintos. Brandon and Gina had come from Texas to Palm Springs for the weekend so that Brandon could attend a conference for financial planners. They planned to hang out at the ridge-top bar, kill some time, and pick up where they'd left off the night before, when they'd partied hard till 3:00 a.m. Boarding the tour bus at the hotel early Saturday afternoon, Brandon wore a T-shirt and shorts, and Gina had on two layered tank tops and yoga capris. They carried lip balm, a one-ounce tube of sunscreen, and a pack of gum.

At the top of the tram, they left the building and walked out onto a well-marked path that changed from asphalt to dirt. Then they thought they heard a waterfall and the couple left the path.

Brandon and Gina missed the chartered bus back to the hotel. No one noticed anyone missing that night, or when they missed their flight back to Texas the next day. Both nights the temperature in the San Jacintos dipped to freezing.

The first phone call to Mountain Rescue was placed on Monday at 6:00 p.m. Knowing that this couple was facing a third night exposed on the mountain, the unit threw everything they had into the search. There were six teams in the field by 9:30 p.m., their shouts ringing out at popular waypoints in the San Jacintos: Hidden Lake, Carumba Camp, and Tahquitz Canyon. "Brandon!" "Gina!" But the searchers called it quits at 2:00 a.m. Bedding down, many were already beginning to think the worst. *Is this a search to find bodies?*

GINA ASKED BRANDON, "Are we lost?" It felt like only moments before that she thought she'd heard a waterfall and they'd chased the sound like a butterfly flitting in the breeze. They kept moving, kept thinking they heard other hikers' voices. But their steps carried them farther and farther from the tram station, even leading them to slide down a rough scree slope. When the sun began to dip they'd started yelling, "Help! Is there anyone there? We're lost!"

They spent the night on a rock slab at the top of a fifty-foot waterfall in a canyon. As the temperature dropped and the wind picked up, Brandon insisted they stand and jog in place every thirty minutes. When the sun rose they waited to hear the sound of a helicopter, but all they heard was the roar of the waterfall that blocked their downward path. Around midday they scratched a big X in the dirt and left Gina's bright orange tank top nearby, then climbed into a parallel canyon and headed downhill. It was a scramble in and out of a stream, over huge boulders, down ten-foot drops, and through dense vegetation that cut and scraped. Gina screamed when she set her hand next to a brown-haired tarantula.

The second night was more miserable than the first. Brandon's shoes were soaked so Gina gave him her socks. On Monday morning they continued downhill, squeezing through crevices and helping each other down cliffs. The chaparral was thicker and even harder to penetrate than the day before.

Late in the day, now their third without food, they came upon a foam mat and a green tarp tied between two trees. The two began yelling—"Hello? Help! Anybody here?"—then they spotted a pair of sneakers, a fork, and a spoon. The sneakers were ten feet apart and the utensils were rusty. Something was wrong.

They found a yellow backpack and emptied it quickly. There was a fleece pullover, socks, and a ziplock baggie containing a wallet. They found maps with journal notes written in the margins. Gina saw the date, May 8—that was today's date. *Someone must be here*, she thought and glanced quickly around. Brandon's voice quavered: "Gina, that's May 8, 2005." The journal notes had been written one year before. They opened the wallet and looked at the name on the driver's license: John Donovan.

Down the canyon they spied another waterfall, this one with a hundred-foot drop. Dejected, they prepared to survive another night. They knew they were too exhausted to climb back up out of this canyon.

Back at Donovan's campsite, Gina scrounged through his pack a second time. She found something she had missed—twenty-five matches. In the dusk, Brandon tried and failed to get a fire started. But for their third night on the mountain they had a small mat to lie on and a tarp to block the wind. Gina pictured her own funeral in her head.

At first light, they tried the matches again. This time, Brandon lit what quickly turned into a half-acre blaze, with flames shooting from the tops of massive cottonwoods. After forty-five minutes the fire subsided and burned out. The two knew that was it; they'd used their last match. Gina thought, *I'm glad I finally wrote out my will.* Moments later, they heard the sweetest sound from overhead. Flying around a bend, right at eye level, was a helicopter.

They waved and jumped. From the sheriff's helicopter came a booming voice: "Brandon? Gina? Are you okay? Stay there." Gina hugged Brandon tight. She wanted to cry, but she couldn't. She was so dehydrated she couldn't generate tears.

John Donovan's matches had saved them.

A MONTH LATER, on June 4, 2006, Glenn Henderson, Jim Manues, and Patrick McGurdy were dropped near John Donovan's final campsite. Down near the hundred-foot waterfall, they found his body. Using a cargo net, a helicopter was able to retrieve his remains—John Donovan was finally starting his journey home, well over a year after he'd left Virginia.

John Donovan had helped countless men and women during his time as a social worker. On the PCT, it turned out he had one final service to perform: John Donovan had saved two more lives.

14

Who Smells the Worst?

LEAVING BEHIND THE San Jacinto summit and their mountaintop frolic, Blazer and Dalton soon entered the treacherous, tight switchbacks that cling to Fuller Ridge. It was a dreaded spiral maze, a no-holds-barred slug-fest, twisting downhill over two miles. When it's covered in snow, it would be folly to hike it without an ice axe. Some hikers get lost and turn back, retracing the 11 miles to Idyllwild. Still others avoid it altogether, opting for a lower road walk. In this historically low snow year, it did not require an ice axe, but that didn't make it easy.

Once off Fuller Ridge, the two walked through sunset, watching the day's colors bleed out. Trailside conifers faded to silhouettes and then shadow sentinels as their world narrowed to the small pools lit by their bobbing headlamps and the sliver of moon in the sky. They'd promised themselves they'd cover 15 PCT miles that day. No dinner till late. Night hiking was the price they paid for that three-hour break on the peak.

When Blazer woke the next morning, they had already conquered part of the 7000-foot descent from the San Jacintos. Operating on less than six hours of sleep, she and Dalton started out leapfrogging, but then each settled into their own pace. As Blazer found herself hiking alone, she unsheathed a mental cat-o'-nine-tails. *I was so needy in Idyllwild. I asked Dalton and Stomp to do everything.* A nasty litany set up in her head. *My feet hurt. I'm hungry.* And when that faded, her mom's voice rang out: *Pass the whiskey.* And then she added the latest, *When Ian's friend made specific vacation plans to join us, what do I do? I whine and ask him to change it.*

This 13-mile descent was the endgame of a 21-mile waterless stretch. Between several liters of water and four days of food—enough to get her to Big Bear City—Blazer's pack was heavy. She wouldn't reach the next water source until the base of the mountain. She had gotten much better about reading the Water Report and mining information from other hikers. Eventually she spied a large white boulder far below that signaled the location of a lone water spigot.

With the spigot still a few miles away, Blazer caught up to another pair of hikers. It was like flipping a switch: The next sounds were laughter, excited chitchat, and then songs. They were curious how she ended up with her trail name. "See these scars?" said Blazer, her smile flashing. "I ended up upside down in the dagger bush!" Blazer gratefully rode the pair's coattails. Eventually she noticed that her tortured feet were beginning to hurt less. Those new shoes from her brother were helping.

Leaving the comparative comfort of the Snow Creek water spigot was harder for Blazer than leaving a soft trail-town bed. She and Dalton pulled themselves away from the boulder's precious ingot of shade and she checked her mini-thermometer—it was stuck on one hundred degrees. Stretching out in front of her was the miles-wide floodplain of the San Gorgonio River, a wasteland of loose sand. The PCT was marked by five-foot-tall posts, each intended to be within sight of the next, bearing the trail's emblem and a white directional arrow. But many were tipped over and, with no evident path, Blazer kept walking forward on faith. With headwinds flinging sand that could have pitted a windshield, it took Blazer two hours to cover the four miles to the next shade—a dusty, unpaved underpass of Interstate 10. A Good Samaritan, a "trail angel," had left two couches for hikers. They were so ratty that they couldn't have even been given away on Craigslist, yet Blazer gladly sunk down onto the torn, sour-smelling cushions. She was fast learning that comfort, indeed, is a relative term.

"Hot! Hot! Hot!" Blazer wrote the next day in her journal. "We started walking at 5:00 a.m. The heat destroyed us in the afternoon." They were climbing into the San Bernardino Mountains—a range that was king in Southern California, one of the section's largest PCT sky islands. The trail ran through the San Bernardinos for the equivalent of five marathons—132 miles, much of it above 7000 feet in elevation.

Hikers in years prior had described the next section—Mission Creek— as picturesque: multiple easy stream crossings along an idyllic willow- and-cottonwood-laced canyon floor with desert chaparral hanging from the walls. Horned toads, rattlesnakes, jackrabbits, bobcats, mountain lions, and even a few bears made this landscape their home. Hiking for miles next to reliable water sources was a drastic change from the trail thus far.

But this year, Mission Creek was not picturesque. Just ten months before, at 8:30 a.m. on July 9, 2006, lightning struck. The Sawtooth Complex Fire would go on to devour 90,000 acres as nine hundred fire- fighters beat back flames that torched fifty homes and two hundred vehicles. The fire also consumed 14 miles of the PCT, reducing the lush cottonwoods and willows to burnt stubs, the stream crossings to charred tangles, the shrubs and cacti to black ash circles in the gravel and sand. Blazer's footsteps raised puffs of cinder dust.

When the burnt smell finally disappeared the next morning, it was as if ten pounds had been lifted off her back. Rising above seven and then eight thousand feet, the trail undulated between thick woodlands of pin- yon and Jeffrey pines, and sparse slopes of mountain mahogany, manza- nita, and junipers. Blazer had views to the south of now-distant Mount San Jacinto and views east to the Ten Thousand Foot Ridge in the San Bernardinos. *I just walked from there to here!*

This climb into the San Bernardinos was harder than any soccer prac- tice she'd ever endured. So many areas of her skin chafed: Her hiking pants, made of double-layer nylon Supplex, had rubbed her thighs red. Her hiking shirt rubbed the skin over her ribs stiff. Alternating between sweat soaked and blown dry had left the soft fabric of her shirt feeling like a starched collar.

The day before heading into Big Bear City, Blazer hiked 27 miles—her longest day so far. *June ninth, June ninth*, pulsed in her head. She and Dalton made camp 10 miles from Highway 18, where they hoped for an easy hitch 5 miles west into the town.

"Glad to be here." Blazer packed a great deal into those four journal words. It felt like Christmas at the Big Bear City post office when she picked up her resupply and bounce boxes. Checking into a Motel 6, she headed for the shower, scrubbing a tiny bar of soap repeatedly over her crusted skin as frothy brown water circled down the drain. She pulled the emery board from her bounce box and smoothed her ragged nails. Afterward, wearing only her rain jacket and a pair of shorts, she pressed quarters in a coin-op washer's slots and looked forward to clean clothes.

Two years earlier, *Backpacker* magazine ran an article titled, "Showdown—Who Smells the Worst?" The three finalists: skunks, stinkbugs, and Pacific Crest Trail thru-hikers. With medical journal precision, *Backpacker* detailed the science underlying thru-hikers' "suffocating reek," but the article completely ignored the worst offender—a thru-hiker's shoes. In trail towns, you can pick out thru-hikers' motel rooms by looking for dirty shoes lined up *outside* the front door. Nothing takes the edge off the reek of thru-hikers' shoes. In the end, *Backpacker* declared the skunk the winner, but it was a tough call.

That evening, Blazer had her town chores mostly done—her body cleaned, her clothes washed, fresh food (cheese, bagels, and an apple) purchased to supplement her food box, her toilet paper supply and hand sanitizer topped off, and any repairs tended to. Eat and rest, and eat again, and somehow find time to contact family and friends. Blazer took her cell phone from the bounce box and punched at the keys. Reception was never a given in far-flung trail towns—often hikers made do with the anachronistic pay phone—but Blazer had enough bars in Big Bear City to check her voicemail. The first message, from a friend, wished her good luck on her hike, but Blazer froze at the second one. *Damn. How did he find out?* The voice was her father's.

In college once, she'd braced herself and tried to write him a letter. With a box of tissues clutched in one hand, she wrote for over two hours, nearly tearing the paper under the force of her pen. She had had almost no contact with him since age twelve, when he'd stormed out of their lives. "You robbed me of my childhood," the letter opened, but she never sent it. A few months later she started a second letter.

I am writing not to uncover the lines of communication, but out of obligation as your daughter.... The only way I know how to do this is bluntly. You hurt me! You might have told me that you loved me, but I know you didn't mean it, because anyone that loved me would not make me feel that bad about myself. Several times growing up I tried to kill myself.

IT, TOO, NEVER made its way into a mailbox. Now, with the phone glued to her ear, Blazer listened as her father's message ran its course. Sitting on a cheap patio chair, she tried to shake off the feeling that she'd been hunted down.

It wasn't long before her reddened eyes gazed across the Motel 6 courtyard to see Dalton walking toward her. She didn't want anyone to see her crying, but he sensed something was wrong. Standing still, Dalton waited for her to speak. Blazer muttered, "Oh, just my dad."

"Okay," said Dalton, sitting down. He didn't ask any questions. Had he persisted in the slightest, Blazer would have resented it. Instead, Dalton lingered, simply being there for Blazer. In that single word, he'd stumbled on the perfect response. Blazer thought, *I really have to talk to Dalton soon. I'll speak to him tonight. I have to tell him how I feel.*

Later, the pair joined a dozen hikers as they walked almost a mile from the Motel 6 to Thelma's restaurant. That year, Thelma's was so well known Yogi lauded it in her handbook: "Anyone who is in Big Bear and doesn't go to Thelma's should be forcibly removed from the trail." But Blazer barely picked at her side salad while others gorged on full dinner plates. Across a series of tables lined in a row, the hikers toasted each other. Blazer tried and failed to mirror their enthusiasm as they chanted, "We're Section C hikers!"

FOR YEARS THE Wilderness Press guidebooks had broken up the trail into an alphabet soup of sections. But the heralded "Section C" and the rest were actually arbitrary designations. In fact, the first *Pacific Crest Trail Guidebook* had no sections. Five years later in the second edition, guidebook author Jeff Schaffer imposed them on the trail. Section H is the longest, 175 miles—Mount Whitney's Crabtree Meadow to Yosemite's Tuolumne Meadows—while Section L is the shortest, 38 miles—Donner Pass at Interstate 80 to the gold country's Highway 49 near Sierra City. When hikers rip up the guidebook, it is usually into these sections— Schaffer's divisions had proved a handy and lasting convention.

Section A had been from the border at Campo to Warner Springs, while Section B was from Warner Springs to the Interstate 10 underpass. Since then, they'd all been Section C hikers.

AFTER DINNER, DALTON and Blazer found themselves walking back from Thelma's arm-in-arm on the shoulder of the mountain road. One moment they were joshing, the next their arms were coupled. Days before, Blazer's gouges from hanging in the thorn bush would have made it painful, but now the two were leaner, harder, more muscular versions of themselves.

The other hikers set a quick pace, and soon the two were walking alone. Blazer opened her mouth to speak, her voice softly rising from deep inside. "I feel so close to you, Dalton . . ." Blazer had realized how much Dalton meant to her, but she knew that could evaporate in a moment. He might become just one more date to turn down. She knew what she needed to tell him.

Four years had passed since Blazer had last dated, in her junior year of college. She'd thought he was the bee's knees, and beamed when he asked her out. But within a month she realized that he drank too much, which made him aggressive and angry. One night in his dorm room he pounded back a few, then got more than pushy about wanting to have sex. He made a hard grab and Amanda flipped: she slapped his face, a resounding smack. He was so drunk he fell to the floor when she shoved him. Then Amanda ran out of the room and slammed the door. Bee's Knees came out, yelling and shouting to the dorm crowd, "It's her fault!"

That's when Amanda decided: No dating. And she'd kept to the rash promise, just like she'd held true to the pledge to shave her head and hike the Pacific Crest Trail. Now, with her arm entwined with Dalton's, Blazer felt more comfortable than she'd felt in such a long time. Above them, the wind gently swished through the road-hugging pines. "I feel so close to you, Dalton. Really." A passing car lit up Dalton's face; Blazer's was invisible, inscrutable. "I almost feel like you're a brother." It was so rare for her to care about a guy in a nonromantic way. *Don't blow it. Can't we just keep it this way?*

In the darkness, Dalton answered, "Yeah, I feel the same way." That night in the Motel 6, Blazer and Dalton shared a bed, but did not touch.

15

Tony's Promise

FOR THREE NIGHTS running, it felt like Nadine and Tony's relationship would remain similarly platonic. They were leapfrogging with an eighteen-year-old hiker who had the trail name Whisper. The hike had been his parents' idea. Nadine thought he looked like a Cabbage Patch Kid with his dark, curly hair. Whenever she and Tony were alone, when the next few moments might bring their faces together, along came Whisper. Even when they'd set up their camp, and were easing their way into an intimate conversation, he'd show up and set up camp two feet from their tents.

But by the time they reached Big Bear City, Nadine and Tony were sharing a bed. Of course, Gaby and Ryley were in the same room in two other beds—the Nature's Inn slept six to a room for fifty dollars a night. On their second night, the two owners treated Gaby and Ryley to BBQ steaks and chicken. They even packed them all goody bags filled with protein bars and candy bars to take on the trail.

In town, Nadine got to see a side of Tony that she hadn't seen on the trail. When they were hiking with Pacha, Tony was effusive, downright charming, often telling stories just to hear her laugh. But in town, around groups of hikers, he was the opposite. *He's only open with me when we're one-on-one.*

This was now Nadine's fourth town stop, and the same problem surfaced in Big Bear as in the other three. *No matter what I eat, I never feel full.* She'd been a vegetarian for seventeen years, but surely that couldn't be the problem. She confided to Tony, "I think I have a tapeworm." They went to Thelma's for breakfast with Gaby and Ryley, and Nadine ate for three hours straight. She ordered three full meals and ate all the boys' uneaten sides, toast, hash browns, and fruit—and still had hunger pangs. Then she called up a friend who was a naturopathic doctor. "What's wrong with me? I ate six or seven thousand calories in one sitting and I'm starving."

Her friend advised, "Buy a couple of avocados and eat them." That did the trick—the oleic acid in avocados makes your brain think, *I'm full.*

BEFORE STARTING THE PCT, Tony had made a promise that now threatened to plunge a dagger into his relationship with Nadine. On October 7, his best friend of twenty years, Tarik, was getting married and Tony had pledged to be his best man. That meant he had to reach Manning Park by early October. Completing the PCT in five months was doable—actually the average thru-hike time—but he'd have to stay focused and hike efficiently. On the Appalachian Trail he'd dawdled, but here on the PCT he wanted to hit 25 miles pretty much every day. He wasn't opposed to a zero day, but couldn't take three or four days off in a row to hang out with friends. And Nadine wanted to hike her own hike, on her own schedule.

As Tony, Nadine, and Pacha put Big Bear Lake behind them, heading back to the trail to tackle the remainder of the San Bernardinos, Nadine started to talk about her plans for farther up the trail. They were glaringly different from Tony's. She was meeting her friend Lori in one place and so-and-so in another, all at different spots along the trail. But even as the two talked about timing, between Nadine's laugh and Tony's stories it was all so easy to gloss over and ignore.

16

Naked Bucket Brigade

SATURDAY, MAY 19, 2007

THE PCT EXITS the San Bernardino Mountains astride two dramatic features—the Tunnel Ridge earthquake fault and flood-carved Deep Creek. Cutting a 400-foot vertical cleft in the earth, Deep Creek runs northwest out of the mountains and then skirts west, paralleling the Mojave Desert before disappearing into flat, baked wasteland. For nearly seven miles the PCT clings precipitously to the canyon wall high above the creek.

For Blazer and Dalton, their 6:00 a.m. start made little difference. Like a griddle on full flame, the day heated fast. Looking down, Blazer thought it was such a tease, the sight of cool water tumbling far below as they walked amid shrubs, scattered ironwood, and needle-leafed grease-wood. Only eight years before, intermittent spruces and pines would have provided beach-umbrella shade, but the Willow Fire of 1999—which scorched 64,000 acres—ended that. Now the guidebook warned, "Expect the entire gorge to be shadeless." It had also appended a bland geologic note, about the "friable" cliffs above Deep Creek—the cliffs buttressing the trail could crumble in an instant.

The two passed mile 300 without comment, but soon along the catwalk they spied a string of eight prayer flags hanging limply above the trail. Blazer knew this was coming, but it was still a shock. One year before, sixty-three-year-old No Way Ray had come to this same spot while thru-hiking with his wife, Alice. He was just out of view when Alice heard the skittering tumble of rocks. She raced around the corner, but he was no longer there—it was as if he'd fallen through a trapdoor. No Way Ray had tumbled to the base of the 250-foot escarpment. He was pronounced dead at the scene.

Blazer had been preoccupied, chewing over two things, when the flapping prayer flags jarred her from her reverie. *I'm not invincible,* she thought. *I need to be careful.* But she had to balance being careful with moving quickly. One of the two things tag-teaming for her attention was her brother's deadline. Dalton heard about it every day. There were only twenty-two days to cover the 400 miles to Kennedy Meadows—there was no slack. Most hikers planned three, four, or possibly five zero days in that time; Blazer could allow perhaps one. *Will my feet hold up till our June 9 meetup?* She wouldn't even think about the Sierra Nevada that followed, reputedly the PCT's roughest stretch.

The second thing on Blazer's mind was nearer at hand: Deep Creek's much-anticipated hot springs. When first mapped in the 1930s, the PCT had two on-trail hot springs, Deep Creek in Southern California and Kennedy Hot Springs in Washington. But in 2003, a hundred-year flood wiped Kennedy Hot Springs off the map. Deep Creek's hot springs were now the only ones left along the trail. Composed of a mélange of hot pools circling a set of cold-water swimming holes, Deep Creek featured a swimming hole with huge rocks well suited for jumping.

Only two miles from the nearest road, Deep Creek attracted a mélange of visitors as well. Arriving midday Saturday, Blazer and Dalton found ten thru-hikers and a few dozen others. After lunch, when Dalton took a dip, to his left were old Dead Heads tripping out, and on the rocks above older men wore nothing but sunhats. In the water, two gentlemen from Israel insisted on calling him Dolphin. Dalton, who was wearing a cutoff Hawaiian shirt he'd bought for fifty cents off the sales rack at a Big Bear City thrift store, fit right in.

A KABOOM broke the revelry—Dalton and Blazer felt the sound in their chests. Soon after, a Chinese man came down the wooded bank yelling, "Fire!" His propane stove had exploded, setting the brush ablaze.

With the fire only seventy-five yards uphill from the river, Blazer, Dalton, and the other thru-hikers quickly secured their gear, making sure that no matter how fast the fire spread their packs would be safe. Then one of them called out, "Everyone grab your water containers!" Grabbing their pots and bottles, they ran to scoop up water, then rushed upslope to the fire. One hiker's never-used ice axe was employed to dig up smoldering roots. Water carriers tripped on loose rock—someone was going to get hurt.

But their efforts were inefficient and futile, and the flames grew larger. Then a voice hollered, "Make lines to pass water!" Two lines formed, one passing full water containers uphill and one passing the empty ones down. Hikers muscled about in skivvies pressed into service as swimwear, interspersed with a passel of buck-naked men.

Two hours later, the last smoldering roots were finally drenched. A loud cheer rose from tired bodies blackened with soot and ash. After that, the party started up again, louder and wilder than ever. Blazer and Dalton decided it was time to leave. As they walked away, the sun falling behind the horizon, they heard conga drums blasting and a woman screaming "ay ay ay ay" at the top of her lungs.

That night, as Blazer drifted off, her thoughts returned to another fire, this one long ago.

SHE'D BEEN IN sixth grade. Though still skinny, Amanda had already shot up, her body showing hints of maturing. Against a backdrop of thick, black curls, she'd been experimenting with lipstick. Recently she had confided in her diary, "Soon I'm going to get a sports bra without Ma knowing."

Amanda had been hanging out with an edgy off-and-on-again friend, Lila, who definitely managed to get in trouble. Amanda's mom discouraged their friendship, but that made Amanda want to hang out with Lila even more.

They were in the girls' bathroom at school when Lila pulled out a lighter. She asked Amanda to hold a piece of paper and then lit it, grabbed it out of Amanda's hand, and threw it in the garbage can. Everyone ran except Amanda. *I have to put it out.* As the others shrieked in the hallway, Amanda willed her hands to move faster as she scooped water from the sink next to the garbage can, but flames kept shooting up. "Out of the way," a male math teacher shouted as he ran in and put it out. Then he grabbed Amanda by the ear, twisted it, and marched her straight to the principal's office. She was suspended for ten days. From that point on, her school peers looked at her differently. She felt labeled, tarred as a bad seed, she wasn't Miss Goody Two Shoes anymore.

Looking back, that fire was the moment she veered off on the wrong path. Amanda started hanging out with the older toughs at Kaulmont Park. They were mostly high school kids and she was by far the youngest. She'd babysit after school and not tell her mom when she got off. Instead of going home, she'd go to the park. One day someone in the group brought tequila and they started drinking straight shots. The toughs thought it was hilarious to egg on thirteen-year-old Amanda as she chugged them down. Competitive even then, Amanda downed seven. She stumbled in late and drunk to a friend's house. When her friend's mom saw her, she told her to stay away, yelling, "You can't play with my daughter anymore!" Amanda had become the bad influence, the one that mothers warned their daughters to avoid.

At age fourteen, Amanda was still hanging with the toughs at Kaulmont Park. That summer, a charismatic eighteen-year-old guy, just out of high school, started hanging out with the group. Amanda, about to enter ninth grade, was drawn to him, fascinated by his stories. She was flattered when he flirted with her. One day he turned to her and asked, "Do you want to go for a ride?"

"DALTON, THERE'S SOMETHING I have to tell you."

She had his full attention. "Dalton, off the trail, what I did, well, I'm a physical therapist. That's what I do." Blazer's brown eyes pleaded with him. She was afraid he would look at her differently, that it would change the way he, and everyone, treated her. They'd only see her as someone who could mend their physical injuries. She just wanted to be one of the hikers. She wanted to fit in.

Having started, Blazer told Dalton about her traveling contract job— telling it as if it were already hers—about how she switched positions every three months, how she'd get to see the world, and how she was paid a great premium. Caught up, she found herself feeding Dalton the happy story, just like she'd done with her college chums. She didn't tell Dalton about the tests she'd failed, but she had unwittingly transferred a burden to him. *Keep this a secret.*

AFTER FOUR MILES, the PCT left Deep Creek behind and raced to an open flat. Briefly dipping a toe in the edge of the Mojave Desert, it quickly veered away from that storied wasteland into low, brown, rolling hills. Heading west past Silverwood Lake and onto Cleghorn Ridge, the PCT then dropped into Little Horsethief Canyon before leaving the San Bernardino Mountains for good. There, between sky islands, a trail legend loomed— the one set of Golden Arches on the PCT, a trailside McDonald's.

Like many of our fellow hikers, Frodo and I had not been inside a McDonald's for years. But on the PCT, almost every hiker stops in—even vegetarians. Near Cajon Pass at mile 342, right before the trail passed through a puddled culvert under Interstate 15, hikers could turn right and in the distance of two city blocks walk into McDonald's. For hikers who wanted even more civilization, just three blocks farther were two gas stations, a Best Western motel, and a Subway sandwich shop.

Inside the McDonald's, thru-hikers occupied half the restaurant tables. Frodo and I crammed with six others into one booth against a windowed wall. Food soon occupied every square inch of the table. Among the hikers in the next booth, one young woman stood out. "Blazer," she said, chewing, and flashed us a bright smile before eagerly getting back to work on the food arrayed in front of her—Egg McMuffins, hash browns, coffee, orange juice, apple pie, and cinnamon rolls chased with a full cup of icing. We all played musical tables so we could hear everyone's stories.

Hikers usually linger to stay out of the intense heat, but we couldn't fall back on that excuse because it was a cool, foggy morning. None of us could believe how long we stayed, but every time we'd think about leaving, another hiker whom we hadn't seen in days walked in. Somehow, in the crush of smelly bodies and our food-induced comas, I didn't meet or talk to Dalton. Ultimately, Frodo and I were there four hours. Blazer and Dalton stayed for five.

McDonald's is certainly an air-conditioned oasis in what's usually ninety-degree heat, but there is another reason hikers flock there—food.

Town food. Thru-hikers constantly run a calorie deficit, as 20-plus-mile days chew through five thousand to six thousand calories. In her hand-book Yogi writes, "Long-distance hikers are different from any other ath-lete. We typically hike for 10 to 14 hours per day, 6–7 days a week, for 5 months straight. The amount of energy required to keep our bodies going like this is unmatched in any other sport."

On trail, hikers repeatedly face decisions about what food to pack: sim-ple or flavorful; calorie-rich or ultralight. Most hikers cook one-pot trail meals, such as Top Ramen. Yogi's all-time favorite trail dinner is Idahoan mashed potatoes. Blazer's favorite is Kraft macaroni and cheese. Frodo's is our home-dehydrated chicken paprikash. Mine is Stove Top stuffing mix with freeze-dried chicken. All are prone to be bland.

Town food is a huge contrast from what hikers eat on the trail. Frodo's favorite town combo was milkshakes and onion rings—far from her nor-mal fare. Nadine's favorites were a big salad and watermelon—on trail she fantasized about the red flesh and black seeds.

"Did you score any condiments in town?" A deft snatch of a hand at a fast-food restaurant could reap a rich reward. Hikers pocket packets of salt, pepper, ketchup, mustard (yellow or Dijon), mayonnaise, relish, salsa, soy sauce, horseradish, crushed red pepper, and barbecue sauce. Taco Bell's Border Sauces come in three flavors, mild, hot, and fire, all spicing up the one-pot backcountry meal. Then there's olive oil. Many hikers spike every warm meal with olive oil, to load up on calories. Some even add it to oatmeal.

AFTER MCDONALD'S THERE was a long slog as the trail rose into the San Gabriel Mountains. Dalton's birthday was the next day, and Blazer had a plan. Fourteen miles after they crossed under Interstate 15, they camped high on a foggy ridge with Big Cat, another thru-hiker. Dalton woke the next morning to the sound of voices singing. Louder than a rooster's call, Blazer and Big Cat pumped out a rousing version of "Happy Birthday." Then Blazer stuck both hands under Dalton's tent flap. In one hand was a lighter, which she flicked into a birthday candle flame, and in the other was a McDonald's apple pie. Beaming wide, Dalton thought, *This is what it feels like to have a surprise birthday party.* Blazer's effort filled a rare gap in his childhood. As Dalton exited his tent, Blazer thought: *Mission accomplished.* She loved to see Dalton smile.

Seventeen miles and a 2200-foot climb brought them to their next trail town, Wrightwood, population 4000. The handbook advised, "Good place for a zero day." But Blazer's schedule allowed her only a single overnight.

NADINE HAD STARTED her hike a mere six hours after Blazer. She overlapped Blazer in Big Bear City, staying with the boys—Tony, Ryley, and Gaby—on the opposite end of town. Now, twenty-six days after they began the trek, Nadine and Blazer would meet for the first time.

Three days before, Nadine was delayed when the resupply box Lori sent to the Best Western motel near McDonald's was late. The boys hadn't waited, expecting her to catch up later that day. Even with their newly intense bond, Nadine and Tony clung to a thru-hiker's fierce independence, heeding the call to move ever-quickly on.

After 56 miles, Nadine still hadn't caught them. On her third night apart from the boys, she was camping at Cooper Canyon Trail Camp, midway through the San Gabriel Mountains. Unknown to her, Tony, Ryley, and Gaby had set up camp just a few hundred yards ahead.

It had been a long day. All days were long at that time of year—over fifteen hours of daylight. Blazer used all those to hike—fifteen hours lugging ten pounds of water piled on her thirty-plus-pound pack. She had already covered 25 miles on her second day out from Wrightwood—"Another big up, big down, exhausting day," she journaled. Dalton had fallen behind her. She was alone, but on the PCT "alone" is a relative term. Thru-hikers tend to bunch into a loose-knit bulge, and she was about to catch up to "the herd," an ever-moving and changing clutch of hikers near the center of the class of 2007.

When Blazer walked into Cooper Canyon Trail Camp, which a sign described as "primitive," she was pleasantly surprised to see mainly women. Amid the relative luxury of the camp—picnic tables, a seasonal stream, and wide, flat, soft ground—there was a pair she'd heard so much about: Nadine and Pacha—stories about the lone thru-hiking dog were readily passed along.

Blazer's mind raced the moment she saw Nadine set up her and Pacha's tent nearby. *I can barely take care of myself out here*, she thought, *and Nadine is out here hiking with her dog*. From trail scuttlebutt she had built up Nadine as a mysterious superwoman, and Pacha as her steely super dog. Nervous, Blazer snuck sidelong glances from a dozen feet away as she settled into her evening routine. She laid her Tarptent flat to cowboy camp, set each piece of gear in its place, and started doing yoga planks.

Nadine thought, *Incredible, is this woman doing push-ups every evening on the trail?* She noted Blazer's close-cropped hair, her crisp execution, up, down, up, down. Just as with everyone else, Pacha broke the ice, bounding over to Blazer, who dropped down mid-plank and reached out a hand to stroke behind Pacha's ear. Nadine laughed, "Hah!" And with that Blazer relaxed.

Around them were five other women, all 400-trail-mile veterans—Breeze, Sage, Heidi, Munchkin, and Feather—and one guy, D-Bone, out-numbered and quiet. Blazer told her trail name story. Those who had been there regaled Nadine with the Deep Creek Hot Springs fire tale—"We called it the naked bucket brigade." As spirited voices rose and fell, Nadine's laugh boomed off the hills and Blazer's woes blew away like pine needles in the dry breeze. The night could have gone on forever. But tomorrow was another day—20 more miles to hike.

17

Hiker Heaven

HIKERS PACK SO much into short on-trail conversations. "Where is the next water?" "Who left the trail?" "When's your next mail drop resupply?"

Hikers chatter about trail towns: California's Idyllwild, Wrightwood, Sierra City, and Etna, Ashland and Bend in Oregon, and Washington's Trout Lake, Skykomish, and Stehekin. They chatter about danger spots: Fuller Ridge, Forester Pass, Evolution Creek, and the Suiattle River. There's trail chatter about stellar landscapes: the infinite desert views off the San Jacintos, Bighorn Plateau's 360-degree wild Sierra panorama, Crater Lake's impossibly blue water, and Goat Rocks, so grand with its Mount Rainier backdrop that it's memorialized on a US postage stamp. There's trail chatter about the trail angels who open their homes to hikers: Girl Scout, Bob Reiss, and Frodo and me at the start, Joe and Terrie Andersen in Green Valley, Bill "Pooh" Pearson on Donner Lake near Truckee, the Braatens in Belden, Georgie Heitman at Old Station, Lloyd Gust in Bend, Oregon, and, finally, Jerry and Andrea Dinsmore at Skykomish, Washington, only 175 PCT miles from the Canadian border. But in 2007 no place was the subject of greater trail chatter than Agua Dulce, the home of trail angels Donna and Jeff Saufley.

Located 454 trail miles north of the Mexican border, the Saufley's home was only a 45-mile drive northeast from downtown Los Angeles.

Set in jagged-rock high desert, their two-acre compound was outfitted entirely for hikers. They dubbed it Hiker Heaven. No trail destination shy of Canada was more storied.

WITH A DOZEN miles left till Agua Dulce, Blazer's footfalls were picking up speed. This was high desert—the landscape interchangeable with what she'd seen for much of the last four weeks. But she knew today would be different: by midday, she'd reach Hiker Heaven. All week, she'd heard people getting excited about this place, but she had little idea why and was embarrassed to ask. Yogi's handbook said the place was a trail angel's house, but Blazer wasn't sure what to expect. *Do folks really open their home to hikers they've never met before, to hundreds of them, and for no charge at all?* It was hard for Blazer to grasp, and she reacted by tamping down her expectations.

It had been three days since Blazer last saw Dalton. And four days since she'd last showered—four days of alternating between sweat, rest, and sweat again. She was trying not to think about what her skin felt like. Her bare legs jutted from blue Adidas running shorts and looked tan, but they were really just layered in dust, pancaked like rock strata. She knew a shower would work miracles on her skin, and she was equally confident that Dalton would catch her at Agua Dulce. This was the longest she and Dalton had been apart on the trail, and she was surprised by how eager she was to see him.

By late morning Blazer was in the tunnel under the Antelope Valley Freeway, just four miles from Hiker Heaven. Her footfalls echoed in the blessed shade of the high-ceiling culvert as six lanes of traffic roared overhead. When she exited she found the expanse of Vasquez Rocks, a jumble of slanted slabs reaching toward the sky. Nestled low in those rocks, Blazer saw the oddest sight—a six-foot pink snake that looked like a big ball of intestines. The rare rosy boa quickly sensed Blazer and, startled, burrowed out of sight.

Soon enough, after briefly getting lost in a confusing maze of trails, Blazer reached Agua Dulce's outskirts. Following roads as the trail wound through town, a walk that was reminiscent of heading home from school in Kersey, Pennsylvania, she turned left onto Escondido Canyon Road and then took a quick right onto Agua Dulce Canyon Road. She was walking the second-longest road stretch on the PCT, almost four miles. The small hamlet's downtown district featured a "Welcome PCT Hikers" banner hanging from the Sweetwater Grocery. At Darling Road, Blazer turned left off the PCT—in one mile she'd be at Hiker Heaven.

Blazer could hardly believe what she found. The garage had floor-to-ceiling shelves with hundreds of hiker resupply parcels and out back were racks of clean loaner clothes in all sizes. Donna Saufley personally did every hiker's laundry. There were ten separate hiker boxes, organized by category: shoes, clothing, gear, fuel, toiletries, and maps and books, toys, and three boxes of food. She would soon learn that you could find just about anything in the Saufley hiker boxes, including, once, a live goldfish in a plastic bag. Out back was the ranch house—the Saufleys' sole private space—and a two-bedroom single-wide trailer, a twenty-one-foot RV camper, and six twenty-foot-by-ten-foot catering tents with thirty-six cots that housed the visiting hikers.

The trailer, more suited to a mobile home park than a backyard, was well equipped. In addition to the bathroom and shower, it had two bedrooms, a full kitchen, and a living room with a large couch, as well as two computers, a television, two phones for hikers, an upright piano, and hanging on the wall, a guitar. All the Saufleys' water—for washing clothes and taking long showers—came from one three-thousand-gallon tank, with a new load trucked in daily during the height of hiker season. It was all free to hikers; Donna and Jeff dipped into their pocketbook and a deep reservoir of love. This massive operation, in organization and scope, was unparalleled anywhere else on the PCT.

It was here that Blazer allowed herself a gift. She was going to take a zero day, the only one she'd allow herself to take over the 520 miles from Idyllwild to Kennedy Meadows, a month of hiking. But, like a pulsing migraine, Blazer's deadline demanded attention. *Whatever it takes, I'll be there.* Soon Dalton hiked in and, with the flash of his smile, Blazer finally began to let go. Dalton unlimbered his Martin guitar. She felt as close to comfortable as she had for a long time.

Late afternoon found Blazer resting on her cot, amazingly clean, full of town food, and with her thrashed body on the mend. She was sharing the high-roofed, white canvas tent with five others. The front flaps were tied open, giving her a direct view of the nearby campfire circle surrounded by ten bales of hay. Beyond that were barbecues, chairs and tables, and bicycles for hikers to borrow. If that wasn't enough, on the street the Saufleys had two loaner cars—hikers only had to provide the gas.

FRODO AND I were well settled into Hiker Heaven by the time Blazer arrived; we'd taken long showers and Donna had washed our filthy clothes. But even before showering I'd spotted the guitar hanging on the wall of the trailer. It called to me for much of the day before I finally brought it outside to tune it. Blazer was twenty feet away in her tent when she heard me pluck the strings one by one. Sitting on that hay bale, I wasn't aware of anyone. Stretching fingers that hadn't handled a guitar for a month, I thought of my own guitar back home. I quietly lit into a late-'60s standard, "Leaving on a Jet Plane." "All my bags are packed, I'm ready to go . . ." What I really hoped was that any hikers listening might come over and sing along.

Blazer's ears perked up. She had been watching me from her cot and immediately recognized the tune. She knew all the words, not just the chorus, and, unconsciously, her lips began to move. Sitting up, she was hit by a wave of exhaustion. The weight of the 270 miles she'd hiked over the fourteen days since Idyllwild rooted her to her cot. *Should I get up and join in? That's Scout playing, isn't it? But I'm so tired*, she thought with resignation. *If I get up and join in, I'll just embarrass myself.*

THREE HOURS BEFORE Blazer, Nadine arrived at Hiker Heaven with Pacha and the three boys. She caught them the morning after she'd first met Blazer. That day they'd celebrated Gaby's twenty-first birthday, with Ryley whipping out a can of Guinness he'd been carrying for 50 miles.

Here at the Saufleys', Nadine was once again experiencing PCT déjà vu. She'd first met Donna in 1998, in the days when Donna would head into town searching for hikers. She'd stopped Nadine and her boyfriend on the street and offered them a place to stay. That was the second year that

Donna and Jeff hosted hikers, and Nadine and Will were the only ones there. Back then, the total number of thru-hikers didn't even come close to one hundred.

While the scope of the operation had become huge, Nadine thought Donna hadn't really changed all that much. She was still trim and pert, with short-cropped brown hair that fit in with the hiking crowd. Donna remained a no-nonsense gal, but Nadine observed she would drop everything to help a hiker who expressed even a small need. Donna mothered all, whether the hiker was twenty-one or sixty-five. But one thing had changed about Donna in the intervening years: she'd acquired a trail name—Lightning Rod, or L-Rod.

At Hiker Heaven, Nadine focused on the serious tasks of town chores and resupplying; she also found herself watching Tony closely. This frat-like hiker bunch-up generated a frothy party atmosphere. When hikers headed to the store they often returned with six-packs to share, and Nadine had hoisted her own. Watching Tony, she wondered, *He's eighteen years clean and sober. Does this ever tempt him?* Nadine, for her part, was beginning to experience the faint stirring of a long-lost craving, brought on by the never-ending sizzle of beef on the Saufley's barbecues. Worse, she was going to Agua Dulce's Mexican restaurant for dinner, where the air would be redolent with spiced carne asada. She still mouthed off often about her constant state of hunger, but unlike her 1998 boyfriend, Tony never once pressed her about eating red meat.

THE WOOD OF the guitar felt good in my hands, but I was unusually nervous. Each summer for three years, I'd stood on the All Nations lodge porch and faced down a hundred yawning campers hungry for breakfast. The last thing on their minds was singing with sleep-scratchy throats. Yet in moments I'd have them serenading the day in a loud, joyous chorus. At night, I'd walk into a still-rowdy cabin of early teens, sit on an empty bunk, and start playing. So few of those kids ever got tucked into bed at home. Fewer still had parents sing to them, whether it be "Blowin' in the Wind" or "Puff the Magic Dragon." I can still feel the wonder of that moment, when squirming and giggling died down, and the silence of rhythmic breathing began. Two things I love most: voices rising with mine in melody and singing others quietly to sleep with a guitar. So how could I sit there with a guitar feeling nervous?

In the month since I last played at home, I'd grown a half-inch-long salt-and-pepper beard. The backs of both my hands bore trail scratches that resembled spiderwebs. Yet my right hand still had a set of carefully maintained, eighth-inch nails, perfect for strumming. On my thigh I felt the full weight of the guitar pressing on a nasty cut, a souvenir from when I'd tripped on a tree root a day out of Wrightwood.

But I wasn't thinking of the pain from the two-inch gash on my leg, or the lack of sleep over the past nights, as I started in on "Leaving on a Jet Plane." I was thinking, *If I sing, will anyone notice? Will anyone join in? Everything I play is so mired in the late sixties and early seventies. They're all so much younger. What might they know?*

I saw Bull look up from his gear. Built like a college lineman, Bull had two ball-bearing studs that thrust out from his lower lip. He's a carica-ture of the person you don't want to meet in a dark alley, but scratch that hard exterior and underneath is a gentle soul. Twentysomething Bull was newly married to City Girl, his slender-as-a-rail opposite. Whereas Bull had thru-hiked the Appalachian Trail, City Girl's first night sleep-ing outdoors was their first night on the PCT. Their unlikely adventure had started less than a year ago, when City Girl found out she was preg-nant. The two had laid out a life full of extensive plans centered around their new baby. But City Girl miscarried, leaving a gaping, empty space. They filled it with Bull's dream—thru-hiking the PCT. Now 450 miles into their PCT hike, Bull got up from his cot, came over, and sat on a hay bale. I watched as he moved his mouth along with the song.

Out There was next. Near my age, he came over and sat beside Frodo on a hay bale covered by a horse blanket. Then came Cloudspotter and Mr. Smiles. If PCT hikers had a BWOC—Big Woman on Campus—in 2007, that woman was Cloudspotter. She was two years younger than Blazer, outgoing to a fault, had thru-hiked the John Muir Trail the pre-vious summer, and was always organizing something. Mr. Smiles, a retired high school band director, had dreamed of this hike for years.

They didn't know all the words, but with little urging on my part, they all joined in at the first chorus. My gaze drifted over the shoulders of

Frodo and Out There—there was movement on another cot. *I know that girl. Didn't I meet her at McDonald's? What is her name?*

BLAZER LOOKED DOWN, feeling embarrassed that she wanted to sing. It was a beautiful moment and she wanted to be there, but it took more motivation than she had. *The other hikers are so awesome,* she thought. Some had been at the Saufleys' two or three days, and acted like brothers and sisters. In the crowd, Blazer was so uncertain about how to fit in. She had heard others talk about the two of us, Scout and Frodo, just like she'd heard others talk about Nadine. Something about us reminded Blazer of the friends' homes she'd hung out in, the ones with parents she'd pretend were her own. She saw Frodo, singing and looking at me from close by.

Then something of the spirit of hiking 450 miles kicked in. *I walked here just like everyone else.* Blazer got up and met my gaze with a soft smile, different from the sassy smile I'd seen at McDonald's. I hoped that Blazer saw the gratitude shine from my eyes as she sat on a hay bale next to Out There and joined in with a strong alto voice. When she looked at me for a brief moment, I saw the eyes of my own children when I tucked them into bed.

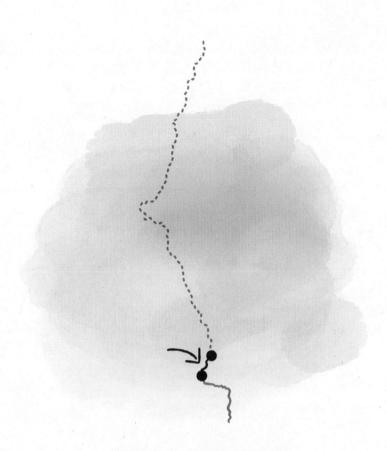

DIRT

Agua Dulce to Walker Pass

203 miles

18

Hikertown

WHEN SHE LEFT Agua Dulce, Blazer had felt like a million bucks. But her confident air soon dissipated, just as the desert's furnace heat vanished the moment the sun dropped. All too soon, she reverted to her negative mantra: *My feet hurt, I'm hungry, I'm thirsty.* Her Kennedy Meadows deadline was grabbing her by the throat, and the landscape wasn't helping. Yogi's handbook uses capital letters and three exclamation points to sum up the 250-mile stretch from Agua Dulce to Kennedy Meadows: "WARNING!!! The hike out of Agua Dulce is dreadfully hot. This hot, hot, hot hiking continues until you reach Kennedy Meadows." The guidebook was like a second vulture tearing the same rotten flesh: "The Mojave Desert stretch of the PCT can broil your mind, blister your feet, and turn your mouth to dust." Sky islands had broken up the desert before this, but now it felt like the mountains had up and fled. We hikers lived for the moment the shadows lengthened, which presaged the moment it finally cooled down enough to crawl into our sleeping bags.

IN THE DESERT, Frodo and I carried our two-pound Squall 2 Henry Shires Tarptent, but in the High Sierra and the North Cascades we would carry our bombproof four-pound Big Agnes Seedhouse SL3. Most hikers didn't have the luxury of alternating tents, but courtesy of our daughter Jordie and the US Postal Service, we could swap scrunched shoulders for more headroom, bug protection for open air.

Twice in the desert Blazer and Dalton had shared his Marmot EOS single-person tent, cramming themselves under its narrow canopy. With the pair having agreed to straightjacket their hormones, such tight quarters tested their platonic pledge.

Tony and Nadine had us all beat. On nights when wind or mosquitoes drove them inside, Nadine's Seedhouse SLI resembled a circus clown car with the two of them and Pacha, plus their three packs, meshed together like well-folded origami. At seven feet long and close to a yardstick wide and tall, it was essentially the same size as the average funeral casket. There was no platonic pledge to heed—one night when we camped nearby Frodo and I heard their giggling—but narrow confines can test any relationship, especially one only a few weeks old.

SIXTY-FIVE MILES AFTER Hiker Heaven, the PCT entered the Mojave Desert. Highway 138 was the official transition, but what signaled the start of the Mojave for hikers was one of the oddest resupply stops on the entire trail: Hikertown. The six of us passed through over three successive days, first Frodo and me, then Blazer and Dalton, and finally, Tony and Nadine.

Hikertown was a desert retreat on a large lot, a pale yellow ranch house with a front yard and a white picket fence encircling a mulberry tree with grubbing ducks and roosters that crowed at any hour. Hikertown was a twenty-plus motor vehicle museum, with a spit-and-polish 1950s Rolls Royce, a red Ferrari, and a forklift. Hikertown was a seedy back-lot western movie set, reduced to three-quarter-size, so that a four-foot-tall Wyatt Earp would feel right at home. Sometimes Hikertown's owner was there. Sometimes only the caretaker. Sometimes they charged to stay. Other times not. We slept in the front yard along with the restless fowl.

Frodo and I had arrived in the evening after a 22-mile day and lit out before sunrise. Over the next 16 miles, the PCT crossed a wide finger of the Mojave Desert. Farther northeast was Death Valley, an arm of the Mojave, which not only holds North America's crown for the lowest and driest place, but also holds the world record for extreme heat, 134 degrees. Neenach, a farming community a mile from Hikertown, had a record high of *only* 114 degrees.

All the while I was dripping sweat and thinking, *We've come 500 miles, why are we still coping with blisters?* At every break I lanced both my blisters and Frodo's—she called me Dr. Blister. I had press-ganged a sewing needle into serving double duty, dipping the point in our alcohol fuel bottle, and carefully, forcefully, piercing the edge of a swollen bubble. Some popped like geysers and others had to be squeezed. What pained Frodo worst were those blisters under her toenails, each a harbinger of a blackened toenail that would fall off in a few months. She practically sighed with relief after I drilled one. Our socks were sweat soaked, even though we aired them and our feet out at least once an hour. The Mojave grit chafed puckered skin inside shoes that felt like toaster ovens. It didn't matter that our feet were already callused, when confronted with this frying-pan desert floor.

Finally, having seen only two other hikers all day, we arrived at the Cottonwood Creek Bridge, the end of the Mojave on the PCT. We took another break, tended our blisters, and then trudged on into the dark, heading into the Tehachapi Mountains. Scalding heat blisters, shoulder and hip pain from packs, scratches, cuts and bruises, chafed skin, joints and muscles complaining from constant overuse—you have to really want to be out there to hike on.

BLAZER ARRIVED IN Hikertown hours ahead of Dalton. Tired and fully absorbed with hewing to her brother's deadline, she went to sleep early, planning to start at 4:00 a.m. Around her clumps of thru-hikers slept, scattered across the grounds. Dalton huffed in late, well past hiker midnight. He set up camp quietly, to keep from disturbing the other sleeping forms, and didn't notice Blazer. He was still asleep when Blazer headed out before dawn the next morning, her eyes focused on the circle of light cast by her headlamp.

IRONY IS UNCOMMON on the PCT, but on this section it takes a baton and beats hikers senseless. Directly under us in the Mojave was a river sufficient to quench an entire city's thirst, the gargantuan pipes of the Los Angeles Aqueduct. In the 1970s, PCT hikers lifted the covers off the aqueduct's intermittent access manholes, climbed down steel pegs, and stole

L.A.'s finest. They weren't in danger of dehydration; they were in danger of drowning. Now the covers were locked, so we carried over ten pounds of water apiece, all the while listening to that cold flow gurgling southward.

Midday found Blazer and two dozen other scruffy hikers crammed under the Cottonwood Creek Bridge, the only significant shade in this scorching landscape. Despite its name, the dry gulch showed no evidence of cottonwoods, let alone water. Yet, one of Blazer's companions journaled that "without that bridge I think we all would have died." In the shade of the bridge, Blazer's thermometer topped one hundred degrees, but when she held it in the sun for a moment the poor device redlined, having maxed out at 120 degrees. As the sun slowly moved throughout the day, the shade moved across the ground. Hikers on the west side, eventually finding themselves back in the sun's rays, would then pick up and move their gear twenty feet east. It was a slow, macabre dance, a dystopian tango, repeated so many times Blazer lost count.

One pleasant surprise intervened; Dalton caught up. With cracked lips and sweating faces there wasn't much talking, but the two were content to share weary smiles. Finally, around 6:00 p.m., the temperature back in the nineties, Blazer broke free from her six-hour confinement under the bridge. The two hiked out together, taking it slow. Dalton was trying to hide that he'd started to favor one foot, but her professional eye saw it right away. He was grateful that Blazer wasn't pushing the pace. They hiked nine more miles before calling it quits. The moon rose, fat and bright, sharpening the hard edges of the stark landscape. It was Blazer's second full moon on the trail.

ALMOST FROM THE get-go, Nadine and Tony were at cross-purposes about food. For him, no trail meal was complete without a side of junk food, while Nadine's on-trail culinary watchwords were "healthy" and "vegetarian." But Tony never needled Nadine about meat, even though he knew she was beginning to have cravings. An incident with a trail angel put a temporary end to that.

At a desert trailhead, a trail angel had appeared with a passel of McDonald's chicken sandwiches to give away. The smell of fresh white bread and fried patties wafted through the air. Tony and others wolfed down the fast food. It had been days since the last town stop and would be days more till the next. Nadine found herself picking one up. She cradled it, unwrapping the crinkled, grease-stained paper, then took one bite. Next thing she knew that first one was gone and she had a second in her hands. She ate that just as fast. They tasted greasy and wonderful, then merely good, and finally she was left with a thick, cloying aftertaste.

When she and Tony hiked on, however, the two sandwiches started a wrestling match in her stomach. They stayed with her for about two hours, when she vomited the partially digested food into a scrub oak.

19

Tehachapi

PITY THE TEHACHAPIS. If these mountains had been set in Blazer's home state, Pennsylvania, or anywhere on the East Coast for that matter, they would be celebrated, the stuff that national parks are made of. The range's peaks dwarf Mount Mitchell, the highest mountain east of the Mississippi, by a thousand feet. The Tehachapis' curse is to abut the south end of the Sierra Nevada, lost in its shadow. No John Muir, Ansel Adams, or Teddy Roosevelt championed these mountains.

Where's the trail? Blazer thought. *This was supposed to be easier.* Blazer and Dalton had climbed out of the Mojave into the Tehachapi Mountains, and were traversing barren, eroded slopes. The ensuing tripping and sliding wasn't helping Dalton's foot. Dirt bike tracks crisscrossed the trail, obliterating it in places. Worse, most trail signs were defaced or plain missing. The guidebook fingered the culprit, noting that there once had been ample "brown PCT posts, but some dirt-bikers have made a project of uprooting them."

For 24 miles, from the Cottonwood Creek Bridge to Tehachapi–Willow Springs Road, Blazer and Dalton trudged through these mountains. An incessant wind set their teeth on edge and they passed a second time through miles of wind farms. Surrounded by what felt like thousands of turbine towers, Blazer and Dalton endured an ear-cringing, aural assault—humming generators, buffeting gusts, and a psychotic whir from a legion of blades.

TEHACHAPI WAS THE next trail town. With a population of 14,500—triple that of Big Bear City—it was by far the biggest town Blazer had seen in five weeks. It even had a multiplex theater and a Kmart.

By sheer coincidence, while Frodo and I were dropping off a cooler of drinks for hikers at the Tehachapi–Willow Springs Road trailhead, Dalton and then Blazer hiked in. The day before, my cousin Linda had driven the two hours north from Los Angeles and had waited to meet us at the trailhead with our van. Linda was staying the weekend, so we had wheels in town.

Effusive and grating—that was Dalton's first impression of me. Thankfully he waited a week to share the thought. We chatted briefly at the trailhead and then Blazer popped out. It had been six days since we'd sung together at Hiker Heaven—that had made my day—and I was so excited to see her that Dalton felt like a third wheel.

Tehachapi has two claims to fame. Arriving hikers were already quite intimate with one—those five thousand wind turbines on the surrounding windswept slopes. Once in town, big-throated blasts heralded the second: Tehachapi is home to one of the "seven wonders of the railroad world." In the 1870s, Southern Pacific Railroad engineers faced an impossible uphill grade. In an exercise of brute strength, three thousand Chinese laborers with picks, shovels, and blasting powder cut a four-thousand-foot-long upward spiral, the Tehachapi Loop, a circular track that crosses over on the top of itself. Railroad buffs from all over the world make the pilgrimage to Tehachapi just to see it. Dozens of times a day, often with railroad buffs taking photos, an engineer on a pulsing diesel exits the loop and looks down at his train's rear cars directly below.

With limited lodging options, Blazer and Dalton stayed at the Best Western motel. Blazer parted with a twenty-dollar bill for one night to share a room near ours with Dalton and two others. The time crunch was on; no zero day here. She'd hiked 14 miles today and would hike at least that the next. Somehow, in between, she'd squeeze in all her town chores.

In Tehachapi, Blazer made time for something besides town chores—something that she and Dalton would hide from their roommates. She'd seen his limp, no matter how hard he'd tried to keep it from her. Alone in their motel room, Blazer set her hands on Dalton—the tools of her trade were always with her. Callused and strong, her hands were now covered in a maze of healing cuts and, even after showering, the dirt in her knuckles was ground deep. But Blazer's fingernails were town-clean and neatly clipped. She asked Dalton the same questions she would have asked a patient: "Where exactly does it hurt? Describe and rate the pain." After listening to his answers, she went to work.

She didn't think about failing her licensing tests, or whether anyone would find out. Silently, working her fingers, Blazer tried to communicate with her touch—*Dalton, I've grown to love you. I'm so grateful for your company on the trail.* Just as silently Blazer gave a gift to herself: self-respect.

SOMETIMES WHEN FRODO and I took a break on the trail, she'd lay her head in my lap or nestle in against my shoulder. It wasn't just that touch is wonderful per se, and it wasn't just that we'd both come into the world hardwired to need it, but out here—in a land with no couches, cushions, or beds—we each were the softest thing available. As skinny as I was— and I was getting bonier by the day—if she wanted something soft to lean against outside of town, I was the only game around.

One morning in the desert, I thought to myself, *What's the most ridiculous question I can ask her?* Frodo and I hadn't spoken for a half hour, our feet moving rhythmically but mechanically, sweat blossoming with the first brush of warm air, thighs sticking together and underarms a gluey mix of grit and perspiration. We'd already hiked three miles that day, and were slogging in the loose sand of a dry wash. We needed a pick-me-up, and— even though I knew her answer would be zero—at least I'd get a laugh. "How many times have you thought about sex this morning?" I asked. She didn't even turn her head as she called back, "Three times."

After thirty years, she still surprises me. From that day on, at random times, both in front of others and on our own, I'd say, "So, how many times today?" Frodo would chuckle and give an answer. Did other hikers ever wonder about it? Blazer surely heard Frodo giggle at the question at least half a dozen times.

"A HALF POUND," I said. Frodo interjected, "No, get him a pound." At Tehachapi's Rocky Mountain Chocolate Factory, we bought Ryley a brick of fudge for his twenty-seventh birthday. Frodo insisted we get him enough to share with the three others in his room at the Best Western: Gaby, Tony, and Nadine. Blazer and Dalton had just checked out to hike more miles, but Frodo and I, in sheer decadence—and to build up battered bodies and spirits—were taking a second zero day in Tehachapi.

While Blazer and Dalton hitched back to the trail and started up a 3000-foot climb, Frodo and I went to the movies. Ryley, Gaby, and twenty other hikers joined us, taking up at least half the seats at a late-afternoon showing of *Pirates of the Caribbean: At World's End*. Our fellow moviegoers were clad in clean but sweat-stained shirts or in rain jackets as their clothes twirled at the laundromat; scruffy beards were abundant. We occupied whole rows, calling out to each other across the parlor-size Hitching Post theater. As we waited for the movie to start, Frodo asked Ryley and Gaby how they had liked the fudge. Ryley looked embarrassed—in the three hours since we'd given Ryley his birthday brick, he'd downed the whole thing.

Moments before the lights dimmed for coming attractions, a woman—nicely dressed, obviously from the town—sitting in the row behind us leaned over. She whispered, "What is all this, some kind of club?"

FRODO AND I always got a room for ourselves, so I once asked Tony how he and Nadine worked out sharing a room with two guys. "Do you arrange some sign with Ryley and Gaby? Hang a towel in the window, put your shoes on the front step upside down?"

"We never spoke about it," Tony said, "but surely they must have thought we need to give these two some space because otherwise they're just going to have sex right in front of us." Gaby and Ryley were with us at the movie; Tony and Nadine were not.

THE MONEY'S RUNNING *out.* Luigi was frantic as he went through Tehachapi's neon-lit Kmart, a jarring juxtaposition to the trail's sage, juniper, and mountain mahogany. A wan smile crossed his and his brother Mario's faces as they found Top Ramen packets priced twelve for $2.99. But even as they scrimped and the food in their shopping cart rose, the dream of a complete thru-hike faded. There was no mistake—funds were in a tail-spin. Kmart was a salve, not salvation. Could anything save the rest of their hike?

Frodo and I saw the shopping cart emerge from Kmart. We recognized the off-kilter, this-is-my-only-shirt look. *Thru-hikers*. Twice before, we'd seen these young brothers, both near twenty, as youthful as Gaby but narrow faced and lean bodied. The older was bearded and short-haired. The younger was clean-shaven with stringy, shoulder-length hair. One day, early on the trail, both wore T-shirts—one was a Nintendo print and the other *Super Mario Bros*. Hence their trail names, Luigi and Mario. While Blazer hiked on a shoestring budget, the Mario Brothers were doing it on a single thread. In thirty-five days, Blazer had spent a grand total of eighty dollars on lodging, four twenty-dollar nights sharing a single bed. As long as Mario and Luigi could camp, they didn't stay in towns. They avoided zero days and went to great lengths to stretch out their money. Their only goal was to stay on the trail.

20

Trail Magic

"WHERE CAN I help you guys?" Dan asked in 2006, a year before we started the PCT. "I have a Jeep. I'll go anywhere." Dan Gizzo, thirty-three, lived in San Diego. We'd been Boy Scout leaders together.

Frodo consulted maps, conferred with me, and we replied a few days later. "Dan, meet us north of Tehachapi and south of Walker Pass at a dirt jeep track called Road SC47. Make us one of your famous homemade Italian dinners. There may be more than two of us."

It was spare high desert where Road SC47 intersected the PCT, 65 miles past Tehachapi and 26 miles before Walker Pass. Army Rangers might hone their survival skills in this moonscape. It was all hard-baked shades of tan, dotted with shaggy Joshua trees and with scattered dirt truck trails that might not see a single vehicle in an entire week. The spot was 15 miles into a 20-mile waterless stretch. And it was only 20 waterless miles thanks to two man-made water caches. Otherwise, it was 35.5 waterless miles.

Even before reaching Tehachapi, Frodo and I had put out the word: "Trail Magic—Mile 625.9—Italian dinner—2:00 to 5:00 p.m., Wednesday, June 6." Soon after my cousin Linda picked us up in Tehachapi, we called Dan Gizzo to warn him: "Plan on two to fifteen." After we attended the movie in Tehachapi with Ryley, Gaby, and the rest, we called Dan again: "Plan on two to twenty." I told Dan I'd give him the money for this feast. Even over the phone I felt his glare—I wasn't going to mention paying for his trail magic again.

It took us two hard-charging 22-mile days out of Tehachapi, with significant sweat-drenching climbs, to get within fighting distance of where we'd meet Dan the next day. That was the price we paid for our town days.

Everyone rose early, whether they had 16 miles to go like us, 14, 18, or, in the case of Gaby and Ryley, 24. Even the closest of us would have to hoof it to get there by 2:00 p.m. Gaby and Ryley started walking at 4:45 a.m. Far to the south of us in San Diego, Dan Gizzo and his compatriots rose earlier still.

By the time Ryley and Gaby started hiking, Dan had been loading his Jeep for forty-five minutes. He'd enlisted his brother Joe, so they made a two-vehicle assault team. Olive skinned with strong chins, both men were as playful as forest elves. In front of Dan's house, his Jeep and his brother's Hummer sat with doors and tailgates open like gaping maws.

In the dark, Dan's wife, Monica, had watched the loading through sleep-rimmed eyes. "It won't fit," she said, glancing from the open Jeep and Hummer to the stacks of supplies. The night before, she'd said the same thing when she measured four gallons of homemade marinara sauce against their Tupperware supply. Joe piled boxes in willy-nilly while Dan carefully placed each one, assembling a 3-D jigsaw puzzle visible only to him. In addition to banquet tables, Coleman stoves, and a dozen folding chairs, the pile included a tow chain, shovel, and wooden blocks just in case he spun out in the sand. On the seat of the Jeep lay a map with a large circle around the junction of the Pacific Crest Trail and Road SC47. Uncharacteristic of Dan, they were running late.

The hike to the rendezvous was through wind-whipped sand, and even in the desert sun, jackets and watch caps were the norm. Every canyon notch funneled the wind into bulldozer gusts. Blazer found she had to run through each one to keep moving forward, ducking her head to lower her profile. At least twice I reached out to grab Frodo to steady her in the wind. By 1:00 p.m., the scene on the PCT at Road SC47 looked like a refugee camp. We huddled in patches of shade in the windbreak of a tight clump of Joshua trees, with our dirt-streaked faces and weathered satchels.

At that moment, the going was getting rough for the Jeep and Hummer. They'd left smooth pavement, hurtling boldly onto the first of six dirt roads. First it was merely bumpy, but then they hit the first deep gully— gear went flying, the marinara sauce spilled, and a shovel hit Dan's head. Next they got lost. It took miles to get back on track, but finally they entered that scrawled circle on the map. Dan and Joe saw figures crawling out from scraggly brush. Standing taller than the rest, I waved my arms wildly. And Dan said, "There's my old friend, Scout."

In minutes, the Jeep and Hummer were fully unloaded. With the scratch of a match and *whoosh* of pressurized gas, the Coleman stoves started humming, and the temperature rose in commercial-kitchen-size pots, one for the pasta and one for the marinara sauce. Yard-wide bowls of salad, veggies, and fresh fruit and a wickerwork basket of fresh rolls with butter filled the banquet tables. Cooler lids opened again and again, yielding up beer, soda, juices, and water. I'd last told Dan to expect twenty, but twenty-four thru-hikers were here. Even Ryley and Gaby made it. They'd never before hiked 24 miles in a single day, much less by 2:00 p.m. Basin after basin of sauce and pasta flowed off the Colemans. Blazer discovered how good cherry tomatoes and grapes tasted together in a single bite. "Oh, you must try it," she said.

A football emerged from the Jeep and an impromptu touch football game started. But it soon ended when the ball got stuck on a yucca spike. Out There approached Dan and asked if he could buy his hat, after his had literally blown away that morning. Dan took his hat off and gave it to him.

In no time at all Dan felt these strangers were family. As hikers jostled around the tables, setting up the banquet and pitching in, he saw how much they looked out for each other—no one wanted to eat first. He envied the fraternity and thought, *I want to hike on with them.* Watching Frodo and me, Dan was so happy to see his good friends basking in the experience of thru-hiking. *As long as I live, I will never forget this meal in the dust and wind.*

With the football flat, four gallons of marinara sauce gone, platters of fruit consumed, and the roll basket empty, we took a group photo. Ten of us posed in front of Joe's silver Hummer with Blazer stretched out across the hood. At her feet, Dalton kneeled, bare-legged in shorts, jacket on, red hair flung about wildly by a gust. We all wore large, full-bellied smiles.

And then it was over. At 5:15 p.m., the same trail-hardened hands loaded everything back into the two vehicles. Afterward hikers hoisted packs, left the Joshua tree windbreak, and met the gale that had built up while they'd been eating. Joe and Dan drove off, dust clouds dissipating so quickly it was as if they'd been a mirage, but for the food still warm in our bellies. The site looked as it had that morning. Like fabled Brigadoon, Dan and Joe's Bistro Gizzo shone, faded, and was no more.

It was five long miles to Bird Spring Pass, the next campsite and hoped-for windbreak. Blazer, even with her jacket tightly zipped, felt the nylon beating a violent tattoo. Anything loose in the air, whether grit, sand, or hair, flew horizontal to the ground, defying gravity. Blazer stayed close to Dalton, the pair trying to make headway together.

DRINK, DRINK, DRINK. Keeping hydrated was so important, and doubly hard in the desert. The harsh winds made it harder, wicking moisture away. To carry water, thru-hikers used Camelbaks, Platypuses, and soda bottles, only rarely carrying that backcountry staple, the wide-mouth, thick-walled Nalgene bottle. Camelbaks and Platypuses are water bladders, card-stock-thick plastic bags that expand when filled and when empty fold down to almost nothing. A two-quart Platypus bag weighs just over an ounce. A one-quart Nalgene bottle is four times that weight. A quart soda bottle weighs about the same as a Platypus. Thru-hikers have to drink often, much more often than they take breaks. The bite valve—the end point of a straw-diameter tube that is squeezed with the teeth—is one easy means to do so. The tube runs from the bladder in the backpack over a hiker's shoulder. Water on tap—almost as good as home.

TEN MILES BACK, Tony and Nadine had settled in, and were making one-pot meals over tiny alcohol stoves. Tony had instant mashed potatoes and Nadine had angel hair pasta that she'd spiced up with a sliced clove of garlic. Tony chased down his meal with a Snickers bar and Pringles potato chips. That night they read out loud to each other from The Long Walk by Slavomir Rawicz. It's a survivor's account of an escape from a Siberian Soviet Gulag camp and the escapees' subsequent 3000-mile walk to India. The scenes traversing the Gobi Desert particularly intrigued them.

Tony read a description aloud that could have been the two of them under the Cottonwood Creek Bridge, "We sweated it out for about three hours in throbbing discomfort, mouths open, gasping in the warm desert air over enlarged, dust-covered tongues." But as much as they related to the story, what they really enjoyed was listening to the sound of each other's voice.

Like the *Long Walk's* hero, both of them had lost weight. Nadine was down nearly ten pounds, Tony almost fifteen, but the one in the worst shape couldn't speak about it at all. Pacha had thinned and was showing real signs of suffering.

Once before, Nadine had considered taking Pacha off the trail. It was around mile 200, on a zero day, while visiting a friend's house in Palm Springs. They had plied Nadine with margaritas and Pacha with burgers. After eating, Pacha lay on the floor and didn't move for twenty-four hours. Nadine thought she was broken. Thankfully on the second day, Pacha got up and started running around like herself. But now, three days out of Tehachapi, her condition was deteriorating. She'd started giving Nadine a nasty look when she put her pack on. Nadine thought Pacha needed a long rest, an idea she brought up with Tony. He described the game Pacha had started playing with him, her "I'm hurt" trick. She'd act hurt and then Tony would carry her for a while. But when he set her down, she'd be off chasing the first lizard.

Tony, Nadine, and Pacha had been pounding out 22-to-25-mile days. This was what Tony wanted, but discussing Pacha's condition cut him to the quick. He loved that dog, no matter what he'd once thought about dogs on the trail. She seemed at home in the wild, with other hikers and especially with Tony. He felt increasingly torn. Finding Nadine and hiking with her had filled a hole he'd felt since parting with his wife. But he'd promised himself that he wasn't going to repeat what he'd done on the Appalachian Trail. He wasn't going to hike slow and dawdle.

He wasn't opposed to a zero day but he wasn't going to take multiple zeros in a row to hang out with friends, especially given the hard deadline of Tarik's wedding date. But often when he tried to talk about it with Nadine, it felt like a third person was in the conversation, as if Nadine wasn't talking to him, but to her ex-boyfriend from 1998. And it riled him when Nadine would say something like, "You're doing it the wrong way," or, "You're not stopping and looking around." Tony wanted to help Pacha, but he wanted her old boyfriend off his back and he wanted to make his miles.

Nadine's feet were really hurting—more so than at any other time on the trek. When she took her shoes off, Pacha would nuzzle her feet. She underplayed the issue in her blog: "The new shoes that I picked up in Tehachapi were a half size too small which didn't become a problem until the second or third day out." She was about to ditch them and hike 50 miles in her Crocs, lightweight plastic clogs usually reserved for camp.

21
Night at Walker Pass

BLAZER AND DALTON arrived at Walker Pass at 5:00 p.m. with 21 miles under their belts. Blazer was desperate to stop, but there were still 50 hard miles between her and Kennedy Meadows. In a day and a half she was supposed to meet Ian and Scott there, and then attack the Sierra Nevada. But with screaming feet, Blazer was tempted to rest before crossing Highway 178, one of the handful of paved roads since the Saufleys'.

Rest wasn't the only thing tempting her—there was also trail magic. Three trail angels had set up camp chairs, snacks, and coolers—beer, cola, and juice—at the small Walker Pass campground. There was excited chatter as they walked in. "We're almost out of the desert." "In the Sierra Nevada there will be water everywhere." With every fiber she wanted to stay the night, but she felt compelled to press on. *I should get in five more miles before dusk. Get that hard climb out of the way as the sun goes down.*

Voices around her joshed like schoolchildren on recess. Everyone was so relaxed and awash in good cheer—and the pile of empty beer cans was only partially responsible. On that last crest, before dropping to Walker Pass, the promised land, the Sierra Nevada, was arrayed before them. Crossing that ridge, they'd enjoyed a brief splash of Jeffrey pines and black oaks before the trail thrust them back into the hot embrace of sage and chaparral.

Blazer unbuckled her pack and dropped it. Her dirt-streaked fingers pried her damp shirt away from her sweaty skin. Once bright blue, it now bore permanent grime, with stains to rival a dirty bathtub. Darkened concentric circles plastered her back, underarms, and collar. Dalton's shirt was the same.

Not for the first time, Blazer thought, *Ian's deadline is so harsh*. As impossible as the deadline seemed, it held one saving grace—it smothered her other woes like dirt shoveled on a campfire. Failing to pass the state exams: buried. Worrying about money: buried. Telling anyone besides Dalton about her career. Making it to Canada. Her father's phone call. That Ian was only her half brother. All buried. With her horizon pulled in so tight, she couldn't see past the next two days.

But what lay underneath it all, behind the stoutest stone wall, deeper than a Stygian cave, was that frozen image of a fourteen-year-old. Some part of Blazer was always linked to that budding, pixie-faced girl, and what happened to her. Two words, a poison worse than nightshade or hemlock; two words that could curl the hairs on the back of her neck: *Kaulmont Park*.

As tired and conflicted as she was, Blazer's heart still pulsed thru-hiker blood and she wasn't going to ignore the trail magic bounty. Just one cold drink, not beer—after all, she still had to hike out. She hoped that a jolt of cold refreshment might shift her mindset, but it utterly failed. Even thoughts of Kennedy Meadows weren't enough to stir her.

Kennedy Meadows is legendary on the PCT—the gateway to the High Sierra. Beyond it are hundreds of miles of snow-filled passes, cascading streams, dangerous river crossings, soaring crags, and slab-sided granite peaks. But for Blazer, Kennedy Meadows meant one thing—the deadline that hung like a millstone round her neck.

JOHN C. FRÉMONT, explorer of the American West, was so well known he was called "The Pathfinder." Kit Carson, Frémont's lead scout, was perhaps more famous still. He's the subject of a dozen books, including *Kit Carson and the American Frontier* and *Blood and Thunder: The Epic Story of Kit Carson and the Conquest of the American West*. Even the PCT harbors echoes of his exploits: at mile 1075, the trail crosses a highway at Carson Pass. But another of Frémont's scouts, Joseph R. Walker, if noted at all, appears only in footnotes. The first was his 1833 overland expedition, where he pulled a mountain-man version of Wrong-Way Corrigan. Setting out to map the Great Salt Lake, he instead rode 1700 miles out of his way to the California coast and back. Walker's second footnote was that, well before reaching the coast, he may have been the first European explorer to lay eyes on Yosemite Valley. And his third footnote is that during his return he discovered a serviceable southern Sierra pass. Today, at 5246 feet, the open-saddle pass that bears Walker's name is split by a four-lane highway.

THOUGH THE SUN'S angle had decreased, Blazer remained stuck, riven helpless by indecision. She felt the tug to head out north, to plunge ahead into terrain that would soon morph into hulking, sawtooth mountains. Squinting behind dark sunglasses, she set her gaze west toward knuckled ridges that resembled a backlit layer cake. To the south, she saw what she'd put behind her, the hills rippling like sheets in the furled sweep of desert winds. But to the north, ahead, were the mountains of the Sierra Nevada.

Dalton had picked out a campsite and unpacked—like Old Faithful, his gear had again erupted onto his groundsheet. Afterward, he'd come down from the spare, scrub-oak-covered slope where he was cowboy camping, and had begun playing guitar in a circle of hikers around the trail magic bounty. Blazer had to make a decision soon. If she didn't, the passage of time would make the decision for her. One more song and then . . .

FOR FOUR WEEKS, since her town stop at Idyllwild, the same scenarios had played out in her mind, over and over. *What happens if I'm late?* She pictured Ian and Scott standing on the rough wooden deck of the Kennedy Meadows store, watching hikers arrive, none of them Blazer. Excitement and enthusiasm would fade from Ian's lean, bespectacled face, replaced by a stern visage. Next, Blazer pictured the look on his face if she was "only" hours late—eyebrows pinched, glowering. *What if I don't drag myself in till the next morning?* Which would he feel more, anger or worry? As each scenario played out in her mind, she saw the opportunity for her and Ian to grow closer fade away.

Back in Idyllwild, Ian had told Blazer over the phone what their options would be if she was late. "Scott will hike solo or Scott and I will go without you. Or, we'll go relatively slow and you'll try and catch up." To her, all those possibilities sounded awful. "I'll do everything I can. I'll be there. I will." The duct tape on her feet, her aching back, her too-tight calves, her lack of rest, her leaving Dalton behind twice—all gave proof to Blazer's pursuit of that promise.

THERE IS AN Ernest Hemingway short story, "The Old Man at the Bridge," where an army scout tries to convince a seventy-six-year-old man to get up as the enemy advances toward a pontoon bridge. *You have to get up and move out of danger.* The sole action in the 731-word story is this—the old man stands up, gets to his feet, and then sits back down.

Dalton had stopped playing. In the silence, the shuffling between songs, Blazer got to her feet. *Is it this late already?* She hadn't meant to let that happen. There was the first promise of coolness in the air, along with a tang, the time of evening when the sun's shadows grew long. Blazer's outline cast out twenty feet along the ground. Across the pass, the hills and Joshua trees were in the first grip of dusk, the greens, olives, and tans changing to grays. Blazer sat back down, defeated. It was too late to hike another five miles tonight.

As she lay on her groundsheet that night, Blazer was beyond tired. She started sobbing, but was bound and determined that no one would hear. She didn't want to disturb anyone, especially Dalton who was cowboy camping nearby. *I've bothered him with my complaints enough already.*

Among her worries was her camaraderie with Dalton. They would do anything for each other, but their platonic relationship was near cracking. Blazer had laid hands on Dalton to massage his feet. And she'd listened to his songs, which were as close to a caress as she'd allowed in four years. It was time to decide to close the last distance, or part ways.

In the still night, Dalton stayed awake for hours. Not giving any sign, not speaking, he watched over Blazer, listening to her faint sobs. He didn't really think that she'd need him, but just maybe she'd sense his presence. Finally, so deep into the night that the three-quarter waning moon had climbed well into the sky, rhythmic breathing replaced stifled crying.

Before dawn the next morning, Blazer silently dressed, packed, and hiked out. Dalton was asleep. She didn't wake him to say goodbye.

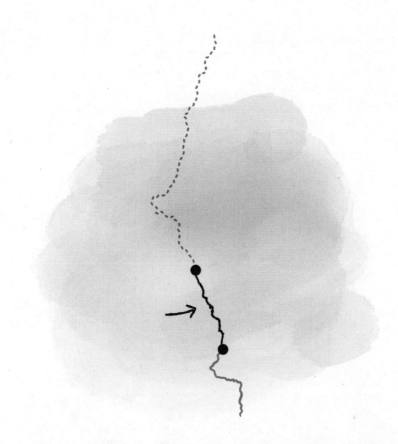

GRANITE

Walker Pass to Lake Tahoe

442 miles

22

Kennedy Meadows

FRIDAY, JUNE 8, 2007

THE TRAIL RAN through high open hills between Walker Pass and Kennedy Meadows. For the first 30 miles, hikers' only water was a uranium-tainted cow trough or sketchy, seasonal Spanish Needle Creek. In 2007, the desolate southern Sierra Nevada endured a drought the likes of which hadn't been seen in decades. For a year with less precipitation, you'd have to turn back the clock to 1924, more than eighty years earlier.

Blazer was blowing through this stretch. She wasn't the only one up at 4:00 a.m. at Walker Pass—Ryley was awake and already moving, so she adopted his pace. *He's a fast hiker. I'll draft off him.* Eighteen hours later, at 10:00 p.m., she was still walking, her headlamp beam bouncing on the trail. Finally, she let herself scout for a campsite. The next morning, just before her second pre-sunrise start, she scratched away in her journal: "Grueling 28 miles. Freaking crazy. My body was so sore. I shivered and shook all night."

SKETCHY WATER SOURCES, grazing cattle, and drought are a witch's brew. For hikers, fresh cow patties are not just booby traps for plodding feet— they signal waterborne pathogen risks like giardia. If backpacking has a boogeyman, it's encapsulated in that one word. Treat your water on the trail or get sick. Helicopter-rescue sick. Yogi said it best: "Many people are afraid of bears. I'm more afraid of giardia."

Giardia is a single-cell protozoa that likes to make a home in the human gut. It can be found in contaminated water or passed through fecal-to-mouth contact, such as when you touch your food or face with your poorly cleaned hands after you relieve yourself. On trail many heed the rule "Never eat anyone else's food," and they use Purell, or another alcohol-based hand sanitizer, right after pooping. Cows, deer, and forest denizens poop anywhere they choose, throwing off giardia in ten-to-whatever-power quantities. If even the smallest portion ends up in a sip of water after flowing into a river or stream, a hiker is at risk.

In the city, giardiasis is debilitating and merits a visit to a doctor's office. In the backcountry, giardiasis can be hike threatening—even life threatening. But a substantial percentage of people are immune. Another significant number are only carriers—expelling giardia cysts without experiencing symptoms. Some who become infected experience only mild symptoms. For the rest, it takes as few as ten giardia cysts to make them sick, with an incubation lasting one to two weeks. A full-blown case of giardiasis drains body fluids rapidly. Hikers spew at both ends, vomiting and enduring explosive diarrhea, often in a cottage cheesy, astonishingly noxious, sulfur-fumed flow.

For gross-looking water sources the decision is easy—treat it. There's plain old boiling, as well as adding chlorine or iodine or exposing water to ultraviolet light. And there are filters, a slew of them, from hand-pump, to gravity-feed, to in-line straws. But what about that lake, pond, cascading creek, or fresh spring? One study found that the water from most Sierra Nevada sources tests better than what flows from the average U.S. city water tap.

Since she hiked out of Campo, Nadine had been frying giardia with ultraviolet light. She had a SteriPEN, a lithium-battery-powered wand that was simple to operate: Turn the clear bulb on, immerse it in a pint for sixty seconds, and presto! Treated water.

Blazer chose a Katadyn filter. It was the size of a soup can with a hand-pump plunger that she pulled up, and pushed down, over and over. At first it was easy for her, but when it got clogged or if there was silty water, it was so much harder. At first a liter took a couple minutes, then it was more like five or ten minutes. Blazer never liked that camp chore.

Frodo and I chose Aquamira. For every two-liter water bladder, we counted out fourteen drops of solution A and fourteen drops of solution B and combined them together. After five minutes we poured the mix into our bladder. After another twenty minutes our water was ready to drink. When we were thirsty, with a cold lake staring us in the face, that wait was a drag. But sometimes we drank straight from a spring or small side stream.

One of my fellow hikers journaled that at Chicken Spring Lake in the Sierra Nevada, he was chemically purifying water with Aquamira when next to him he watched another hiker pouring solutions A and B together and immediately pouring the mixture into his water. He debated *Should I mention that the two solutions need five minutes to react before you add them?* When he finally shared that tip, he was initially met with a blank stare. Then the other responded, "So, what you are telling me is that I haven't purified *any* water on the trail?" And they both burst out laughing.

What did it mean to rely on one cow trough and a clutch of trickles running off Spanish Needle Ridge when hiking through this cattle country? A 2008 article in the *PCTA Communicator* by two doctors and a National Park Service ranger puts it in perspective: "One cow, if infected with giardia, can produce enough cysts in one day—over 100 million—to infect the entire city of Los Angeles."

"YOU DON'T LOOK so good." Those were Cloudspotter's first words upon spotting Blazer at Manter Creek under the noon sun. The two were at the foot of Rockhouse Basin, and what Cloudspotter couldn't get over was how Blazer, usually so upbeat and spirited, seemed completely demoralized.

After a slow morning hiking by herself, Blazer was near collapse. She was crouched down, her head hanging, as limp as a sock puppet with no hand inside. "I think I'm going to throw up," she muttered. "Will you tell my brother Ian that I'm coming?" In the eight hours since 4:00 a.m., Blazer hadn't once stopped to eat and she hadn't had near enough to drink. Cloudspotter was the first person she'd seen.

Over the last two hours Blazer had descended over 2000 feet. With no energy to spare, she'd taken little notice of Rockhouse Basin, arrayed before her during the long slog down to Manter Creek. This miles-long depression was a jewel at the eastern edge of the Domeland Wilderness. Half the horizon was dominated by stately domes and clustered granite fins with crowned headlands topping every gully and canyon. Each spire, dome, or spike was perched shoulders above emerald-robed slopes choked with scattered oaks, white fir, juniper, and pinyon, sugar, and Jeffrey pines. Or they had been.

THE FIRE THAT changed it all started July 22, 2000, and wasn't contained until August 10. Burning 75,000 acres, two-thirds of the Domeland Wilderness, the Manter Fire was so hot that it sterilized the earth. Gone were the green-clad slopes, pines, firs, oaks, and junipers. In their place were charred skeletons. Nadine had seen it in 1998, two years before the fire. When she saw it again in 2007, she practically mourned. But the peaks and domes endured and were now even more visible.

Blazer was squeezed into a narrow swatch of shade from a single dead tree near Manter Creek. All morning she had dreamed of water, but when she reached the creek's sandy bank all she wanted to do was lie down and sleep.

Cloudspotter had been completely absorbed with getting to Kennedy Meadows, eager to see trail friends she knew were already there. Now that would wait. Taking Blazer's yellow paisley half bandanna, she walked the few steps to Manter Creek and dipped the threadbare cloth into the fresh flow. Dabbing the back of Blazer's neck, Cloudspotter decided, *I can't do what Blazer asked.* Instead, she stayed with Blazer, encouraging her to drink and helping her get to her feet. Then Cloudspotter walked with Blazer the entire 10 miles to Kennedy Meadows.

With less than a mile to go, Blazer and Cloudspotter hit a paved road. It was past 5:00 p.m., hours after Blazer was supposed to meet Ian and Scott. She pictured her brother at the rustic Kennedy Meadows store, waiting impatiently. *What's he thinking? And what about his friend?*

Blazer had never met Scott. But she knew some things about him: He'd thru-hiked the Appalachian Trail, his trail name was Shamus, and he was a newly minted doctor, now a first-year resident at George Washington Medical Center in Washington, D.C. What she didn't know was that this week of backpacking was so important that he was using half his annual time off.

"There's Ian." Blazer spotted her brother and got her first glimpse of Shamus—a wide face with a grin of Crest-bright white teeth. His expression was striking alongside Ian's own half smile. Though both were pushing six feet, Shamus had soccer-build legs and longshoreman arms, while Ian, lean bodied and limbed, looked more suited for an office than a cargo hoist. Close as brothers, and both equally driven and determined, the two had been physical opposites since meeting ten years before as undergraduates at Johns Hopkins University. As Blazer drew close, even though she'd lost weight from her torrid pace, she looked like she could join Shamus on a soccer pitch and play stifling defense. If the three of them—Blazer, Shamus, and Ian—stood side by side and random strangers were tasked to pick out the two siblings, the vast majority would pair up Shamus and Blazer, not Blazer and Ian.

What Blazer hoped for in these four weeks was simple: She wanted to become closer to her brother. It was why she'd been pushing so hard since Idyllwild, for over 500 miles. Amanda had been only twelve when Ian left their Kersey home for college. As adults, they'd never spent time together like this, and she worried they might never have the opportunity again. *I don't want to be this mess. What if I blow it? We've got this next month together and then what?*

THE HEART OF Kennedy Meadows is the store. Often called "The Gateway to the Sierra," it's more than a trail icon, more than hot food, a shower, and a cold beer. It heralds the end of the desert. It's where thru-hikers ship themselves ice axes, crampons, and snowshoes. It's where they cram two-pound bear canisters with five, seven, or thirteen days' worth of food. If a canister has a small crevice left, hikers fill it with fun-size Snickers bars or M&M's.

For hikers, Kennedy Meadows is what Independence, Missouri, was for wagon trail pioneers. And like those Conestoga drivers, travelers here bunch up, often choosing to hike out in small groups. They also have to decide how much food to carry: *Do I carry one more day's food to take the day-long side trip to Mount Whitney? Do I get off at Trail Pass or Kearsarge Pass to resupply? Do I stop at Muir Trail Ranch or Vermillion Valley Resort? Will I hike 45, 95, 155, or 175 miles to my next food drop?*

BLAZER STUMBLED OVER the packed dirt of the store's driveway toward the wooden porch. Then she straightened, admonished herself—*Muster some energy!*—and powered in the direction of her brother and Shamus. She didn't want them to think she was weak. She didn't want them to think she wasn't happy to see them. Shamus, the doctor, saw through her immediately. With a glance, Shamus delivered his professional diagnosis: "You look like shit." Shortly after, he and Ian were plying Blazer with Gatorade from the store.

The Kennedy Meadows store was so classic it could have been a movie set. Wares were hawked from glass-fronted wooden cases while a Ben Franklin woodstove burned; elk antlers perched over the main entry competed with an outsized stuffed rainbow trout hung over the cluttered counter. There was a full freezer of Ben & Jerry's ice cream, 1300-calorie, one-pint bursts of sugar and fat, the perfect size to hog for yourself. When Blazer arrived, the back room was filled to the gills with hundreds of resupply boxes. There was a single open-air pay phone and a full waiting list on a nearby clipboard.

In the summer of 2007 cell phones were not yet ubiquitous on the trail. Indeed, hikers were embarrassed to be seen with one. Coverage along the PCT was rare, and many trail towns were serviced by only one major carrier—in one place it was Verizon, and in the next T-Mobile or AT&T. Though many hikers had cell phones, most shipped theirs from town to town in a bounce box. For the few hikers who carried them along in the hopes that the next hilltop just might have coverage, their screens all lit up with the same message in Kennedy Meadows: "No Service."

The fluids hit Blazer like an elixir. Equally reviving was the reality of finally seeing Ian and Shamus. But it was something else that really buoyed Blazer, and she felt her spirits rising like a kite. The air was redolent with it, palpable like ozone after a lightning strike. Every hiker, whether standing, sitting, or lying down, silently shouted from every abused, dust-clogged pore, "I HAVE MADE IT TO THE KENNEDY MEADOWS STORE."

Blazer was relieved to finally be with Ian and Shamus, but all too quickly the three faced their first decision: How soon would they hit the trail? Ian and Shamus could barely restrain themselves, like greyhounds chomping to get under way. Blazer, though weary through and through, still had to pick up her resupply box and bear canister and repack. At least in this low snow year, there would be no other new gear to deal with.

The guys wanted to head out the next morning, no later than 10:00 a.m., but Blazer pleaded, "Please, I just need a little more time." They agreed to delay their start by three hours, to 1:00 p.m. That would give them slightly less than seven days before Shamus's wife picked them up at Kearsarge Pass. If they made the miles, they could take that side trip to Mount Whitney. If they didn't, the three East Coasters might never have a chance to summit it again.

Blazer couldn't put on the brakes any more than she had—Ian and Shamus were ready to hike. That first day, even limited to the afternoon hours, they covered 11 miles. Camping under the South Fork Kern River bridge, the trio dodged dive-bombing cliff swallows whose gourd-shaped mud nests crowded the girders of the hundred-foot span. Erected in 1986, the rusty bridge eliminated one dangerous snowmelt stream crossing. The swallow village was an unintended consequence.

The next day, Blazer set the tone early. With packs burdened by full bear canisters, she misdirected them three miles out of their way, 2000 feet down and then 2000 feet back up. Ian orchestrated the next screwup, having left behind that morning the poles and stakes for the tent he shared with Shamus. He didn't realize that sorry fact until 15 miles later. It was too painful to think of backtracking that far, so he and Shamus figured they'd guy out the tent with lines stretched to overhanging trees all week. Shamus was up next. He got sick, puking anything that hit his stomach. It was probably the altitude; after all, he'd dashed from Washington, D.C.—high point 409 feet—and was now at 10,000 feet. Blazer certainly sympathized with his plight, but she also found some comfort in his distress. Shamus had been so energetic it was hard to keep up.

That evening, Ian spilled his spaghetti dinner on the ground. In the Sierra especially, that's a double-whammy mess. Not only was the food lost with no way to replace it, but even after they tossed the greasy, smell-laden dirt far away, they worried it was going to attract bears. Yet with all that, Blazer went to bed thinking, *Even a bad day on the trail is better than a good day in the real world.* She was so glad to finally be with Ian and Shamus.

The two guys were so close that they quickly fell into well-set patterns, but all three got along famously. Shamus openly admired Blazer for being out there on her thru-hike. Recalling his own months on the Appalachian Trail, he was jealous because this time he was the one who would soon be going home.

They were a trio, but at times it felt like a foursome. Blazer talked about Dalton a lot. An awful lot. At Deep Creek with the fire and the naked bucket brigade, eating greasy food at McDonald's, Dalton's apple pie birthday before Wrightwood, and that horrid hide-and-seek from the sun under the Cottonwood Creek Bridge. Dalton playing his guitar. Ian and Shamus not only welcomed the stories, but started to feel a nostalgic loss, wishing Dalton was hiking with them.

Most nights were topped off with Shamus's signature dish, his Appalachian Trail chocolate pudding. With no refrigerator, no whisk, and only nonfat dry milk powder, even instant pudding is a challenge to make on the trail. One of Shamus's secrets was to add crumbled Oreos or candy bar bits. Blazer watched closely as he said, "You let it set up, and when it's ready, you go make some friends."

Every night Ian and Shamus rigged a half-dozen lines to overhead limbs in an effort to prop up their sagging tent. While the two were as inclusive as could be with Blazer, the reality was that they left little open ground for Blazer and Ian to talk alone. Blazer thought back to her college years at Wheeling Jesuit University, about the times she'd made a huge detour to pick Ian up in Maryland while heading home to Pennsylvania. The two of them had been best buds before Ian left for college, but during those awkward car rides, she felt like more and more distance was growing between them. It was a gulf far beyond their five-year age difference. Blazer had even given that gap a name, calling it the "Wedge." She didn't know how to talk to Ian, or ask him the million questions that she wished she could.

THE THREE SUMMITED Mount Whitney on their fourth day out. Leaving their packs at Crabtree Meadow early in the morning, they took just enough supplies for the ascent and return—a strategy thru-hikers refer to as slackpacking. They climbed 4100 feet in just over eight miles to the top. Blazer wanted to shout, "I am standing on the highest spot in the Lower 48 states!"

On the way back they retrieved their packs and hoofed it another four miles. No one complained that of their twenty miles that day only four were on the PCT, but they did loudly bemoan the rampant mosquitoes. Even growing up on the East Coast, Blazer had never seen so many mosquitoes in her life. She sat in her tent and refused to exit until it was time to pack up the next morning.

The next day, the three crossed Bighorn Plateau, where the magnificence of the Sierra hits like a pile driver. Up on Mount Whitney, half the view is over desert, but from Bighorn Plateau, the 360-degree view is pure Sierra. Strung out to the east are Mounts Hitchcock and Mitchell, while to the west the sharp ridgeline of the Kaweahs is banded by red and brown granite. The circling peaks seem countless, making it the grand hall of John Muir's Range of Light.

ON THE NEXT day, the trio's penultimate, they crested Forester Pass. At 13,180 feet, this small notch is the highest point on the PCT. It was hard to imagine a trail that could climb the near-vertical face leading up to it, but one had been blasted out of the mountainside. After hearing so much about Forester, Blazer, Ian, and Shamus had built it up in their heads. More than once each thought, *Where is the pass?* Walking toward it, everyone was silent.

The next day they only had ten miles to hike, including eight miles off the PCT over Kearsarge Pass. There, Shamus's wife would pick them up and take them to town. Blazer and Ian would resupply; Shamus would go home. When Shamus met his wife at the trailhead he was so happy to see her. Then he peeled the duct tape off his feet and looked in horror at how few toenails he had left. He was battered, bruised, and sunburnt, but the first words out of his mouth were, "It was a great vacation."

For Blazer, the week with Ian and Shamus had been a great distraction. What with the other two's banter, the gigantic mountains, and abundant, fierce-flowing water, she had broken free from her self-destructive cycle, free of that mantra that had dogged her the first 700 miles: *My feet hurt, I'm tired, I'm hungry. I need to eat.* And, except during the wee hours of the night when she tossed and turned, for that entire week the dark places Blazer had hidden away were kept at bay. But she'd still not had any real chance to talk to Ian. The Wedge was still there, a gulf as big and wide as it had been when she sat next to him in the car.

DALTON WAS MORE than a day behind Blazer. He had mulled over their split as a hiking pair: By far, she'd been the most important person to his hike. *Should I have done more to stay together?* Once again being the tough guy, he rationalized, *I guess it was time. We did hike a long way together.* He had known Blazer was hustling to meet her brother. He didn't want to butt in on that. Also, Dalton did want to meet more people and he didn't want to fall into a rut. But having thought all that, Dalton looked ahead with this certainty, *One day I'll catch up with her.*

23

Shower Buddies

TONY, NADINE, AND Pacha hiked into Kennedy Meadows the day Blazer hiked out. With the touch of a shoulder, warm glances, and shared, private one-word jokes, they were the very picture of an enthralled hiking couple, but the seams holding them together were increasingly under stress. Tony wanted to pack out twelve days of food and hike, uninterrupted, most of the length of the High Sierra, all the way to Vermillion Valley Resort. Nadine wanted to break up the 190 miles with town stops.

But it was Pacha, whose coat had lost luster and who desperately needed rest, that put their continued hiking partnership most at risk. Dogs are prohibited on national park trails, and just north of Kennedy Meadows the trail ran smack through three of them—Sequoia, Kings Canyon, and Yosemite—over the next 200 miles. If they brought Pacha and were caught, they'd be cited, fined, and, worse, forced to hike to the nearest trailhead. Nadine journaled, "The trail between here and the Ansel Adams Wilderness is chock full of ranger stations and we're sure to get caught. In Sequoia it might be as much as a three-or-four-day detour."

If that weren't enough, Nadine's too-tight shoes were now deadweight lumps in her pack. She couldn't even limp along in them. By the time the Kennedy Meadows store came into view she had been wearing her Crocs for 50 miles. As strong as she was, Nadine no longer tried to downplay the severity of her feet problems. Before embarking into the Sierra, new shoes were an imperative. But 20 miles of near-deserted mountain road and 30 miles of open highway separated Nadine from the nearest shoe store.

For Tony and Nadine, the Kennedy Meadows store made them forget everything they'd been struggling with, at least for a while. Nadine sat in a dusty white patio chair on the store's wooden deck with a de rigueur pint of Ben & Jerry's. She had a chocolate-lipped smile, a sunburnt nose, and an open packet of raw hot dogs in her lap. There was only one left; Pacha had wolfed down the other seven.

Soon after arriving, Nadine got a puzzling surprise. "Nadine, are you all right?" The question came from Breeze, a thru-hiker Nadine knew well, one she'd been leapfrogging with. But the woman had been a couple hours behind, and even that small amount meant they hadn't seen each other for three days. But Breeze had known Nadine was a short distance in front of her by the shoe prints on the ground—most thru-hikers learn to recognize the various tread patterns on dust in the first 700 miles. But after a while, she had seen Nadine's shoe print disappear as the Croc sandal prints started. Two other thru-hikers had also noticed the change in Nadine's shoe prints and from that alone realized she was hurt.

Thru-hikers are not the only ones with a keen interest in shoe prints. For a search and rescue team, shoe prints can be the difference between a found hiker or a dead one. One search and rescue website advises that hikers can increase their odds of being found by creating a sample of their shoe print at home using a piece of aluminum foil and a folded towel. I have never, ever, heard of anyone doing this. However, there was the case of a lost woman who called the local sheriff's office on her cell phone. All she could tell them was the county she was in and the name of the trailhead she'd left hours and miles behind. With her cell phone she sent them a photo of her shoe print, which led them right to her.

NOTHING ON THE trail was quite like the Kennedy Meadows showers. The two stalls stood side by side on a rise behind the store. There was no roof, only a sheet of plywood for a center wall, and the sideboards didn't quite reach the rough concrete floor. All afternoon, guys and gals, their ankles, calves, and feet exposed, luxuriated in limitless hot water before cycling out to allow the next hiker in. For this privilege, and a tattered towel, hikers exchanged two dollars at the store's counter.

I closed the shower curtain, stripped, and picked up a misshapen bar of soap. Allegheny, a sixty-five-year-old who had previously hiked the Appalachian Trail, was in the adjoining stall. If I ever started feeling proud of myself—*I'm thru-hiking at age fifty-five!*—I thought of Allegheny. During the five minutes that we overlapped, I listened to a rundown of his three marriages from the other side of the plywood wall. Wife number one had given him a choice: "What's it going to be—me or your guitar?" Sitting around the campfire at the Saufleys', Frodo and I had heard Allegheny still singing and strumming. When it comes to divulging life stories, a psychiatrist's couch couldn't hold a candle to these shower stalls.

"Scout, is that you?" The voice was Tony's. He'd stepped into the stall vacated by Allegheny.

I rubbed the soap hard against my flanks as I tossed a question over the partition, "Hey, Tony, were you ever married?"

"Scout, I was married for fourteen years." I'd had no idea. He said he had changed and his wife hadn't. The marriage ended and he'd gone off to hike the Appalachian Trail. They were still friends.

Before I knew it, I'd told Tony a capsule version of Frodo's and my marriage. Under the warm jet of the shower, the next step felt easy. Without a pause, I told Tony the second great story of our marriage. "Tony, did you know Frodo and I were separated for three years?" *Did I really just say that?*

"Really?" Tony said, and then he was quiet as I shared the details in a deadpan voice. I squeezed shampoo into my hands, ground my nails into my scalp, and clamped my mouth shut.

Tony continued with his story, "I was a landscaper once. I loved the planting and the feel of good soil in my hands." There was pride in his voice. "But after ten years they moved me up to sales. It's what I was supposed to do. Everyone expected it." Tony's hands lost their calluses and he manned a desk indoors. "I was in sales for five years." The flat tone said it all. "Scout, those were the last five years before I left my wife." He stopped abruptly as if someone had hit pause. Birds wheeled overhead, Steller's jays and Clark's nutcrackers. Something felt off-kilter. Tony's baritone skipped a few more beats as pine needles blew inside the shower stall.

Through the splintered plywood, Tony continued, "So, there was this day, I was in the kitchen. It was a Saturday and I was alone. It was before I split up with my wife. I looked down and saw I was holding a knife. It was in my hand. Scout, I have no memory of how it got there. I can't remember what happened next. Maybe my wife called me from her work. But whatever it was, my next thought was, *I'm not doing this now.*" The birds still wheeled about on the breeze. Rinsing myself clean, I pictured Tony setting down the knife.

I shut the water off; the shower jet dribbled on the floor. As I dried off and dressed, the cement slab rasped like a coarse file against my bare soles. It felt so good to be alive. I left our confessional stall, and another shower buddy entered.

Tony and I walked out again into the brilliant Sierra sun. He had felt safe enough with me to speak of a knife in his hands. And in that moment I had felt safe enough to hear it.

24
Sacrifice

BOTH TONY AND Nadine had started the trail in Campo with something to prove. For Nadine, this hike was going to be about her and not some guy. She'd set dates to meet friends. The only schedule would be her own. Tony had started his hike adamant that this would not be a repeat of his Appalachian Trail hike. He was going to finish, not dawdle, and he'd make Tarik's wedding.

Tony knew he was in hip-deep with Nadine. This relationship might be what he'd been seeking the entire Appalachian Trail. Nadine, for her part, was now willing to bend or even break the rules she had made for herself. In times of darkness, it was her nature to grab a candle and strike a match. So she had concocted a plan—she would sacrifice 45 miles of trail.

IN THE SUMMER of 2004, one of Yogi's feet was killing her. She was at the start of her fourth thru-hike in as many years, and had hiked "only" the first 500 miles. She wasn't about to stop, so to cut the pain she soaked her feet in every stream. She took ibuprofen, popping the pain deadeners like candy. When she finished—over 2000 miles later—her podiatrist stated the obvious, "You've overused them." When she told him how long she'd been in pain, he bluntly told her, "You shouldn't be able to walk on them at all." Her annual regimen was a Wonder Woman feat— five months pounding out 20-plus-mile trail days and seven months waitressing fifty-five hours a week. The diagnosis was premature osteo-arthritis and high arches. The cure was custom orthotics, to the tune of four hundred dollars. Relief was palpable within months, and the pain was gone after a year.

Nadine's custom orthotics cost five hundred dollars. Without them, she feared that the same knee injury that she had in 1998 would reappear. It was that injury that had started the arguments with her boyfriend.

NADINE WAS LOOKING forward to seeing Tony. Three days earlier she had left him at Kennedy Meadows to hitch the 50 miles to Ridgecrest, the nearest place with a car rental. Then she'd driven south to Newhall, a Los Angeles bedroom community. She had arranged to leave Pacha with good friends there for two weeks. They were going to pamper her with sirloin and treats and then drive Pacha to Vermillion Valley Resort for a grand reunion. Nadine also bought new shoes, which was a huge relief. After a full day in L.A., Nadine retraced her steps, driving for hours and seeing signs for the places she'd already hiked past. During that same time, Tony took a full zero at Kennedy Meadows before hiking forty-five miles north to Trail Pass trailhead. When he walked the two miles off the PCT to the asphalt parking lot, Nadine was there waiting to pick him up in the rental car. She was beaming.

Back together after three days, Nadine and Tony were both looking forward to sleeping together that night. At the Dow Villa Motel in Lone Pine, they had a bed and clean sheets, their first since Tehachapi. All their fears about Pacha were allayed, they were going to climb Mount Whitney, and they'd agreed to a schedule—for the next two weeks at least. After their recent rough patch, it felt like they'd recaptured the magic of their first weeks together, reminiscent of that first night outside of Warner Springs. Not long before turning in, Tony set out to complete one final chore: cleaning out the rental car.

That night, the stars stood out in the moonless high desert sky. Not even the parking lot lights or the bright motel sign could dim them. As he opened the trunk, Tony spotted the new shoebox, now containing Nadine's cast-off trail runners. *Good riddance,* he thought. Those dusty shoes had only caused Nadine grief. *I'm doing her a favor cleaning all this out.* Then he saw something else in the shoebox. *Those are some crazy insoles.* There was a garbage can next to the parking lot. Tony opened the lid and pitched the box with its contents into the trash.

25

Getting Naked

THE SUMMER SOLSTICE is Hike Naked Day, a bigger holiday on the PCT than the Fourth of July. Like trail names, this was an Appalachian Trail custom that had jumped coasts. Thru-hikers chewed on the challenge, wondering who would do it. But when the day itself came, most gave it a pass.

Ian was adamant. "I'm with my sister. It's too weird." But the two needed a jolt. In the four days since Shamus and his wife flew home, Blazer and Ian had spiraled downward. She had pictured them having long talks and being spontaneous and jumping into lakes. Instead, he was focused on miles. Blazer wanted to sledgehammer the Wedge.

The terrain of the High Sierra was more challenging than that of Southern California—up to a pass, down to a river, over and over, usually with at least 3000 feet elevation difference between the two. Blazer summarized each pass in her journal. Kearsarge Pass: "Am I cut out for this?" Glen Pass: "Brutal." Pinchot Pass: "Stupid hard." Mather Pass: "Great pass."

One morning Ian surprised Blazer by pulling a whiskey flask from his pack. They alternated, toasting each other with shots. But the buzz was short-lived. Worse, it reminded Blazer—like a scab ripped off a wound— of her mother's code, "Whiskey," and those phone calls.

After their whiskey break Ian set out on another of his jackrabbit starts. Blazer fumed as she followed his shoe prints, trying to catch up. Ian had effortlessly shifted from a Washington, D.C., office to thru-hiking mode, galling Blazer's competitive nature. And he would be the one to arbitrarily decide, "Let's break here," treating her like a kid sister. When she whined, he chided her.

The next time he jackrabbited out, Blazer tried a game. *I'll think about the good times with Ian.* Those rare good times at the Kersey house. In winter they'd break off the three-foot icicles hanging from the kitchen window. She and Ian would lick them, sucking them like lollipops. In autumn, weeks before the ice popsicles formed, the four kids—Amanda and Ian, Jeremiah, and Arwen—always raked the leaves together into a huge pile. Together, they'd dive in again and again before heading inside with twigs and leaf bits stuck on their clothes. Waiting for them, their mom would pick the leaves off and then make hot cocoa. For Blazer, those moments raking together were her best memories of that house— except for the time she took the rake, hit her sister with it, and broke her finger. In the Kersey house, good times always had "excepts."

The bad times didn't have exceptions. Every Sunday, Amanda's dad dragged them out of bed, pounding on the walls down the hallway, before church. He would start drinking immediately afterward. Sunday dinners were a fright show. He'd yell at Lois over nothing, start up an argument that could escalate to him throwing chairs. Amanda might end up hiding in a closet, fingers in her ears, clutching her bear, Cheerio. Nothing shut out her dad's yelling. Her birthdays were no better. One year she was in the hospital with a kidney infection. On another, she wrecked her bike, suffered a concussion, and had to get a tetanus shot.

But this trail time, even though things were so off-center with her brother, was peppered with exceptions. When Blazer felt sick on the tough 4000-foot climb up Pinchot Pass, Ian slowed down and was patient and encouraging. Anything that came up—the motel bill, checks for meals—Ian paid, no fuss. And those few times that Blazer paid a check, Ian offered her a gracious thanks.

But no matter the glow of good memories or aged whiskey, the Wedge remained intact. The gap felt as strong as on those long drives from college. Blazer held her tongue in check as she wondered why she had punished herself, racing through those 700 miles. Their senses were drenched with the High Sierra that surrounded them. There'd never be a better time. What would it take? They'd never have four weeks like this again.

Near noon on Hike Naked Day, the two crested Muir Pass. They'd endured 10 miles of uphill trudging during the 4000-foot ascent. *This is taking forever*, Blazer thought. At the top, Ian paused. This Sierra pass had a structure—Muir Hut. At 11,995 feet, it's an icon, a turret with no castle, 20 feet around and 20 feet high with a beehive dome made from layered, native rock that had weathered three-quarters of a century. He looked around. No one was in sight. He heard a voice, like a mischievous angel on his shoulder—"Ian, go ahead." He felt like a playful ten-year-old.

If Ian had shouted for joy into the broad bowl of granite massifs, there might have been an echo. But even in the silence, as Blazer saw her brother pulling himself up hand over hand, rising higher on the side of the hut, she heard something faint. It was an echo, not off the mountains, but an echo from long ago. *"Amanda, look, there's a leaf pile. Let's jump on it."*

Blazer squeezed the camera shutter. She wanted to holler, "Be careful!" She wanted her voice to touch him, protect him, hold Ian safe. He looked so vulnerable. His bare head was near 30 feet off the ground, his two shoes balanced on a small stone. Muir Hut's caprock, topping forty-two layers of rock, looked like it might teeter or break free. He called out to her, "Blazer, come on, get yourself up here." The granite cut her fingertips, but she didn't notice. She clambered up stone by stone and joined her brother on the pinnacle. They stood together as a breeze flapped the fabric of their matching navy-blue shorts. Each squeezed one foot onto the capstone and thrust their fists in the air.

At Evolution Lake two hours later, after descending five miles and losing 1100 feet, they found themselves sitting on a narrow beach of grasslike sedges and chatting. The mile-long body of water, a gouge ripped in granite by a long-vanished glacier, was illuminated by the solstice sun. In front of Blazer and Ian, in full view of their grassy cove, was a rock island as tall and wide as Muir Hut.

Their conversation was spiraling around one subject—a cluster of five hikers who were having so much fun. The two of them and Shamus had summited Mount Whitney with Germinator, Festus, Neptune, Bounty Hunter, and Figaro, but Blazer realized that when she asked herself, *Why are they having a blast?*, she was really asking, *Why aren't we?* Both siblings took a hard look at themselves. Blazer didn't bring up Ian's resolve—to end his hike near Lake Tahoe. They both knew that meant 400 miles of hiking at a harsh clip in harsh country. Under the Muir Hut's spell, Ian brought up the possibility of stopping at Sonora Pass or Tuolumne Meadows, 50 or 100 miles fewer than he had planned. He could hitch or catch a bus and still get to an airport. And once Ian had started, the possibilities swept them along. "We can take a side trip to Yosemite Valley, we can spend a day climbing Half Dome, we can . . ."

When the talk finally subsided, Blazer lay thinking, *This is one of my favorite days.* They watched the water shimmer in silence until Ian, staring at that little island, said, "You know what? Let's go skinny-dipping."

A granite peninsula jutted out from the beach. Ian took one side and Blazer took the other. They stripped off their sweat-stained clothes. There was nothing subtle about the water—it was freezing snowmelt. Blazer jumped in and jumped out quick. Dabbing herself dry with her half bandanna, Blazer saw the note on her side of the rock. Ian must have written it before shedding his clothes: "Take out the camera."

Blazer looked up. *He can't be doing that.* Her brother's arms rhythmically rose and fell as he swam toward the island. The water was so cold that Ian found himself in shock, but as the shoreline receded, he thought, *This is amazingly uncomfortable, but I'm not going to die.* In one hundred yards he reached the island and hauled himself onto the rock. Then, shaking, he climbed to the top. He waved his right hand at his sister and covered himself with his left. Blazer snapped two photos.

An unexpected climb, a glacier-gouged lake, and a freezing water plunge—that was the combination that spun the tumblers and opened the lock. After that day, they both focused on being happy, making memories, and letting the miles come as they may. The Wedge was vanquished.

In the ensuing days, as they kept on talking, it finally began to dawn on Ian what it had cost Blazer to keep his Kennedy Meadows date. He'd been so confident she'd be there, and she didn't make a big deal of it at first, but gradually everything came out. His respect for her increased. Far more than any verbal declaration, it drove home how much Blazer loved him.

The two rarely spoke of their parents or childhood—an old habit. Blazer also never asked Ian about his biological father. She had no idea if Ian even knew who he was. And Ian never mentioned Blazer's lack of a romantic life. He figured she had her reasons. Blazer appreciated it, but even if Ian had asked, Blazer would have deflected. "No guy's good enough," she'd have played it for a laugh. One time, while hiking, when they each had grown serious, she said to him, "You're still my brother." Immediately, he said to her, "You're still my sister." To each it mattered that they had said those words out loud.

FIVE DAYS AFTER the summer solstice, Ian and Blazer reached Reds Meadow. They had hiked through the heart of the Sierra Nevada, over 200 roadless miles. Boarding a Forest Service shuttle, they headed to Mammoth Lakes, a substantial village of eight thousand built for winter skiers, now at loose ends in the summer season. Stepping into their room at the Motel 6 felt to Blazer like a time warp—the paintings, furnishings, and bedspread looked exactly like her room in Big Bear City, 600 miles back. With Dalton well behind her, she and Ian shared the room with two hikers from the East Coast.

For the two hikers in the room next door to Ian and Blazer, staying in a motel was completely out of character. But checking into the Motel 6 didn't mark an uptick in the Mario Brothers' dire financial straits; it signaled their last hurrah. Word had already circulated—they'd run out of money and were getting off the trail.

Blazer hadn't heard. Not that she could have done much—she'd come down roaring sick. The giardia cysts she'd picked up just north of Walker Pass two weeks ago had multiplied, leaving her feverish, aching, chilled, and nauseous. She couldn't eat—that was how bad it was. Fortunately, she was in town, with clean sheets and a soft bed. She took to bed at 4:00 p.m. and slept straight through till 10:00 a.m. the next day. There was no choice but to take back-to-back zero days, a first for Blazer.

Only after she awoke did she hear the Mario Brothers' news. It was a hit to the gut—if not for Ian, this could have been her. Right here in Mammoth Lakes was where her cash would have run out. Heidi had been right; Blazer hadn't had enough money. She'd never have known the trail's gifts that lay ahead.

More than a quarter of the class of 2007 had already left the trail. Usually hikers only hear about it afterward, often long afterward, but in

Mammoth Lakes the trail casualties were happening front and center. One of many deeply affected, Cloudspotter reported the loss of Mario and Luigi in her online journal like a Civil War reporter listing the latest battle deaths: "This morning I received news of friends quitting the trail. Foots-Aflame and Walk-It-Off are rumored to be finished. The Mario Brothers confirmed that they would not be continuing on."

But during the eighteen hours that Blazer slept, a set of knuckles had rapped on the Mario Brothers' door. Dust motes rose from the low-pile carpet as a hiker stepped into their room and asked, "Is it true?" Mario and Luigi slowly nodded. He continued, "You're leaving the trail? You've run out of money?" They exchanged glances. Mario, the older of the two, answered somberly, "Yes." They didn't know this hiker well and were puzzled. *What does he want? To offer sympathy? That's nice, but it doesn't change anything.*

The hiker proceeded, gingerly. "There are two of us with a request we'd like you to consider. If you're set on getting off the trail we understand, but would you consider letting us fund the rest of your trek? We thought four thousand dollars might be enough. There are no strings attached." Completely drained by the trail and the hard decision they'd come to, neither brother could muster a response in that moment. But the Mario Brothers had been tossed a lifeline.

Is it too late? the hiker thought as he walked away. He passed a lineup of worn running shoes outside another room—Blazer was asleep on the other side of the door. After the last two months, many hikers were increasingly drawn toward the soft beds and hot showers of life off the trail. He thought about the look he'd seen in the Mario Brothers' eyes— they'd begun thinking about home, about not being dirty all the time. He'd done what he could. It was for them to decide.

LATE THE NEXT morning, Blazer and Ian left Mammoth Lakes carrying only two days of food. Given their light load, they'd forgone the usual thru-hiker fare of mashed potato buds, mac and cheese, or bland noodles. In her journal, Blazer gave their gustatory lineup more play than a Sierra pass: "Bell peppers, onions, tomatoes, salsa, rice, spices, lime chips, jalapeño tortillas, oh yeah, and cheese." They even made fresh guacamole after the first eight miles—she could get used to resupplying with Mexican feasts. But even as they both reveled in this "short," 37-mile jump to Tuolumne Meadows, for Ian it would be the end of the line.

BACK IN MAMMOTH LAKES, the Mario Brothers talked it over—home or trail—and made a call to share their decision: "Luigi and I are willing to accept." The next day they received an envelope full of cash. A second envelope was waiting for them near the halfway point at Old Station, a small town in Northern California. The Mario Brothers and their bene-factors never spoke about it again.

ON THE DAY of the full moon, Blazer and Ian reached a milestone, proba-bly the most photographed spot on the PCT: iconic Thousand Island Lake backdropped by Banner and Ritter Peaks. Seven miles later they crested Donohue Pass, the last time northbound hikers are over 11,000 feet. With the fixings of their Mexican feast nearly exhausted, Blazer was back to journaling about their food: "Brie, Triscuits, strawberries, wine, orange Milano cookies, and whiskey shots!" At the pass, the two tried to outwit the resident tag-team marmots. Fat and sassy bandits the size of fuzzy footballs, and nearly ten pounds each, marmots are the offensive line-men of rodents. And these particular marmots acted as if they owned the place. When one darted out, skittering, they cooed over him, "Oh, he's so cute." Meanwhile, the other snuck up behind them. No Triscuit was safe.

The next day they reached Tuolumne Meadows. Before Ian departed, the pair hopped on a bus to Yosemite Valley. For two days, they played at being tourists among crowds of people in clean clothes with cameras draped around their necks. They viewed waterfalls, Bridalveil and Yosemite, and the sheer sides of El Capitan and Half Dome before eating themselves silly at the Curry Village buffet. On their second day, they trekked the 15-mile round-trip up Half Dome, 4800 feet up and down.

Then it was Ian's final morning, time for him to board a bus west while Blazer headed east back to Tuolumne. There was no putting it off, no casual "bye," no small wave. The two hugged tightly. Blazer waved madly and tried to hold back her tears.

FOUR MILES NORTH of Tuolumne Meadows, Blazer could have camped with others, but chose not to. This was only the second time in her life she had slept outdoors by herself, but she didn't want to be with other people just yet. For Blazer, the hike could end now. Everything she'd been through, she'd do it twice over again, just for those weeks with Ian. After all these years, she'd gained his respect. The Wedge was gone, but Blazer now felt more alone than she had since San Diego.

That night, tears dampened her sleeping bag. But these were different from those shed at Walker Pass—she was wistful, not frightened, grateful instead of frantic, and her hurt came from grief, not from the pain of abused, battered feet. Blazer drifted toward sleep as the moon rose. She had come 940 miles. Canada lay 1710 miles ahead.

26

No Good Choices

NADINE'S RUDDY COMPLEXION drained until her freckles stood out like pebbles on a beach, startling Tony. They had just been dropped off at the 10,000-foot-high Trail Pass trailhead and had been bubbling, raring to get to the High Sierra. Not even the prospect of carrying six days of food had dimmed their spirits. Minutes ago, they'd gratefully thanked Nadine's friend who'd given them a lift. The dust from the SUV had just settled. Except for the two of them and their packs, the expansive tarmac of the parking lot was deserted.

Tony's chest clamped. He knew right away that something really bad had just happened. Without knowing the reason, he surmised that they were not getting any miles in today.

After wearing sandals the day before in town and during the ride out, Nadine's green eyes were laser-focused on her new shoes. "Tony, they're gone. I can't find them. I can't find my orthotics." Tony reached out to hold her. As he did, scattered dots coalesced in his brain. He saw himself the night before at the motel. *No, not that. It's those insoles, those crazy insoles. They were orthotics!*

They'd gone to such lengths to hike together again. Tony had sacrificed his twelve-day-straight carry and Nadine had given up 45 miles of trail. After three days apart, when Nadine had picked Tony up in the rental car they were so happy to be together. It was like recapturing the magic of the beginning of the trail. Now this. Tony was abject, apologizing, "Nadine,

I'm so sorry. I did it. I cleaned out the car last night. I didn't know what they were. I threw everything out. They're in the motel garbage can next to the parking lot." What Tony fervently hoped was that they were still there. There was nothing to discuss—they were going back.

Sitting on the shoulder of a narrow road, the two tried to hitch back. In three hours, two cars passed—neither stopped. Even while apologizing to Nadine, Tony was already thinking, *How do we solve this?* We. Two people. One team. The next grinding Sierra ascent could wait; their challenge was to get back to the Dow Villa Motel. Sitting next to their packs, they worried, *Will the orthotics be there? Should we start walking? It's 23 miles. Do they empty the parking lot garbage cans daily? What if they've tossed them in the motel dumpster?* Tony would happily go dumpster diving, if only he could find them. *What if the city garbage truck has come today?*

After they'd been waiting for three hours, a driver took pity and stopped. When they made it back to the Dow Villa parking lot in Lone Pine, Tony practically jumped out. He ran to the garbage can and pulled the top off. *There's trash*, he saw, letting his hopes swell. *Blessed trash.* He rooted around, shuffling past orange peels and empty cups. His hands got sticky. Tony didn't care. Then he uncovered the shoebox—and under it were the orthotics. Tony held them aloft, showing them off like pirate treasure to Nadine.

FOUR DAYS LATER they climbed Mount Whitney. Imagining front-row seats as the sun first peeks over the White Mountains, the two contemplated hiking to the top before sunrise. It would be romantic, but it meant starting by 3:00 a.m. They were unanimous: "Naaaah." Instead, they set out from Crabtree Meadow at a more civilized hour, leaving most of their weight in camp: bear canisters, food, tent, sleeping bags, and pads. Setting out they thought, *It's a picnic*—one with a 17-mile roundtrip hike and a 4100-foot climb. *Piece of cake!*

Tony began to feel lightheaded as they rose into thinner and thinner air, so crisp and clear, walking carefully on the loose rocky tread. But it wasn't only lack of oxygen that made him feel so giddy. *I'm summiting Mount Whitney. I've heard of this mountain all my life.* Right here, this was what Tony had sought—adventure, wilderness, and to feel so remote.

One more thing accentuated his pleasure. On the Appalachian Trail, he'd not only sought adventure, but also a person. *And just maybe*, he mused happily, as Whitney's summit hut came into view, *just maybe, she's walking by my side.*

On the summit, Tony stood near a white enamel plaque bolted flat onto granite: "Mount Whitney 14,496 feet." Steps east was a 2000-foot vertical drop; this was the mountain face visible from the Owens Valley. From this aerie perch Tony saw the thread of Highway 395 splitting the desert valley. Down there it was Sunday. Down there it was June 17. Down there, scattered families drove to be together for Father's Day. Tony had never felt so far from home as he turned his camera on, switched from photo to video, and pointed the lens at himself: "Hello, Dad." As he spoke, the small screen recorded how much Tony had changed. A faded bandanna corralled his grown-out buzz cut, his beard was a thick, black mass, and he'd hardened, flesh lost from his cheeks. Tony was a Hollywood-screen image of Robinson Crusoe. "I'm doing great, Dad. I'm on top of Mount Whitney. Love you. Happy Father's Day."

WHEN FOOD STARTED running low six days into the High Sierra, Tony and Nadine left the PCT for their next Sierra town stop. It took eight miles of non-PCT hiking to get up, over, and down Kearsarge Pass, a resupply route used by two-thirds of thru-hikers. Only seventy-two hours before, Blazer, Ian, and Shamus had trod the same path.

Tony was used to various odd aches and pains, but lately his cheek muscles had been hurting—from smiling all the time. How could he not? They were in the High Sierra, and covering miles at a fast clip. The lost orthotics had become a fun story to tell others, with a bonus ending because they got to spend another night in a hotel. He especially loved listening to Nadine's voice as she told the story: "So then Tony thinks, *What are these crazy things?* And he tosses them in the trash." Each time she punctuated the tale with bouts of infectious belly laughs and giggles. It was music to Tony's ears.

That night in town, scrubbed clean of the week's grime, they went for dinner at a nice restaurant. What joy—the amazing smell of town food that someone else had cooked! But Nadine felt tormented. The smell of meat was becoming harder to resist.

A PROSPECTIVE THRU-HIKER once wrote on a trail forum, "I am hiking the PCT this spring and am hoping to stay vegan during my hike." Yogi responded, "Don't be surprised when you eat your first cheeseburger! In 19,000 miles of hiking, I've met very few vegetarians who last an entire thru-hike without eating meat. Vegans are even more rare. Eventually your body will tell you what it needs. The main problem is that chickadee in the Sierra. It sings *cheese-bur-ger* all day long. You cannot escape it."

But Nadine had, at least in 1998. Then, even her boyfriend's jabs hadn't cracked her resolve. She just wasn't tempted. So what was different now? The vegetarian dish in front of her was fine, but she wanted to blog about Tony's steak, describing even the grill pattern. Seventeen years of vegetarianism—dating all the way back to her freshman year in college—weighed on her. Amid all the partying and straight As, she'd been grabbed by Francis Moore Lappé's *Diet for a Small Planet*. She'd read how meat production was at the root of world hunger, the cause of cancers and disease. After reading that, no meat had crossed her lips for nearly two decades.

Nadine started to pick at the food on her plate. She thought, *I need to ask for an avocado. I need to get up, step outside, and get a breath of fresh air.* Instead she said, "Tony, can you cut me a piece?"

Tony cocked his head and gently asked, "Are you really sure?" He wasn't her judge, and it wasn't for him to stop her. But he was uncomfortable playing the enabler role. Nadine lifted her fork. That one piece tasted good.

While Nadine chewed, savoring the flavor of charred beef, Tony watched her and thoughtfully chewed his own. Wine flowed all around them. Stemmed glasses were filled, sipped, and emptied. And Tony was with Nadine, a woman who made her living off fermented grapes, even earning a master's in viticulture from the University of California, Davis, six years ago. If Bonny Doon Winery hadn't curtailed operations, Nadine would still be managing their vineyard, not thru-hiking. But Tony wasn't tempted. No matter the passage of time, he knew that for him a single glass of wine led to hard liquor; he had no built-in stops to rely on. Awash in a sea of casual drinking, Tony was the one nonswimmer.

FIVE DAYS LATER, Frodo and I had just left Muir Trail Ranch—one of the few places to resupply in the High Sierra without detouring off the trail for miles. Normally, I hiked right behind her, the gap ten feet or less, but I had purposefully dropped back over fifty feet because I couldn't trust my tongue. I knew if I opened my mouth nothing good would come out.

This was our eighth straight day in the Sierra backcountry, an eleven-day version of Tony's original twelve-day plan. For fifty dollars, Muir Trail Ranch had packed in our sealed five-gallon bucket on horseback. Frodo had mailed it two months ago and I'd gotten it into my head that she must have packed a few non-trail goodies. I'd dreamed of cans of fruit cocktail. Days of nuts and dried fruit made the prospect of diced pears, peaches, and pineapple floating in fresh juice seem fit for a king. When we pried off the lid, I was salivating. But the drum had our usual rations: dried, dehydrated, and freeze-dried food.

The ranch's tepid reception only increased my feeling of disappointment. We'd been greeted nicely enough, there was a picnic table for hikers, and they sold us alcohol fuel by the ounce. But the guest ranch kitchen was not far away, and the array of produce boxes was a teasing reminder that the kitchen's bounty was forbidden—ranch guests only. Feeling like a second-class citizen didn't sit well.

I was also dreading the climb to Sally Keyes Lakes ahead. Four years ago we'd hiked it downhill—and even that was tough. Now we were headed up a 2500-foot gain over six miles while monotonously crisscrossing a slope clad with waist-high manzanita. Without tree cover, I saw the two of us baking again, just like in the desert. I felt miserable, hungry, tired, and downtrodden. I knew my reaction was exaggerated, but that just made it worse. Wallowing in self-pity, I dropped farther back, focusing on the one thing I hoped I could control—*Don't lash out at Frodo.*

Frodo was feeling the weight in her pack from our resupply. Her hair was greasy and her scalp felt itchy from more than a week without a shower. From my silence, from the scowl I was trying to hide, Frodo was quite aware that I was in a black mood. She felt guilty even though nothing was her fault. Then we heard a shout. "Scout!"

It was Nadine's voice. She and Tony snapped us out of our funk in an instant. With the sting blunted, I confessed, "Nadine, it was hard seeing fresh fruit boxes." "Hah! Scout, I crave watermelon all the time." Happily, we imagined cold, sweet juice dripping down our chins.

THE TRAIL WAS stuck in a steady climb the next morning, as the four of us hiked up Bear Ridge. "Nadine," I began. She was only a few feet ahead, while Tony was well ahead of us, and Frodo farther back. "What question haven't I asked that you'd like to answer?" I was priming the pump. We'd been gushing stories like spring snowmelt, but our chatter had trickled out. Soon, Nadine and Tony would split off, heading toward Vermillion Valley Resort and a reunion with Pacha, while Frodo and I continued two more days to Mammoth Lakes—our next shower, clean sheets, and town food.

The morning had been perfect, and I didn't want it to end. The trail offered intermittent views, but each one was an Ansel Adams–worthy image. Alongside us was the deep defile of Bear Creek, and, across it, steep slopes topped out with crags and sawtoothed ridges. No doubt the absence of yesterday's depressed funk combined with nine straight days of oxygen deprivation helped encourage my feeling of exultation.

Nadine cleared her throat. "Scout, did you know that I'm Jewish?" I had no idea. Since we'd first met, Nadine had seen the Star of David on a chain around my neck. One of the duets that Frodo and I sing is a Hebrew prayer. In myriad ways, my Jewish roots are exposed, but that was not the case with Nadine. With her revelation I felt drawn closer still, and yet somehow off-balance.

"When my father was little, he and his parents lived in Paris. He was six years old when everything suddenly changed, when the Nazis occupied France," she began. "My father told me this story only once. I was eight years old." Nadine and her father had gone for a long walk near their home, on the route she loved to ride on her bike—along Harvard,

Yale, and Princeton. "It was during the occupation. His parents were called in. They were to report for questioning by the local gestapo."

Is it possible, I thought, *that Nadine is telling me a Holocaust story?* She continued her tale, her voice somber on this pristine Sierra morning. "They had already put my dad into hiding. He survived the war by pretending to be a little Catholic boy. My grandparents went to the gestapo office together and they called my grandfather in first. My grandmother waited in the anteroom a long time. She knew she would be next. Then a nun came in from a side door." Nadine paused and drew a breath. "The nun told my grandmother, 'Your husband is as good as dead. If you want to live, come with me.' Scout, the nun was asking her to abandon her husband." Nadine's grandmother had to choose.

The rhythm of Nadine's feet didn't change as they hit the pine duff. I saw her reach up to adjust her shoulder strap. With no food left, her pack rode light and high. "My grandmother got up and left. She never saw her husband again."

Nadine's dad said his mother was never the same after that. Nadine had only met her grandmother a few times; each time she looked ancient. Nadine's father finished the story by telling Nadine that, except for him and his mother, all their relatives were killed during the occupation. He later heard that his father had been transported to Auschwitz and died there. With that hanging in the air, we were both quiet for a long time.

EIGHT DAYS LATER, Pacha had been back with Tony and Nadine for a full week. The three of them reached Tuolumne Meadows, mile 942. Pacha was resting in the shade under a well-used picnic table—so far, so good. They had had a grand reunion at Vermillion Valley Resort, with Nadine shouting, "Pacha, you look absolutely HUGE." Now they were lazing about outside the Tuolumne Meadows' combined store, post office, and cafe.

The night before they had camped just outside the southern border of Yosemite National Park, poised to hike the eight miles to Tuolumne Meadows before daybreak. Dogs were allowed in the "front country" of national parks, but not on the trails. They planned to lie low here for the day, then start hiking north as daylight ebbed. They hoped to avoid rangers for the next 56 miles, till they passed back outside the park boundary.

Pacha was lying under the table quietly. It was as if she sensed it was best to hang out of sight. During the day they'd seen rangers on horseback, a quaint throwback to simpler times, posing for vacationers' pictures. The broad meadow fronted Highway 120, a popular route to Yosemite Valley. In the late afternoon, a mounted ranger came up to their table. There was gear scattered about, their clothes and packs had stains and rips, and the guys had beards. It had to be obvious to the ranger that this was a cluster of thru-hikers. From his horse he opened up a conversation. "How's your day going?"

Everyone at the table tensed. They were acutely aware of where this could lead. They all knew that Pacha was not allowed in the backcountry. If, as usual, this line of questioning led to "We started at the Mexican border," then it could surely lead to "What about the dog?" As they sat there silently, Pacha burst out from under the table and began barking at the ranger's horse.

At the table, not one hiker looked up. No one met the ranger's eyes. Nadine tugged on Pacha's leash, pulling her up short. She made three quick silent wishes. *Pacha, stop barking. Stay on your horse. Please go away.* Then the ranger asked, "Are you thru-hikers?" The tension rose, palpable, an electric live wire connecting them all. Nobody wanted to see Nadine get busted. No one wanted to see Pacha hauled off to a kennel. One of the other hikers softly started up a conversation with his mate as if the ranger wasn't there. Another reached down and began fiddling with his gear.

Nadine faced away and stroked Pacha behind the ear. "Good girl. Lie down." Pacha relaxed. Nadine was sweating and her hands would have trembled if she wasn't so tense. At the same time, she was so grateful that, to a person, everyone was standing up for Pacha. After an interminable, awkward wait, the ranger pulled at the reins, turned his horse's head, and left. Nadine, who had been holding her breath, almost let out a gasp. She wanted to race around the table and hug each of these stinky, incredible hikers.

At Dorothy Lake Pass Nadine and Tony left Yosemite National Park. There was no sign announcing "Dogs Welcome," but they felt like they'd seen a marquee flashing this message in neon as Pacha entered Hoover Wilderness a free and legal canine.

EARLY JULY IN the north Sierra is the height of two seasons: wildflowers and mosquitoes. Blooms exploded around Tony, Nadine, and Pacha in clumps and singletons—purple shooting stars, blue-and-yellow wild iris, shoulder-high lupine, and a rainbow of columbine. Like exclamation points, displays dotted the landscape in profuse blasts, all apropos near the Fourth of July.

"A bit buggy," Nadine made a note to write in her blog. That trite phrase didn't begin to describe that day's unrelenting mosquito hell. The swarming fiends got into everything, including their food, nostrils, and mouths. Nadine couldn't sit still for more than a minute, no matter how exhausted she was. She and Tony lived for the moment when they'd be safe in their tent, protected by mosquito netting. Anti-pesticide, Nadine tried using what Tony called her "hippie mosquito repellent." But soon she was so desperate she slathered on Tony's DEET.

Appreciating the wildflowers set against the stunning north Sierra landscape and focusing on all the usual trail concerns—where's the next water, is this the right way, where can I camp, do I still have enough food— were blessings for the pair. So much of the time it drowned out what Tony and Nadine knew was staring them in the face. Echo Lake was now less than 100 miles distant. There, Nadine planned to meet her friends. And Tony would have to make a decision.

CASCADE CREEK MADE a lazy exit from Lake Harriett before picking up steam. The PCT crossed it once near the outlet, and then a second time, a half mile from the lake. At the second crossing the guidebook promised a footbridge. No such luck—it was washed out, and only the rock and cement footings remained. Over the narrow chasm, an insubstantial log subbed in for the man-made span. Without breaking stride, Tony and Nadine strode over it. They knew what this signaled, what they would soon see. And there it was alongside the trail. *Have we really done it?* Walnut-size rocks sketched four numerals in the dirt: "1000." Tony and Nadine had hiked 1000 miles. In sixty-five days they'd walked from New York to St. Louis and then some.

Nadine's plans for Echo Lake dated back to before she started the PCT, and before she met Tony. Nadine's friend Lori, who was mailing her resupply boxes to various spots on the trail, was meeting her at the Echo Lake Youth Camp. Although it had a full complement of kids, long-distance hikers were welcome at the camp, situated on a densely wooded hill a quarter mile above the lake.

Lori was bringing her dog and her young niece, Christy. The plan was to take a full zero before hiking the 65 miles to Donner Pass over six days. Tony knew he was welcome—actually, quite welcome. If he and Nadine had been dating in the city, something like this would be a blip, barely a speed bump. But out here Tony couldn't get past the fact that it would set him back four days.

A full day before they got to Echo Lake, the sky gloomed over and it rained—their first rain since Lake Morena. The brooding low clouds reflected Tony's mood. He didn't want to be irritated at Nadine. But it wasn't just Lori and her dog; there was also that young niece. What was she, fifteen? A group like that would slow him down, and Tony was already exhausted from juggling priorities. Nadine meant a lot to him, but so did the promises he'd made—to Tarik and to himself.

Nadine kept on bringing up ways to try and make it work, but increasingly Tony didn't feel open to any of them. Discussing their options felt like picking at a scab. Nadine offered, "Why don't you wait a day and in a week I'll skip ahead to join you?" She was beginning to wonder if Lori and the niece were just an excuse. They'd fallen into a new pattern during the past week that reminded her of an old married couple fighting. She would be defensive and hurt while Tony withdrew and acted sick of it all. He was having problems separating their budding relationship from his fourteen-year marriage, where he'd felt shackled, beholden, and so afraid that he'd be under those constraints for the rest of his life. And Nadine had baggage of her own, sometimes thinking, *Tony's just like my ex-boyfriend. He only thinks of going forward and not about me.* She kept reminding herself that Tony was not the same man, of how he could make her laugh. How much she loved it when he confided in her.

When they got to the camp, Lori and her niece were already there, as well as Lori's dog, Echo. Nadine ran to hug her good friend. Lori was ten years older than Nadine and the two had met in 1996 when Nadine was a ranger at Denali National Park. Lori herself had 500 PCT miles under her belt, and she knew this neck of the woods in particular.

Later in the day, when Tony and Lori were by chance sitting together, he started asking her questions about herself: "Lori, where do you live? What do you do? How long have you known Nadine?" It felt strange to have a normal conversation, like he was in a city. So many of his interactions with other hikers consisted of: "Where'd you sleep last night? Where's your next resupply? Do you know where you can get alcohol fuel in town?" Tony found that he liked Lori. Apparently Lori felt the same, because afterward she gave Nadine her verdict—"I really like this guy." In the past, Lori had not found a lot to like in Nadine's boyfriends.

As the day wore on, Lori felt like she'd wandered into a movie theater for the climactic scene. There was all this quiet drama around Tony leaving Nadine to finish the trail. Lori worried about her longtime friend. *Her goals have gotten so wrapped up with Tony.*

Tony and Nadine had a tent cabin to themselves. They went about their normal nighttime chores.

Lori and Tony both knew that Nadine was estranged from her family, that she had cut them off clean as if wielding a scalpel. But Lori also knew one thing about which Tony had only a fuzzy idea. Nadine's friends were her family. To Nadine, Lori was like an older sister. That's what made this choice so hard—it was a choice between Tony and family.

Back in 1998, the choice to stay together or part ways wasn't hers. She'd stood on the roadside and watched that boyfriend leave, swallowed in a towering thicket of mountain hemlock and mixed firs. This time she did have a choice, and so did Tony. In the brisk morning air, Tony and Nadine hugged outside the canvas tent. He hitched his pack up on his back, turned, and strode away. Nadine watched as he was swallowed up by a towering thicket of lodgepole pines.

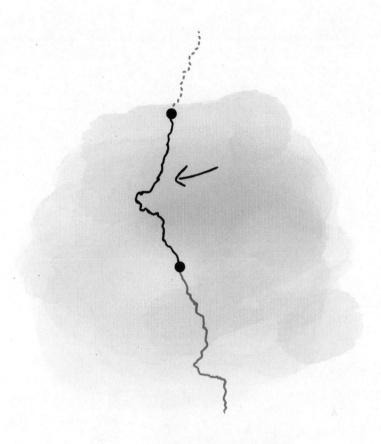

LAVA

Lake Tahoe to Bridge of the Gods

1051 miles

27

Watermelon

LORI WAS STRUGGLING to keep up. It was the second day after she, Nadine, and Christy had hiked out of Echo Lake, and they were climbing 1400 feet up to 9389-foot Dicks Pass—the last time the trail would climb above 9000 feet in elevation. Pacha and Echo were trotting alongside and panting; their tongues lolled as they scampered from one new smell to the next. With the low humidity and direct sun, the eighty-degree heat left them hot and dry.

At the pass they followed a faint side trail running over chipped rock another six hundred feet up to Dicks Peak. At the broad summit, tufts of alpine grass and lingering patches of snow dotted the loose rock. Lori kept reciting, "I can't wait to rest. I can't wait to rest," but once she got to the top, she immediately felt antsy. Nadine and Christy were doing what normal people do—sitting down. Lori called out, "Look there's a big patch of snow," and bounded off, leading the dogs, her shoes crunching on the loose stones. Then she saw something—was it a football? A basketball sticking out of the snow? As she got closer, she shouted out, "Watermelon!" The other two didn't budge. Lori was flabbergasted. *What's wrong with them? Didn't they hear what I said?* Finally, Lori picked up the melon and carried it over as proof. Nadine's eyes bugged when she saw it, a grin splitting her face.

This was not just a watermelon. It was a watermelon on ice in the middle of nowhere, with no footprints in the snow. There was only one explanation: it had dropped out of the sky like a meteor.

They hacked it open and ate piece after piece—pink juice running down their chins, staining their clothes—with the dogs happily eating the rinds. As hikers passed by, they shared the watermelon with them. It was the happiest Nadine had been on the whole trail.

When it was finally gone, they sat spent and full like lions sated from a fresh kill, the chewed-over rinds strewn about them. Only then did Nadine think to herself, *My gosh, I hope we didn't steal someone's watermelon.*

AS NADINE AND Lori set a leisurely pace in the stretch of trail north of Lake Tahoe, Frodo and I logged 21- and 26-mile days, covering it in half the time. We saw no watermelons, but we did have two opposite-spectrum wildlife encounters.

At Miller Creek, as Frodo soaked her sore feet, she saw some twigs moving oddly at the bottom of the cool pool. She bent in close and exclaimed, "Why, that twig has legs!" There were dozens—twigs, seed pods, and tiny pebbles—all with legs the size of tiny hairs darting like miniature hermit crabs. Days later Frodo was able to suss out what they were—caddisfly larvae. Before metamorphosing into winged flies, they were teensy, submerged, armored tanks that bonded bits of plants and other debris to themselves with a sticky silk that extruded from their chins.

That night, Frodo sat next to our open bear canister as she cooked dinner, steam rising from the pot. I was twenty feet away, laying out gear to cowboy camp, when I spotted him. On the other side of Frodo, not fifty feet away, a mass of tawny fur emerged from behind a huge boulder—sleek coat, folds of muscle heavy with summer fat. I had never seen a larger black bear in the wild. Beautiful and the size of a Volkswagen Bug, he hadn't yet seen us. My first reaction—I'm ashamed—was to pull out my camera. Only after I got two shots did I call Frodo's name in a hushed whisper. She put the full pot in the bear canister and screwed the lid shut. Coming beside me she asked, "What should we do?"

"Stand tall and let's sing," I whispered, thinking that it would help us to look large and sound nonthreatening. We sang Leonard Cohen's

"Hallelujah" in two-part harmony. Mid-verse our ursine audience turned his massive head, gave us a long look, and then slowly ambled away. But this was his "house," not ours.

THE ANGORA FIRE started in late June. Extreme winds whipped the fire up into the forest canopy, flames hurtling from treetop to treetop. Million-dollar houses went up like torches. Over two hundred houses burned, reduced to ash and bricks. The conflagration raced to within a mile of the PCT, where it hesitated, as if drawing a breath.

Nadine and Tony had heard about the fire before they parted ways. So often, when they'd hiked together, they'd seen charred slopes, tell-tale blackened husks of oak and yucca, and the skeletal spires of pine and fir. They knew there was a significant chance their hike might be waylaid by this new fire. The year before, in 2006, it had happened to hikers twice—one of the trail closures was only 60 miles from Canada. All thru-hikers could do was cry. Two long weeks passed before the trail corridor reopened.

All it would take was one lightning strike, one campfire ember, or a single cigarette. Nadine knew any of these could spark a fire along the trail. She'd seen so little evidence of wildfire since Kennedy Meadows that she'd been lulled into complacency, but days before they reached Echo Lake, she and Tony began to hear reports from other hikers: "Smoke plumes near Lake Tahoe. Embers and ash falling on the trail." Would the PCT be closed when they got there? Would they be forced onto a detour? Or, worse, would they have to skip a section of the trail?

Yogi, who had hiked right into the thick of it, described the conditions in her online journal, "The air quality was terrible, as the smoke was really thick. Everyone had sore throats. Hikers who were in South Lake Tahoe said that ash and little pieces of burning wood were falling from the sky."

Hammer, who was hiking the PCT with his brother to fill the void left by his father's death the year before, was also impacted. Arriving at Lake Tahoe just before Yogi, he had hitched into town while the Angora Fire burned. Hammer wrote in his online journal, "We talked to a guy who said the house he built 30 years ago burnt and all he managed to save were five pictures. He was all shook up, wandering around." The encounter jolted

Hammer, the man's loss a fresh reminder of the loss of his father. But not an hour later, the two brothers walked into a completely different scene. As they described it:

> *The Red Cross had set up shop in a school to offer relief. They had all sorts of cots and a big lasagna dinner laid out on the tables and ice cream freezers with Drumsticks and really good fruit bars. But the only people there were the volunteers and my brother and me. It was a nice thought and all—but when your million-dollar log home burns down, I don't think you're going to go to sleep on a cot in a middle school gymnasium. But the volunteers were all excited about our thru-hike and kept offering us food and so we kept eating. When we were done they told us to come back for breakfast. So we did—same story— we were the only people there, except for a dude who looked like he also heard about the free breakfast. The lady coordinating the volunteers told us we could take a shower and hop in the pool if we wanted. We got to laughing about how peoples' houses are burning down and we're at the Red Cross, getting in a few laps.*

LATER, YOGI PASSED on the most important news: the fire never crossed the PCT. The trail was still open. Her words—passed via word of mouth in town, through notes left on the trail—spread rapidly, providing relief. Nadine and Tony learned the news before Echo Lake, leaving them with one less worry to fret over.

IT WAS JULY 24, ten days after the watermelon dropped out of the sky. Nadine and Pacha had fallen into the rearguard of the class of 2007 as they plowed on into Northern California. Like most hikers, by this point Nadine had a well-tuned sixth sense for how far ahead or behind other hikers were. She absorbed tidbits from trail registers, gleaned hints from notes left under rocks, read shoe prints, used word of mouth or sheer dead reckoning. Dalton was two days ahead. Frodo and I were six days up the trail. She knew where Tony was, too. In a short span of time, the pair had split far apart. Close to 100 trail miles now lay between them.

The distance between them wasn't just because she'd slowed down to hike with Lori. She'd also taken two more weekends off after good friends drove two hours from her home in Davis. Now, she and Pacha were largely hiking alone. Nadine had started laying down big miles, feeling like a primed fuse, ready to stretch well-muscled legs. Pacha was thriving after those breaks, reveling like a puppy on the consistently softer trail tread. Since resupplying at the last trail town, Sierra City, Nadine had tallied a first, second, and now third 25-plus-mile day. She was opportunistically taking advantage of the easier terrain and still-long July days. The rest of us did the same.

After constant company, Nadine had adjusted to hiking with just Pacha. She read the guidebook more, learning about the mountains she was passing by, and their geology. Now, instead of saying, "Those rocks are pretty," she'd say out loud, "Those phyllite rocks are pretty." And then she'd laugh as Pacha gave her a look. "I'll bet Pacha thinks 'phyllite' means 'pepperoni.'"

Nadine was now eating red meat with relish, enjoying that smoky, rich flavor. Ever since that first bite from Tony's plate, she had wanted more. In Sierra City, with no Tony to ask, "Are you really sure?," she and Pacha had happily ordered burgers. And as she put more of Northern California behind her, she dreamed of more burgers to come, often casting thoughts up the trail toward Tony. As she did, she'd challenge herself—*I'm going to catch him*—and start pumping her legs and lengthening her stride.

Most thru-hikers picked up their pace while passing through this section of trail. Though there was nothing inferior about its landscape, Northern California was like a passed-over wallflower at a dance. The PCT's first seven hundred miles ran through raw desert and sky islands. The next four hundred spanned Sierra passes, countless glacier-carved lakes, abundant waterfalls, and white granite that blinded by day, glowed at sunset, and gleamed by night. Those were hard acts to follow. Northern California, with its volcanoes and weathered lava fields, couldn't help but seem pedestrian by comparison, the plain sister in the mountain brood of the Golden State.

So much of what Nadine saw now was an undulating forest plateau, with shorter climbs and civilized grades. Sure, there was Mount Shasta, the Castle Crags, and the precipitous drop-off of Hat Creek Rim, and sure, every 70 miles or so the trail descended deep into a river canyon. But they were like rhinestone baubles next to the crown jewels of the High Sierra. And after snuggling coquettishly with most every body of water, in Northern California the trail spurned what few lakes it passed. Nadine resigned herself to looking down from afar.

For Nadine, it was fine that the country didn't shout for attention. She had much to reflect on. *I'm in my thirties and I can't help but think, Why haven't my relationships worked? Why don't I trust people more? Why don't I have a better community of people?* Taking stock, she realized that she did have a large circle of good friends. But with that warm glow came a realization: *It takes work. For me, it's not natural. I'm always second-guessing myself.*

Nadine had constructed a family for herself out of a close group of friends and thru-hikers, but the word "family" was anathema to her. Instead, she borrowed a word Pacha might have used if she could talk: "pack." Lori, Frodo and I, and all her friends were part of her pack. There was little or nothing she wouldn't have done for us. And even as Nadine reveled in her independence, she realized she missed chatting and kidding around with other hikers. She thought wistfully of "the three boys" and the games they'd played as they hiked.

Despite that, whether she was negotiating an easy grade or spotting new plants—blue stickseeds, Indian rhubarb, ripe green *Darlingtonia*, and wild gentian—Nadine's thoughts devolved right back to Tony. *Well, if he didn't feel being together was important, then it's not important to me either.* Then she'd remember again how they'd parted. She'd feel that last hug. *It was so sad.* She knew she cared for him deeply. *We'll meet down the road. We'll figure things out. This is just a good break.*

Then she'd recite her challenge again, and pick up her pace.

28

Halfway

PAUL STARTED HIKING the PCT just six days before Blazer. Now, 1200 miles later they'd only been hiking around each other for the last few days. On a day of cold, punishing rain, the two bonded. Single words were muttered as each passed the other in turn, jacket hoods cinched tight, then whole sentences were exchanged, and finally both dished equal measures of gallows humor in the wretched wet and cold. Blazer found his irreverence endearing.

Back at the start, Paul had jauntily penned in the monument register, "I hope I make it to Lake Morena." The entry below his was more traditional: "Fifteen years coming." That's how Paul's hiking partner, Tim, announced his presence on the trail.

Couples on the PCT are scarce, but rarer still, like mountain lion sightings, are a pair of friends starting together. Not ten days passed before the two had acquired trail names. Paul and Tim bore them like proud cowboys jangling first spurs—Bounty Hunter and Figaro—those were their names when Blazer met them; they were part of the fun group of five back on Mount Whitney.

For Figaro in particular the *nom de trail* was apt. He'd spent the better part of his life training to be an opera singer. His high school was a full-time boarding school for the arts. A week after Campo, believing he was alone on a stage of flint-hard sand, he squared his shoulders and burst into song. For ten minutes, amid the brittle tumbleweeds and sage, his tenor voice rang. He had no idea a whole group of hikers was sitting around the bend. When he walked past them someone called, "Hey, Figaro." The name stuck. Perfect as it was, it was also ironic and sad. Figaro didn't let on that four years earlier he had abandoned his dreams of opera.

They were an unlikely pair, a sound bet for dead last in a look-alike contest. At six foot four, Figaro towered over five-foot-eight Bounty Hunter. Figaro had a narrow, chiseled face with deep-set eyes. Bounty's face was a broad oval with a strong chin. Figaro's hair was as dark and thick as a matted bearskin rug. Bounty's had been as thin and patchy as a badly abused pelt—he'd gotten so tired of people pressuring him to use Rogaine that he shaved his head. Figaro had just turned twenty-six. Bounty was near forty.

Despite their differences, the two shared a love of music—Paul first met Tim as the accompanist for Tim's opera lessons—and they shared a gonzo streak of humor. Both thought it was a great idea to drop their drawers and bare their rear ends for a photo alongside the sign for Butt Mountain. They also shared the dream of the PCT, and an abiding confidence in each other. Neither could contemplate what he'd do if the other one quit.

Now, Figaro was off trail for a week to treat a foot infection and see family. Bounty initially welcomed the solitude, but by the time he met Blazer, he was quite ready for company. He told Blazer, "I've known Figaro eight years, but I'm closer to him than to my grade school friends and I've known them thirty years." Bounty's grade school friends told him his hike was silly.

SOON AFTER THAT day together in the rain, Blazer and Bounty shared a campsite. She made Shamus's pudding to share, further cementing the connection they'd formed during the misery of the rain. While they were dipping spoons into the chocolate treat, Blazer lowered her guard. She'd grown to trust him, and it was dark, which helped. He couldn't see her biting the edge of her lip. "Bounty," she said nervously, "I'm a physical therapist." After a thousand miles, it was a relief to tell someone else.

She'd been riding a wave of positives—she was so far along the trail, and her feet rarely hurt. They were camped on a lofty forested ridge with an expansive view that included a glimpse of Lassen Peak, the southernmost of the Cascade volcanoes. Best yet, they were dry—cowboy camping as the stars winked down on them and meteors flashed across the sky. Things were going so well.

In spite of herself, Blazer continued, "It's a traveling job. I get a new assignment every three months." She listened to herself parrot the company brochure, just as she'd done with Dalton, plowing forward in a slow-motion train wreck. "They give me free housing. The pay is great." *What a fascinating way to make a living*, thought Bounty.

The two talked well past hiker midnight. Blazer, in a shadowed corner of her mind, railed at herself. *Why did I lie? What do I have to prove? I have no traveling job. I don't have my license. I failed the tests.* Despite her fears of being reduced to nothing more than her profession, Blazer nodded off without trying to extract a pledge from Bounty not to tell a soul. There was a good reason, something Blazer had already sensed. Like her, on the trail Bounty kept his profession under wraps.

PAUL STARTED PLAYING piano at age seven and he was good. For a short while he assumed everyone played piano as well as he did, but then his piano teacher held a monthlong competition. Each student would keep track of their practice time, with a prize for the one who practiced the most. *I'll never win,* he thought. But Paul won hands down—that's when he learned that it wasn't just skill, it was having the drive. By seventeen, he was the best in his high school and had won bronze in an international piano competition in Palm Springs. But Paul wasn't planning to make piano his life's work; he couldn't picture himself as a starving artist.

And so he went to California Polytechnic and majored in food science. When he graduated, before the ink on his diploma was dry, Campbell's Soup hired him as a quality control manager at their tomato factory. The job involved paychecks and truckloads of tomatoes. Paul suffocated. He hardly practiced piano. *I can't do this for the rest of my life.*

Eighteen months after starting at Campbell's, Paul flew back east to Rochester, New York, stepping into an audition room at Eastman School of Music. Sixty musicians were vying for four slots in the piano master's program. For six months, Paul had spent nearly every non-Campbell's hour practicing his repertoire, but this was Eastman, ranked right beside

Juilliard and Oberlin. Paul played Beethoven and Brahms sonatas and sight-read another piece. Then he flew back home to his Campbell's desk. Eastman sent word—one of the four slots was his. Paul felt released—*I can't wait for the adventure to begin.*

In 1998, six years after jumping the Campbell's ship, Paul graduated with his master's in piano. Ever since, he had made a living performing, accompanying, and teaching. The day he started the PCT, he felt for the second time what he'd felt when he heard from Eastman—*Let the adventure begin.*

Blazer knew about Bounty's piano skills, but she hadn't heard it from him. Worried about being asked to play—and then found wanting—he avoided talking about it. Bounty liked just being a hiker. On the day they all bagged Mount Whitney, Figaro had bragged to Blazer about Bounty's piano playing. She noticed that Bounty sat absolutely still, neither confirming nor denying it. And now, even as Blazer and Bounty grew close, he never mentioned his life's work. She knew her secret was safe.

FRODO AND I next saw Blazer four days after Sierra City, at mile 1265, where the PCT dashed across Big Creek Road. The PCT did that semi-regularly—emerging from the woods, crossing a narrow dirt shoulder, and then scurrying across heated tarmac. Then, on the other side, the path sunk back into wilderness just as if it were 150 years ago on the western frontier. Frodo and I were hiking on, but we'd caught Blazer and Bounty Hunter, whom we'd hadn't yet met, making an off-trail run into town. With the scent of a diner breakfast in their nostrils, they had their thumbs out, hoping to catch a short ride. Four miles distant was a waiting restaurant table at Bucks Lake Lodge.

Glimpsing the blue shorts, black hair, and that hopeful, hitchhiking smile, I shouted, "Hello, Blazer!" Approaching Bounty Hunter, I stuck out a ready hand. But almost simultaneously I thought something of which I wasn't proud. *What's this? Blazer's with* another *guy?* This was the first of two times that morning I'd be quick to judge and cast aspersions.

But on that morning, Bounty was starting to weigh his feelings for Blazer. He wasn't confused about being attracted to her, and he appreciated that she was funny, engaging, and always ready for rapid-fire conversation. Like him, she expressed herself with her hands—professional hands that were strong like his own. He loved that she had no pretense about her, that she cared not a whit about his hair. But as much as he was taken by Blazer, he prized the absolute freedom of the trail more than anything. In the three months since he'd started, he'd seen hiking couples form, grate like sandpaper, and then split. *Don't start something if you're not serious,* he thought, battling himself. *What does Blazer want? Does she feel the same way?* Pulled eight ways from Sunday, Bounty Hunter flailed in a whirl of emotions.

FIVE MILES LATER, Frodo and I took a real break at the next east-west high-way, Bucks Lake Road. We were munching energy bars on the road's south side when a pale green Forest Service fire truck parked nearby. Five firefighters exited, swinging heavy packs on their backs. Then they lined up single file and marched off north on the PCT, tools in hand. *Look at them,* I thought. *They look like the Seven Dwarfs.* Their heads bobbed under burnished hard hats with "FIRE" stenciled on their tallow-colored shirts. Some wore overalls while the rest wore dungarees. Casting aspersions, I started writing down my impressions in my journal. *Snow White's minions couldn't have looked more purposeful and cheery.* They evidenced no urgency, so I felt safe poking fun. *It must be a training exercise.*

Indeed, the Ganser Bar Fire Station crew that morning were in no rush. Captain Matt O'Dell and the four others—James Lico, Collin Holly, Yoni Cohen, and Jason Bates—were on a routine training mission, carrying their fire suppression tools and emergency medical supplies as was the norm. For this particular training session they were coordinating with a helicopter—it would rendezvous with the team soon.

We were perhaps a half mile behind when we started following their deep-soled boot tracks up the trail. Climbing a closed dirt road, the PCT entered Bucks Lake Wilderness with little fanfare. Twelve hundred miles of the PCT passes through forty-eight different wilderness areas that run the gamut of the alphabet, from the Ansel Adams in California to the William O. Douglas in Washington. Nearly half the trail is on federal wilderness, and here, in the most populous state in the country, the norm, the default, was that we were walking on congressionally designated wildlands. No other long trail comes close.

But on this morning, the wilderness looked like a narrow, abandoned jeep road. The bright waist-high chaparral—so unlike the dull greens of Southern California—carpeted the rising slope as encroaching branches intertwined to reclaim the old track. Masses of chinquapin and manzanita leafed out in vibrant greens. Fifty years ago this slope was logged and clear-cut, but now the Jeffrey pines were staging a comeback.

Much of this Northern California flora was new to us. New were the patches of mountain misery, a distant cousin of the dagger bushes that had ensnared Blazer at the beginning of the trail. Mountain misery had a smell hikers loved or hated. I was with those who thought it smelled like tangy witch hazel. Frodo turned up her nose and thought, *Smells like pee.*

As we tracked deeper into the woods, we started to sense a far-off vibration, a low thrumming that rattled our fillings and set us on edge. Soon the far-off drumbeat coalesced into an audible *whumph, whumph.* An hour had passed since our break and we were enveloped by dense forest. *That has to be a helicopter. I think it's circling.* The noise increased as I craned my neck. *Where is it? We should see it.* But a dense canopy blocked the view—red fir, Jeffrey pine, and mountain hemlock thick as a rain forest. In pendulum swings, the sound rose and fell, cycling back and forth.

Then there was a swath of sunlight, and a clearing emerged. Two of those hard-hatted dwarves were laying out wide, heavy plastic strips in a small grass meadow—a large red X. Just ahead I saw a knot of people clustered on the trail. I recognized one hiker, and then saw another lying in the dirt in the middle of the trail. It was a young woman, curled tight, her slim body balled in the fetal position.

Twenty-five-year-old Roswell had spent the night gripped by vomiting, diarrhea, and stomach cramps like thunderbolts. All morning, two hikers, Recline and Monty, had been helping her, each one supporting a side, to head south, the closest way out. They'd managed two miles in four hours, a bare creep, making for Bucks Lake Road.

Between the cruel torture of each step, one frightened thought pierced Roswell's pain. *I'm not quitting my hike.* She felt ashamed that others had to help her, impeding their own hikes. Trying to stay strong, she'd shuffle one foot, lift it, and move it ahead. Often, she would double over from pain for a bit before straightening up and shuffling the next foot forward. When she saw figures on the trail ahead, she thought it was a mirage. Hard hats. A fire crew. Experts taking charge. *Is this real?*

Learning that a helicopter was on the way, she felt another wave of shame. *I can't pay for it. I don't deserve it.* Only when she saw them head into the meadow to lay out the landing tape did she believe it was happening. A day hiker—a nurse—was at the scene and her voice sliced through Roswell's interior monologue. "Relax, dear," she soothed. "Accept the support." It was those words that gave Roswell permission. *Finally, I don't have to be strong any more.* Roswell crumpled to the ground, pulled tight into a ball, and grasped her knees as her body shivered.

That's how Frodo and I came upon her. We got a quick rundown from the two hikers who had helped her reach the meadow. Lightly touching Roswell's shoulder, I said, "Be well," and we prepared to move on. Roswell cocked her head slightly, and through gritted teeth said, "Scout and Frodo, please stay." We'd never met, but we'd heard of each other. The trail grapevine tied us together sure as manila rope. And so we sat by her and watched heaven descend to earth—a white fuselage, thin blades whirling overhead, a bright red aerodynamic tail. Heaven came in the shape of a Bell 212.

No sooner had the chopper flattened the high grass than a stretcher appeared and was quickly carried to where we sat. Frodo and I lifted our hands gently from Roswell's shoulder and turned her over to the five firefighters. They lifted her gingerly but firmly onto the stretcher. Slender and limp, she was more rag doll than thru-hiker. Threading the stretcher through the woods and out to the meadow below, they worked as if with one mind, sure and efficient.

We saw the door slide close. *Whumph, whumph.* The twin turbines revved, rotor blades disappeared in a whir, the skids lifted, and they were airborne. Frodo and I walked off. "Godspeed, Roswell," I whispered. And I followed that with two thoughts: *Who will finish? Will I make it?*

TWO DAYS LATER I put Frodo's capacity for surprise to the test. I'd told several others, "At the halfway monument we're going to shave our heads. It's a secret. Frodo doesn't know." When I told Blazer, her response had mirrored my own thoughts: "Will Frodo do it?" And Blazer also wondered, but kept to herself, *Scout, is this a good idea for a surprise?*

Surprises had already become a special part of the trail for me. Occasionally I'm asked, "What's it take to be able to thru-hike?" My response is to point to my head. You have to really, really want to do it. You have to be mentally tough. Some part of your psyche has to become a clenched steel fist. Surprises help pull me up the trail by giving me something to look forward to, and one by one they mark the progress of my hike.

We rose at 4:45 a.m., first light, and skirted forested ridges for 14 miles before spotting a stub of a cement post. I knew what it signaled: the halfway point! "Hey, I see packs ahead," I said to Frodo. "They don't look like thru-hikers." My best friend from Boy Scouts, Larry, was there with his son-in-law, Rob. Frodo at first thought that he had hiked in to surprise *both* of us, but she realized something was afoot when I asked Larry, "Did you bring the stuff?"

Larry's car was still another 10 miles down the trail—from there, we hoped to make it to town in time for dinner and a night in a motel. No time to waste—there never is during a thru-hike. I set down my pack and turned to my bride, announcing, "I'm going to shave my head." Then I followed that with a quieter, "and I suggest you do so too." I had no idea what she'd do. Even odds, I'd say. But even if she didn't, I'd still shave mine and it would be fun.

Frodo leveled her gaze at me, placed her hands firmly on her hips, and reared up to every inch of her five-foot-two frame. She took a deep breath and gave me her pronouncement. "Absolutely not. No way."

I turned to Larry, knelt down, and laid my bandanna on the ground to catch the falling hair. I might not have known what Frodo would do, but there was one thing I knew after our thirty-year marriage: "Absolutely not" might not be the final answer. I knew there was still a chance, as long as I didn't say a word.

It felt joyful, liberating, to have my hair shaved for the first time. "My gosh, he's really doing it!" exclaimed Larry and Rob while others joshed, gave catcalls, and eagerly snapped photos. As my bare scalp emerged shiny and pale, I looked down at all that hair, a mix of dark gray and silver, and I said the first thing that popped into my head. "It looks like two old badgers got into a fight. And they both lost."

When Larry was finished, I stood up. Even in a faint breeze my scalp felt cold, but a huge grin lit my face. This was outrageous. Where else would I ever do this? And we'd made it halfway! Frodo walked over, looked at Larry holding the now-quiet shaver, and then at me. She said, "You do it."

Frodo knelt, her knees sinking into the depressions mine had left in the duff, before leaning over the bandanna. As wheat falls to a thresher, so too did Frodo's three-inch locks fall as I ran the buzzing blades.

That evening in town Frodo spoke to her parents. They'd seen the photo we'd just posted online from our motel in the tiny town of Chester. Our shaved heads had top billing in our most recent post, even over the halfway monument. "Dear," they said, "you've been too long on the trail." More practically, they added, "After this, you'll have a hard time hitching."

If someone had pressed their ear against our motel room door that night they would have heard Frodo exclaim, "It darn well better grow back soon!"

TWENTY-FOUR HOURS LATER, July 23 was Blazer's eighty-fifth day on the trail. Between her middle and index fingers she squeezed a cigar thicker than her thumb. Her sore feet and those miserable rainy days were forgotten as smoke wisps coiled off a fat stub of ash. She had reached the PCT halfway point earlier that day.

She was camping with four others and in the glow of that lit cigar, Blazer's dust-streaked face shone in the thickening dusk. She stood side by side with Bounty, her elbow nestled behind his back. Bounty held his own cigar, with long sleeves rolled high, exposing muscled forearms fit for a stevedore, or a pianist. One of those arms was draped over Blazer—a pose reminiscent of Blazer and Dalton on Mount San Jacinto on day fourteen. But while Dalton had held back, Bounty clearly wasn't. On the keyboard, notes came off his hands exactly as intended—so too with his hands now, confidently enveloping the shoulder of the pretty girl with the cigar.

Blazer, Bounty, and the three others had reached the monument 24 miles earlier. Emerging from intermittent red fir, they had found the three-foot cement pillar in a small clearing. Inch-tall yellow letters etched into its sides carried a high-watt message, like a huge concrete exclamation point: "PCT MIDPOINT—MEXICO 1325 MILES—CANADA 1325 MILES." Halfway!

The five of them took photos, signed the register, had a brief rest, and moved on. They had hiked around each other all day—Blazer and Bounty, Figaro, who had returned to the trail two days earlier, Allegheny, with whom I'd shared a shower stall way back at Kennedy Meadows, and OJ, a young woman journalist who'd been nearly as inexperienced as Blazer at the start. Views of Lassen Peak grew more and more prominent with each mile and they knew that mighty Mount Shasta would soon appear on the horizon. Only when they'd settled in at their campsite that evening did the celebration begin. It was Allegheny who broke out cigars. He'd hoarded them for this moment, and passed them out like a proud papa crowing about his kid's birth.

With each breath, a cigar glowed and then faded, winking on and off like fireflies. The last gasp of the sun added crimson shades to the scattered clouds. Taking it all in—everything they had accomplished—Blazer started laughing. Amid the wisps of smoke, and these improbable companions, she was giddy, gleeful. She drew in another raw pull of dank, earthy smoke and, as she let it out, said, "There is no place on Earth that I would rather be than right here, right now. And never in my life would I ever have imagined being here." Blazer had just put into words what each of the others felt. For a long while, the five of them sat there in silence.

IN THE END, Roswell stayed off trail for two weeks. Almost the entire time she felt she was in crisis. *Do I get back on or stay off?* She really wanted to return, but she didn't want to be foolish—even after two weeks she hadn't completely recovered from her bout of giardiasis. She didn't want to risk a recurrence. By the time Roswell got back on trail, however, she was realistic. She knew that losing two weeks made a Canada arrival unlikely.

Roswell wasn't alone in her decision. Twenty-five thru-hikers that year contracted giardia. They all returned to the trail, but they knew the time off had hurt their chances of making it to Canada.

ONLY ONE DAY after the halfway marker, Bounty Hunter was hurting. "Leave me alone," he said, leveling his voice at Blazer as if sighting down a gun. His tone brooked no questions. "Blazer, leave me. Go ahead." Figaro had already started walking off.

That day had begun so well. The three of them had hiked past Boiling Springs Lake, pinching their noses as they edged by hissing mudpots and fumaroles that steamed like teapots, the atmosphere redolent with sulfur. Then, within a mile, they walked into a posh hot spring resort called Drakesbad Ranch. Drakesbad's standard rates would outstrip most hikers' wallets, but the resort managers, Billie and Ed, gave hikers a steep discount for meals and also allowed them free use of the showers and the hot-spring-fed swimming pool. Bounty, Figaro, and Blazer stayed for breakfast, then lunch. Blazer wrote in her journal something she had thought was impossible: "Too much food." But gluttony wasn't what took down Bounty Hunter—it was a long soak in the hot pool.

Six miles after Drakesbad, Bounty's water-swollen feet staged a rebellion alongside forest-edged Swan Lake. One toe led the coup, nearly forcing him to his knees. It throbbed like an ingrown toenail. Blazer tried everything, including taping it and cleaning it out with a needle. Especially since she had told him that she was a physical therapist, Blazer felt frustrated and helpless; nothing she did made a difference. Growing increasingly stubborn and sullen at being unable to walk, Bounty told them to go on. In that moment, Blazer got a front-row view of the depth of Bounty and Figaro's bond. The two had made a pact long ago: if one of them said to hike on, they hiked on. No questions.

As Blazer watched Figaro's pack recede from view up the trail, she thought, *Well, I didn't agree to that.* When he realized she wasn't following Figaro, Bounty glared at her. It didn't change Blazer's resolve. *I am not leaving a hobbling man.* They went back and forth, with Bounty telling her again, "You need to leave me now." He stood there, waiting.

Finally, Blazer broke the impasse, "Why are we still talking about this? I'm sticking with you. That isn't an option."

29

Under Lock and Key

THREE DAYS LATER, Bounty breezed by Frodo and me in the early morning. His feet had improved by the morning after Drakesbad, and, with the easier terrain, his limp had abated and he'd gratefully slipped back into his regular pace. Not thirty minutes later, when we stepped aside for Blazer, I thought I might stretch my legs. "Do you mind," I asked Frodo, "if I walk on ahead?" I did this a few times a week. A hiker would overtake us, I'd check in with Frodo, and then surge ahead and chat. Within an hour or two, I'd drop off the faster pace—then Frodo would catch up with me.

I shifted up a gear, staring at the back of Blazer's pack. In my mind I could picture Frodo's—the wide, mesh center pocket bulging with the section maps, a ziplock baggie of Purell and toilet paper, and a ziplock with her ten essentials—matches, compass, needle, thread, whistle, garbage bag, mirror, headlamp, a half of a comb, pencil wrapped with a length of duct tape, a quarter, and a paper list of important phone numbers. Blazer's pack was a contrasting mix of gray and red nylon with at least ten tie-down straps. The tip of her faded yellow bandanna peeked out of a side pocket next to a hanging nifty all-in-one whistle, thermometer, compass, and magnifier.

As we walked together I thought about Blazer's budding relationship with Bounty, and its similarities with the one she shared with Dalton. It concerned me that she kept each one at arm's length. Just as with our own kids, I wanted to picture Blazer happy with a real partner.

The landscape we were walking through seemed stuck in a monotonous loop. The old lava beds between Lassen and Shasta were covered with only a thin layer of soil, limiting the flora to fire-prone grasses and stunted bushes. Someone, somewhere else in the world, had cornered the market on shade. With parched lips, I started to tell a story about myself. Blazer knew how my marriage to Frodo began. She'd heard the story twice, the second time only a few days ago, and had started smiling as she recognized some of the lines. One in particular Blazer took real delight in, what Frodo thought after I'd "asked" her to marry me. "It wasn't a question. He didn't ask me a question."

When I grew up, vinyl records were king, the long-play 33s and 45 singles. But why had they called them "singles" when there was always a song on the flip side? That's where I started with Blazer, talking about the flip side. Every marriage has one, I think. Ours was only different by degree.

I asked Blazer if she knew Frodo and I had once separated. From in front of me I heard, "I don't think so." I continued the story. We were apart for three whole years. One night in the eleventh year of our marriage, we tucked our three kids into bed as usual. Sean was five, Jordie was two, and Nicky was four months old. I was at the keyboard of the first computer we'd ever bought, playing a video game, *Crystal Quest*, which was odd because I'm not into video games. Neither is Sandy, yet she had almost been encouraging me the past few months, mounting no objection as the electro-punk noises of the attackers issued from that Apple Macintosh SE. I had just reached level twenty-four. That was high for me.

That's when Sandy called me over. Sitting on the couch, she asked, "Can you come here? I have something I have to tell you." As I walked to the couch, my stomach filled with dread.

I kneeled on the carpet just across the coffee table from her. In a flat, even voice, I heard the woman I loved say, "I am having an affair with Chris, my lab assistant. I'm leaving. I'm going to move across the country to be with him at Princeton." Each sentence was worse. *Please make it stop. Please hit bottom.* Then it did. "I'm taking Nicky. Nicky is his child, not yours."

She expected me to throw her out. She had prepared to leave. Instead, I asked if we could try to work on it, see a counselor, attempt to save our marriage. But the counselor we saw for the next six months basically supervised a civilized breakup. I certainly bore my share of the responsibility for our drifting apart. We'd had problems for a while and hadn't faced them.

Sandy did take Nicky, and she did move in with Chris, but not across the country. In the end, she couldn't leave our two older kids behind, so he moved back to San Diego. I cared for Sean and Jordie, and she cared for Nicky.

It was one of the hardest things I've ever done. I had to change my answer to a common question. "How many kids?" "Two," not three.

I dated. I moved on. Yet we still shared a blanket at the kids' soccer games. I'd write her long letters, once every month or two, and she would respond in kind. All through that time, we both still genuinely liked to talk to the other. Soon enough, Chris showed his true colors and treated her badly. Sandy tried for a year to make things work and then moved out. Then she did what marrying at age nineteen had prevented—dated as an adult.

Two years and six months after we separated, I asked her out. At that time we were both seeing interesting people, and felt that our personal stocks were running high. We went to a rom-com: *Green Card* starring Gérard Depardieu and Andie MacDowell. My choice—I am and always will be a hopeless romantic. There's usually a point in those movies when I want to hold the hand of the person next to me. When *Green Card* hit that point I thought, *I've worked so hard to rebuild my life. I am really happy with it. If I reach out and take her hand, I put everything at risk. Everything I've built back up, I'll lay on the line.*

Yet, as Depardieu spoke on in the darkened theater, I reached for her hand. Since we had been apart I had been in a handful of relationships, but holding hands always felt uneasy. Do we intertwine fingers? Do we clasp with full palms together? Holding Sandy's hand, her fingers slowly laced with mine, I felt the full weight of all that was at risk. And in the

same moment I felt in my heart—and knew with certainty—that someday I'd be telling this story, looking back on thirty years of marriage.

It had taken me three-quarters of a mile, maybe fifteen minutes, to tell
our story. I finished by saying, "Blazer, I am a lucky man. Tonight, like
every night, I go to bed with my soul mate."

Blazer daubed her face with her threadbare bandanna. I hadn't told her
the story to make her cry; I told it as a gift. *Blazer, someday I hope you'll have a*
partner and you'll remember this story, this day, and avoid some of our mistakes. In
the still air both of us could hear the other's breath. I asked Blazer what
I thought was an innocuous question, "So, what was it like growing up?"

She felt the day's heat magnify. A part of her didn't believe what she
was contemplating. *Should I do this?* She had been asked questions like
this before, but to actually give a real answer was uncharted territory. If
I'd asked this question early on the trail, at McDonald's, the Saufleys', or
even Kennedy Meadows, she'd have sloughed off my query, same as ever.
Maybe she'd have thrown me a laugh line. But Blazer and I were past the
halfway point.

"Scout, my dad was an alcoholic." Hearing the words in the open air
was startling. Equally startling was the relief she felt. "It really was awful.
When I was little I'd go to friends' homes and pretend that their parents
were mine." Even as Blazer spoke, the ground didn't open up beneath
her—her footing was still solid. She had wondered her whole life if this
day would come. From that point, the words flowed like a Sierra stream
tumbling from one granite bench to the next. "Sundays after church were
the worst." He'd start his drinking right at the table. In no time, her heart
pounding, Amanda would be hiding in the closet, clutching her teddy
bear. "When my dad finally left, I was glad." Without pausing, Blazer told
me she was a physical therapist, and that she'd wanted to be one ever
since she could remember.

She paused then, coming up for breath. To the rhythm of our feet pad-
ding on the trail, I leapt forward in time. "When was the last time you
were in a relationship?"

Blazer reached back and pulled the yellow bandanna from the side
pocket of her pack. I saw her dab her face. "Scout, I haven't told anyone. I
haven't dated for four years."

"So, don't other folks notice?" I asked.

"Not really, it just became matter-of-fact. I didn't need to date. It never came up during graduate school because work was so intense. A couple of my friends tried to hook me up with someone, but that wasn't going to happen."

As we continued to hike, she told me how close she felt to her brother Ian, how crushed she'd been when she learned that he was her half brother and how they'd never really spoken about it. Lowering her voice, she circled back to descend into the spiral of her youth. "After Dad left no one was watching me. Mom was at work all the time. I was practically raising myself. I started hanging around with a really bad crowd. They were all older. That was the start of my 'wild time.'"

Blazer was gripping the bandanna, now damp, swinging it in time with her gait, and then reaching up to her eyes to daub off tears mixed with dust. I walked as quietly as I could, not saying a word.

"I was thirteen and fourteen, always the youngest hanging out at the park." She mentioned the park's name once—Kaulmont—and then didn't say it again. "Some of the kids were out of high school. They thought it was great fun to get me drunk. Even worse." Then she used the phrase again— "wild time." She needed me to know what happened. I couldn't see her face, but I could hear her voice—normally so firm and steady—trembling.

At that point she left off, content with how much she had shared. In the silence I paused, but I knew there were two more questions to ask. I didn't want to push, but I had come clean, and wanted her to have the opportunity to do the same with me. "Blazer, did your wild time involve drugs?"

Pause. Footsteps. The hand with the yellow bandanna went up to her face. "Yes."

Then after another long pause I asked, "Did they involve sex?" Blazer hesitated even longer before answering softly, "Yes."

In my trail journal that night, I wrote,

> *I came on this journey for many reasons and to do many things. Some I knew beforehand—a 30th anniversary to be observed, one (or two) heads to be shaved—and many came as a surprise. Today, I added one more. I had an important talk. For an hour, twice that, or maybe 45*

minutes, I'm not sure, I opened doors with a fellow hiker. We ushered
each other into locked vaults. We spoke of things whose very names we
keep under lock and key. Today, in the open, we named things rarely
acknowledged even to ourselves. This was one reason I came on this
hike. I just hadn't known it.

Blazer's trail journal didn't carry one word of our talk, just as in her journal at home she had never once written about Kaulmont Park.

"BLAZER, WHAT'S THE biggest broken thing in your youth?"

Ordinarily she'd dodge a question like mine, or mention the time she blew the transmission on her ancient Oldsmobile Cutlass Ciera. But, if she was waxing voluble among friends over flowing beer, she might begin instead by describing Big Don.

Big Don was practically an institution in her hometown of St. Marys. Bushy browed with a constant grin, he was indeed big, but short. He'd say, "I'm five foot five on a good day." Bold, zestful, one of a kind, and yet as comforting as a soft shoulder—these descriptions also fit the pizza bearing his name.

Don's Pizza, situated on the busy intersection of South St. Marys and Mill, had been open two years when fifteen-year-old Amanda started hanging out there after school. From the very start, Don mattered to her. She could sit with her books without buying anything—when Don saw her doing homework, he often gave her a free drink. Don went to her soccer games. Amanda's best friend was on the team and worked for Big Don, who attended all his employees' games. Don cheered just as loudly for Amanda. Don might have been only a dozen years older than Amanda, but she looked up to him like a father.

Amanda was envious every time she looked out the huge floor-to-ceiling front window and saw her friend drive off to deliver Don's pizzas. With tips, the money was so much better than Amanda's babysitting pay. The day she turned sixteen, Amanda got her license and a week later she was a pizza delivery driver. She was tickled pink to be working for Don.

Don was just as pleased with Amanda. When they got busy, Don quickly learned that she was the one who rallied everybody. Over the noisy phone orders, the ovens' hum, and the jostling of the busy store, Amanda exhorted her coworkers, "All right, everyone, let's go." Don saw that the busier it got, the more excited she got. He felt she was destined for something big. He knew that she'd leave St. Marys.

The night something broke, Amanda and Don were the only ones left at closing. It was almost 10:00 p.m. by the time the last three pizzas came out of the oven and she ushered them, piping hot, into boxes, and then onto the seat of her Cutlass Ciera. With one hand on the wheel, Amanda looked over her shoulder at the storefront, lit from inside. She could see where she used to sit, green with envy, watching someone else deliver pizzas. She turned the key and a not-quite-tuned engine yielded up a rumble. Amanda threw the car in reverse.

If pizza throwing were an Olympic event, Don would have made the US team. In his deft hands, the swirling dough became an ever-thinning Frisbee. It could reach five feet in diameter, nearly as wide as Don was tall. For youth groups, a tour of Don's Pizza was a popular St. Marys event, and the grand finale was when Don tossed a pizza to see just how big he could make it before it ripped. Each time, the moment it tore, he would toss the dough circle up and out. It usually landed atop at least five kids; they loved it. One time when a group of preschoolers was visiting the shop, Don threw it up in the air and all the kids split except for one girl. The dough landed on her head and drooped to the floor. Don was aghast. He pried up the dough and looked at her, asking, "Are you okay?"

"Silly pizza man," she said. Tears were starting to form—hers and his—but then she burst out laughing.

In Don's world, Amanda was a highflyer, but Amanda knew she was lucky to have Don in her life. She could attract good people, but side by side with that was her penchant for slamming into doors. Don had noticed the way she constantly hit her head on things. When someone opened a door, she'd walk straight into it. He'd see her turn and then *bang!* Life struck Amanda like that—failing the tests, a drunken dad, or "here, hold this paper while I light it on fire." In the end that posed the question: Which would win out, the good people or the doors?

But there was one more thing Don had noticed about Amanda: she wasn't good at backing up her car.

Amanda smelled those three pizzas next to her. The deliveries were all over town so she needed to hurry if she was going to deliver them still hot—Big Don's pride was that all pizzas were delivered hot. She backed up quickly, turning the car to face the driveway, and her bumper tapped an outdoor table. The bumped table then hit the glass window—the ensuing sound was like a cannon shot.

Glass hurled like blown icicles across the front of the shop. *What exploded?!* thought Don. *Did someone throw a brick?* Glass slivers were everywhere. Running as fast as he could to the front door without slipping, Don saw Amanda's car idling near the shattered storefront. He tried to get her attention, screaming, "Hey! Hey!" That's when Amanda took off.

The dark pit in Amanda's stomach got larger and larger with each mile she drove. When she returned, Don was still outside. Shoulders raised, he extended his arms, palms up, and cocked his head as she got out of the car. Everything about his body language telegraphed, *Didn't you see me jumping up and down? Didn't you hear me yelling?* "What the hell were you doing?" asked Don. Amanda looked at the ground. "Don, I knew what I did. But sticking around wasn't going to make a difference. I figured I should make the deliveries. I didn't want your pizzas to be late." They were both near tears. Processing what she'd said, Don was surprised to find himself feeling the same as when he lifted the dough from the little girl's head.

Amanda kept her job. She worked at Don's all through high school, until she left for college. But she was not soon forgotten at Don's Pizza—for many years they kept a sign on the glass out front that read: "Amanda's window."

If ever asked about Kaulmont Park, Don would dispense a curt answer: "That's the bad part of town. When I was growing up my parents wouldn't let me go near there."

"BLAZER, WHAT'S THE biggest broken thing in your youth?" This question was just like one of my old 45 records. It had a flip side, one with the real answer.

Three years before she started working at Don's Pizza, just before she turned thirteen, Amanda wrote in her journal, "Now that Dad's gone we can do whatever we want!" Though Amanda celebrated her newfound freedom, she was also angry and frustrated. With her mom now working the night shift, Amanda felt like she was never home. There was no accountability.

Kaulmont Park was the most dismal of St. Marys' four parks. Small, with no playground or even benches, it centered on an amoeba-shaped oval of scraggly grass. The grass grew in a depression; in happier days, in winters long ago, this was an outdoor ice rink, but now it gathered trash. The merry shrieks of bundled children, a boy and girl's first time holding hands, scenes from Currier and Ives, were long in the past.

Amanda and the older toughs had no inkling there'd ever been an ice rink. They came to Kaulmont Park because it was an open space, with a mat of trees on the northeast side deep enough to hide them from prying eyes. Thick as a witch's woods, the tangle of birch, maple, and oaks ended abruptly at a rail spur line—not deep enough to hike in, or deep enough to feel surrounded by nature. Industrial sites surrounded the park on three sides—a cement and gravel yard, auto part factories—so that the clangs and clanks in the park far outnumbered the sounds of birds.

Amanda spent her first few days at Kaulmont Park because she was curious, but was soon drawn in by the allure of smoking cigarettes and watching others go off into the woods to do drugs. As the youngest, she was initially considered the mascot, a plaything. For Amanda, it became a place to belong, a place she didn't have to pretend to have a perfect family. Days turned to weeks, weeks to months, and even the shock of that night she got stumbling, pass-out drunk—when her friend's mom yelled at her—wasn't enough to drive her away.

She was still spending time at Kaulmont Park a year later, when she turned fourteen. That year, the birthday curse felt like it had abated, so Amanda had nothing bad to record in her journal. Already, even in jeans and loose-fitting clothes, Amanda was budding out. She was taller now, with burgeoning hips, and her hair was a full-bodied mass of curls, long and black. Maybe that's what made her stand out. "He" wasn't a newcomer to the park, he was a man already out of high school and he'd never paid her much attention. *He's in his twenties*, Amanda thought. She was heading into ninth grade.

Six miles separated Kaulmont Park from Amanda's house, a distance she had walked twice. Even then, she wasn't afraid of walking, but when Amanda could, she'd get a ride. So when he asked her to get in his car, she thought he was offering her a ride home. He was cute and charismatic; she felt flattered to have this older guy flirt with her.

Sure she wanted a ride with him. She wanted a chance to listen to his stories. An end-of-summer sun stood two hands' width above the horizon. They started out driving toward her home. He was chatty. She was excited, her stomach flip-flopping. When he took a side road, she tried to focus on just being with him. "Where are we going?" she asked. "Don't you worry about it," he said.

He drove for some time, found a secluded spot, and then stopped the car. Her stomach butterflies changed to unease. He leaned toward her and said, "You're real pretty, you know." She was barely fourteen—scared, confused, desperate to fit in. Pretty wasn't how she felt. He moved closer to her on the front seat.

When he leaned over to kiss her, she was uncomfortable. "What's going on?" He slid himself nearer and pushed his lips onto hers. Amanda started to move back, but the car door limited her retreat. Unease changed to alarm. She pushed him away. "It's okay," he said. Between shoving his lips at her face, he started spreading compliments. "You're so beautiful. I love your hair." She heard the words, from a guy she all but idolized. For a moment, her emotions swung wildly. Then not just his lips, but his hands were on her, grabbing. Clothes pushed, raised, rustling, a zipper lowered.

She shouted, "Stop! Now! That's it!" Cries against a whirlwind. *I'm strong*, she thought. Back jammed into the car door, with all her might she tried to shove him away.

Amanda was nine years old when she wrote what she wanted in life. March 2, 1992: "This is how I want to live. I will have a cute husband. I'll have two children, a boy and a girl. I'll take good care of them." Every morning she'd curl her daughter's hair. Every night she'd make dinner. "I really hope this will come true."

Screams came from the car. It shook and no one heard. "No, no!" The inside was sweltering, the smooth surface of the upholstery sweaty against her legs. She could feel its imprint. She couldn't see straight; his chest and shoulder were jammed into her face. She pushed at his hands and shoved against his face. She was strong. *Listen to me.* "Stop! Take me back! Right now!" He was bigger, stronger. He didn't stop.

When he brought her back to the park, she was deathly quiet. Someone must have driven her home, but she has no memory of it. She'd retreated deep, her mind as well as her body in shock after so much trauma. She took the longest hot shower, then lay on her bed all the next day. Amanda told her mom she was sick. She would be sick for an entire week.

AMANDA WAS IN a hallway at her high school the first time she heard it. "Bitch." She couldn't believe the sneer came from such a pretty face, and was incredulous that it was directed at her. That's how she found out that he'd bragged about what happened. That he had a girlfriend, a senior. Worse still, a cheerleader. Teaming up with her friends, his girlfriend made Amanda's life miserable the whole year—yelling slurs, spitting at her, throwing gum in her hair. Amanda counted the days until the cheerleader would graduate.

Amanda didn't write in her journal until six months after the rape. February 17, 1997:

> *Dear Diary, I have not written in a long time. I guess I only write when times are bad, when I feel there is no one else to turn to, no one else to trust. Behind all my smiles and cheer, there is a lonely, crushed, depressed woman hiding all of her emotions. I do not know how to begin.*

AND SHE DIDN'T. The entry abruptly ended.

During her junior year, Amanda started dating a guy. She'd firmly resolved to not be sexually active, but word traveled to him, too. He threw it at her: "I heard you already had sex, so what's the big deal?" He kept pecking at her, breaking chinks in her resolve until finally she gave in.

All through this, it was unthinkable that she would tell anyone, "He raped me." Amanda wrote in her journal: "No matter how far you run, it still haunts you." She wished she didn't know where he lived, but she did. It wasn't far from a favorite St. Marys haunt, a deli frequented by Amanda and her friends. Her stomach would tie in knots whenever the others started walking in that direction—she always suggested another route. And as for the park, Amanda never went there again. When she went off to college, she shook off St. Marys like a wet dog shaking off rain. But she couldn't shake off the rape.

In movies and books, Amanda could sense a rape scene before it began. "Leave now," she wanted to warn the girl. "Walk away." But the scene would inevitably wind toward the unthinkable. Sometimes Amanda felt the cheap car upholstery again, clammy against her skin. If she was watching at a friend's house, she would excuse herself to make popcorn, or get a drink. She'd walk out of the room and close her eyes. Sometimes she just left their house altogether.

Over the winter break during her junior year at college, Amanda spoke with her mom about Ian as they never had before. For the first time, she told her mom that she knew Ian had another father. She asked how it had felt to marry her own dad that way. Suddenly, Amanda realized why her mom never looked happy, never smiled in their old family photos—even her wedding photo.

Near the end of the same conversation, Amanda told her mom about Kaulmont Park, and about being raped. Her mom was flustered, unsure how to respond. But just by talking about it, Amanda felt as though she had loosened the assault's grip on her psyche.

"Blazer, what's the biggest broken thing in your youth?" Blazer could answer that in one word: "Me."

30

Not-a-Moose

FRODO AND I hitched into the small town of Mount Shasta from where the PCT crossed under Interstate 5, having briskly covered 11 dense forest miles by 9:30 a.m. That night at Casa Ramos Mexican Restaurant, Frodo and I walked in both clean and proud: we had passed the 1500-mile marker. "Look, there's Blazer," I said. We joined Blazer where she was already sitting with five others—Bounty and Figaro, as well as Max, Joel, and Figaro's mom, Jan.

Together, we devoured tacos, well-stuffed burritos, savory cheese enchiladas with baked-on red sauce, and overflowing refried beans, all delivered with, "Be careful, the plate is hot." Frodo loved the enormous margaritas. Beer and talk flowed freely.

The ceiling was festooned with colors of the Mexican flag, while the walls were adorned with outsized photos of the Ramos family. It was hard to slouch in the high-backed chairs, but we managed. Joel was new to us, but we'd hiked before with Max, a lively blond with short ringlets. Her trail name came from the eponymous good luck totem she carried on her pack, a three-inch tall "Max" straight from the pages of the children's book *Where the Wild Things Are*. Joel had a compact wrestler's body and a square face half-hidden by a thick, black beard and mustache. A sweet and gentle soul, Joel had just acquiesced to the trail name Vlad the Impaler. I never found out why.

A nurse, Jan was the epitome of svelte, just like her son, with a narrow face lit by a soft smile and sparkling, bespectacled brown eyes. Jan didn't say much, but the way the others acted, it was as if the table tilted in her direction. She had the gravitas of a mother, and not just to Figaro—Blazer, Bounty, Max, and Vlad had all come under her care. They were her brood. It didn't matter that she'd only met Max and Vlad two hours earlier when she drove them into town with the other three. Everything she did, everything she said, enveloped them within that soft maternal blanket. "Where do you need to go tomorrow? How else can I help?" No one mentioned it, but I knew she was picking up the restaurant tab for the six of them, just as I knew she'd pick up their tab across the way at the Econo Lodge.

There at that table I heard Jan utter a phrase that would enshrine her in my mind. One of the five had just asked a complicated favor. She replied, "I'm on it." I was fifty-five years old, but I wanted under that blanket with the rest.

Blazer had already taken advantage of the Econo Lodge's warm shower, and she was looking forward to the soft bed. Even crammed four into a room, their two nights in Mount Shasta would have set her back forty dollars, but with Trail Mom Jan, that forty dollars was still in Blazer's pocket. Blazer knew that she needed new shoes. Maybe she would splurge.

On the walk back to the Econo Lodge they passed a liquor store and two of the five stopped in. As they sat outside their rooms on the balmy night, a bottle of tequila made the rounds with the hubbub lasting till hiker midnight. As they started to settle in to sleep, Bounty moved close to Blazer.

EIGHT DAYS BEFORE, at Swan Lake, when Bounty had insisted, "Go away," Blazer shot back, "I'm staying." Bounty had wallowed in self-pity. *This is it. I can't hike anymore. It's worse than anything I've ever felt.* Blazer was a buzzing fly, a distraction when he wanted nothing more than to find a corner where he could lick his wounds. He planned to camp, and the next morning he'd manage to walk back to Drakesbad and bum a ride on the road toward home.

Fuming takes energy, more than is sustainable. And with weight off his feet, Bounty's pain lessened. The two eventually started talking, and while cooking dinner, Bounty finally shared his fears about leaving the trail and deserting Figaro. "I've never opened up like this before," he said. Even her mere presence helped others heal.

Without realizing it, Blazer had reached a crossroads. Those miles, the blisters, the stunning terrain she'd traversed had yielded more than calluses: she had begun to feel less angry at men. She'd been annoyed by romantic advances in years past, but that night she found Bounty Hunter was different. He was a gentleman, kind and genuine. Like so many of the men she'd met on the trail, he gave her hope.

And being on the trail had heightened her senses. Her desire to eat was stronger. The scents of nature more intense. What was hard for Blazer to recognize or acknowledge was that that was also true for her libido. She felt healthy and strong.

Bounty made no request of Blazer. He didn't offer a movie and dinner for her to refuse. Instead, Blazer set up her tent for the two of them to share. There was squirming, laughter, and sighs. But when Blazer indicated, Bounty backed off. Soon rhythmic breathing and snores signaled both were asleep.

NOW, SHARING A bed at the Mount Shasta Econo Lodge, under the influence of tequila, Bounty pushed the envelope. They both did. But, when Blazer's laughter stopped, Bounty again backed off. The next morning, Blazer found she was able to write about it in her journal. She summed up the encounter: "Bounty 'uncomfortable.' Don't give in to that, Blazer."

After a chore-packed, full zero day and a second night in town, Figaro, Bounty, and Blazer left the Econo Lodge late, well after 8:00 the next morning. Blazer's thrashed shoes were in the trash—she and Figaro had splurged on new pairs. The three of them had grown into a comfortable trio.

Interstate 5 runs north to south, slicing California like a cleaver into east and west. Originally, the PCT stayed to the east of the interstate, edging close to Mount Shasta before making a beeline north to Oregon's Crater Lake. But in the late '60s and '70s, a new route was engineered that bent west to include the Castle Crags, Marble Mountains, and Trinity

Alps before recrossing Interstate 5 near Ashland, Oregon. Not only did it add another 250 miles, it also made for a maddening day when the trail flipped on its head. *Why am I walking south?* That morning, under the hulking battlements of the Castle Crags, Blazer, Bounty, and Figaro entered the PCT's Big Bend.

Blazer enjoyed Figaro's singing and had even grown used to his pack explosions. The first time had shocked her—she'd thought Dalton was the king, but Figaro's gear was even more flung about. By now she wasn't fazed when even a short lunch break brought out the entire contents of his pack. For Bounty, it remained a source of joy to watch other hikers' reactions when Figaro's stuff spread everywhere within five minutes of a break. He joked that in that amount of time one of Figaro's socks could already be in a tree fifty yards away. But Blazer had come to envy Figaro's relaxed attitude toward his possessions.

As they began to cover ground, the smile on Figaro's face faded. It couldn't have been the trail, which was relatively flat and shaded, and it was still hours away from when the thermometer would soar. The flora included old friends—black oaks, bigleaf maples, and incense cedars—and signs of new ones. The spring seeps of the Marble Mountains promised clusters of carnivorous *Darlingtonia* bug catchers, also known as "pitcher plants," with a hollow tube and business end aptly shaped like a cobra head. And soon there would be gentians, with flowers of startling, unrivaled blues. No, it couldn't have been the trail. And the company around Figaro certainly wasn't the cause. So what had dimmed his smile? It was those new shoes.

Figaro had a thru-hiker's prodigious capacity to endure pain—he overrode the pain from an infected foot for weeks, and like the rest of us he hiked the last miles of each day with some combination of aching knees, feet, shoulders, and back. I myself hid from Frodo a knee gash that probably should have had stitches. On top of that, thru-hikers are out in extremes of heat, cold, and freezing rain, when any fool would be indoors. You have to really, really want to stay on the trail.

So it was doubly surprising that morning, still on the south side of the Castle Crags, that Figaro stopped short after only four miles. "Blazer,

Bounty, I've got to go back. My feet are killing me. These shoes are terrible. I'm going to hike back, hitch to Mount Shasta, and exchange these for different ones. I'll catch you in a few days."

Blazer didn't hesitate. "I'm coming with you." Figaro was just a bit surprised when Bounty said, "I'm going to hike on." Decided in a moment.

To this day, Bounty still questions that decision. The Trinity Alps were wonderful and striking, but more and more, without Figaro and Blazer, he began to miss family and friends. He felt life was continuing on while he was in limbo. He started questioning why he was out there, against a background of physical pain. At the beginning of the hike he'd had all this wild energy, but now it had waned. *Why didn't I go back with Figaro and Blazer?*

AS BLAZER AND Figaro headed back to Mount Shasta, Blazer felt something strange. She wasn't frustrated at not being able to help him. She'd run through her mental checklist before they started walking back. *Can I do anything? Does he really need to hike out?* She drew a blank. A week ago she'd have kicked herself, just as she had with Bounty Hunter. The difference this time was a man named Tazul.

The day after she'd stayed with Bounty Hunter at Swan Lake, the pair hiked to the home of the next trail angel, Georgi Heitman. Like a ship limping into port, they covered 20 miles to Old Station in a section with few views, the trail enveloped in a green tunnel. The two of them got in late, but they got in. With a population of fifty-one, Old Station is a crossroads, not a town.

Similar to the Saufleys' in Agua Dulce, Georgi's place was more compound than house. She had six acres, much of it shaded grass where hikers could camp. She provided meals and hikers were allowed to use the kitchen and expansive living room. When Bounty and Blazer arrived, Georgi herself was away for a few days, but hikers from past years were there to fill her shoes.

Blazer was in Georgi's living room with a dozen others—they'd pop a video in the TV soon—when she first became aware of Tazul. He had a bearded elfin face, with alert green eyes behind wire-rimmed glasses. He was seventy-one and, for a man who liked to smile, his face was surprisingly unlined. Tazul had been a wildlife biologist, but that wasn't why he was out here.

In 1975—decades before he became Tazul—someone gave Jim *The Pacific Crest Trail*, a National Geographic book by William Gray. He fell in love with the idea of hiking the trail. But Jim was married, with two young children, and work didn't disappear just because he'd found a dream. Over time, though, the kids grew up, he divorced, and then he retired. In 2000, Jim set out to hike the PCT in the Sierra Nevada.

Burdened by a pack he'd long recall as heavier than hell, Jim got about four days into the hike and broke down. His back had shooting pains, leading him to bail out over Kearsarge Pass. The next year Jim attended Kickoff, learned about lighter gear, and successfully hiked from Campo to Agua Dulce. The next year, it was Agua Dulce to Kennedy Meadows, and over the following two years Jim made it to Georgi's at Old Station—becoming Tazul in the process. Tazul loved being on the trail.

The fervor of William Gray's book had never left him, but neither had his fear that his back might act up again—even with a lighter pack. So when it flared up at Old Station, on the same day Blazer and Bounty arrived, Tazul almost wasn't surprised. He was about to start on his longest hike ever and he had been looking forward to this stretch, to Crater Lake, the Three Sisters, Mount Jefferson, and Mount Hood. Now it seemed his trek was over before it had started.

There in Georgi's living room, he looked at the circle of faces, the guys with beards, tans, scratches, the makeup-free women. He didn't know them, yet he did. They were hikers, his clan. In a reedy, soft voice, he shared, "I'm so sore. It's my back. I haven't even hiked yet." Reaching behind him, he rubbed along his waistline, his mouth twisting like the knots that growled in his lower back.

I've only told Dalton and Bounty, Blazer cast a professional's eye at Tazul, evaluating his stiff movements, looking closely at how he sat. She made mental notes just as if she was filling out a chart. She was exhausted and especially drained from the last twenty-four hours with Bounty, but her training kicked in anyway.

I can help him. Blazer pictured exactly what she'd do, which muscles to knead, where she'd place her hands, the exercises that would help Tazul.

Then she saw everyone around her. If she said or did anything, they would all know her secret.

Tazul felt he was just going to have to give up. He wouldn't hike this year. Then a young woman across the carpeted living room spoke up. "Maybe I can help you." As she approached, more than one head turned away from the discussion of what video to watch on Georgi's TV, and many overheard Blazer start to ask Tazul her standard evaluation questions. She tuned them out. After a few minutes of back-and-forth, satisfied, she asked Tazul to move to the narrow hallway hung with Georgi's collection of knickknacks.

Blazer knew backs. For the first three months of her job, at twelve dollars an hour, she saw back after back. It was industrial rehab, deep trigger point massage. Tazul sighed in relief. Once those knots unraveled, Blazer patiently guided Tazul through the exercises he would need to do every day to strengthen his core.

For much of her hike, Blazer had felt selfish. She was always thinking about what she needed, her food, her rest, where was she going to stay, whom was she going to hike with, and how much her feet hurt. That night, after working on Tazul, Blazer cowboy camped under the stars in Georgi's yard. Just as sleep neared, the thought came to her. *For the first time out here I feel completely unselfish.* Exhausted, Blazer slept the sleep of the just.

The next day, Blazer's greatest fear—the reason she had been reluctant to tell even Dalton and Bounty about her training—came to pass. She had her own town chores and laundry to do as well as family to contact on Georgi's computer. But other hikers clutched at her when she needed rest, word spreading from one to the next. There were seventeen hikers that day at Georgi's. Many asked for her help.

Teatree was one. Normally effervescent, she was embarrassed to ask about the agony emanating from her left buttocks. It had been funny telling others about it, but now the pain threatened to chase her off the trail. She slunk over to Blazer, and Blazer set to work.

This wasn't the first time Teatree had set out on the PCT. She had thru-hiked in 2003. Then in 2006 her father died; that was one reason she'd set out again, returning to an old friend for comfort. This year, at Kennedy Meadows, on the first anniversary of her father's death, she and another hiker had made a joint confession. They'd fallen for each other. Now, continuing on was doubly important to Teatree. Blazer told her the name of the muscle that had been strained and started a deep tissue massage, leveraging her elbow to apply pressure evenly against the affected area.

Teatree was effusive in her gratitude. Tazul actually bowed to Blazer. "Cut it out," Blazer brushed off their praise, but it also helped her to accept her role. She thought, *This is what it means to serve. It's not just when it's convenient. I have to be willing to sacrifice.* And with that, coupled with Tazul's and Teatree's thank-yous, Blazer began to feel it was okay that others knew.

FROM WHERE BOUNTY left Blazer and Figaro, it was 96 miles to the next trail town, Etna, population 737. Etna's chamber of commerce touts, "It's the last stop in civilization." Bounty may have been hiking this stretch alone, but out of sight wasn't out of mind. Blazer and Figaro thought often of Bounty and, once back on trail, they looked for him around every bend. Walking ahead and by himself Bounty increasingly dwelled on off-trail worries. He didn't know there was another hiker chasing him. Not-a-Moose had been hoping to catch Bounty for over a thousand miles, and she finally did, just before the road to Etna.

Rachel was in her thirties, eight years younger than Bounty, but everyone assumed she was in her twenties. A Canadian with thick brown braids, she had the spirit of Peter Pan, but was a cautionary tale for getting good at something you don't like—in her case, software engineering. Growing up she'd loved piano, but she never thought it could be a career.

The January before her hike, she'd told her boss she wanted a leave of absence. "How long?" She told him five months, and he boomed back, "FIVE MONTHS?" The echo reverberated down the hall. Her planned start was April 15, but it wasn't till the first week of April that he gave her an answer. Not granted. She'd worked for them for ten years—everyone thought she'd simply acquiesce. Rachel quit.

For the first 700 miles, she fought a constant battle with her feet. She saw a podiatrist about the shooting pains and was told they wouldn't go away without physical therapy. Rachel told him, "I'm going to keep on going." The pain in her feet was better than the pain of returning to her software job.

Despite that battle, there were two bright spots for Rachel during those first 700 miles, both involving Bounty. Just like Blazer and her brother, Rachel had been pulled in by Bounty and Figaro and the fun crew around them—for her, at Whitewater River before Big Bear. They'd cobbled together a small dam to create a pool. Sitting there, Bounty told her what he hadn't told the others, about his job playing piano. He also told Rachel that he thought it was possible for her to make a living playing piano. In that shallow pool, Bounty had no idea that he'd just thrown her a life preserver of hope.

The second bright spot occurred soon after, in Big Bear, when Rachel actually roomed right next to the group of five at the Nature's Inn. Sitting on the motel deck, she told them that as a child she'd thought the backside of a Canadian quarter portrayed a moose. "I have a moose in my pocket," she'd tell her mother. No one corrected her. Years later, not long before she started her thru-hike, friends from Banff told her, "That's a caribou, not a moose." It's a small thing, but she felt like the world had betrayed her. The next day, Bounty and Figaro came to her and said, "We're going to call you Not-a-Moose."

For a short while, Not-a-Moose occasionally leapfrogged on the trail with Bounty, seeing him briefly at McDonald's and in Wrightwood. After that, her feet held her back, but she really hoped she'd catch him at Kennedy Meadows. She looked in every trail register for the date of his entry and asked others, "How far ahead is Bounty?" She didn't catch him in the High Sierra, but her foot pain had finally disappeared. Then, in Northern California, Not-a-Moose turned on the afterburner, hiking back-to-back 30-mile days. Arriving at Georgi's one afternoon, she learned that she had just missed Bounty Hunter and Figaro, who had hiked out that morning.

Eleven days later the two of them met again. Bounty Hunter was forewarned—Frodo and I had passed him only twenty minutes beforehand, knowing that Not-a-Moose was moving fast on our heels. But neither he, nor we, had any idea how much hope Not-a-Moose had invested in seeing him again. Instead, we warned Bounty about the often-difficult hitch to get into Etna, and mentioned he'd increase his chances of getting a ride if Not-a-Moose was with him. So when Not-a-Moose caught Bounty, he wasn't surprised.

That morning, the Not-a-Moose who caught up to Bounty was the one who sat in her cubicle for ten years, not the one who told her boss, "I quit." She didn't tell Bounty what his words about making a living playing piano had meant to her, didn't tell him that she was already planning on going back for a master's in piano. Bounty, in turn, didn't share his increasingly gloomy thoughts. That night, writing with classic Canadian restraint, Not-a-Moose honored her thousand-mile chase with one exclamation point. "Midway through this morning's hike I came across Bounty Hunter resting by a stream. It was so good to see him again!"

ALL FOUR OF us successfully hitched into Etna that morning: Bounty, Not-a-Moose, Frodo, and myself. When we arrived, on a Monday, everything was closed except for the Hiker Hut hostel—most of the town had gone to the county fair in Yreka. The day was also Blazer's twenty-fifth birthday and the big question was whether she and Figaro would arrive in time for us to celebrate with her. There was only one open restaurant, Bob's Ranch House, and we'd heard that the pies at Bob's were fantastic. Having faith that she'd make it in, Bounty hiked over and brought back a blackberry pie for Blazer. We also scrounged up seven birthday candles.

Faced with another birthday—and too aware of the birthday mishaps of her youth—Blazer had mapped out the perfect day in her head. She would hike alone, and reflect. Then she would make it to Etna in the late afternoon and celebrate with her trail family. And that's how it happened.

We all went over to Bob's for dinner, but Bounty didn't come. When he had come back with the pie, he hadn't told us that Bob's had an upright piano. If he joined us for dinner, he feared someone would say, "Hey, Bounty, why don't you play something?" That wasn't going to happen. He isolated himself in the hiker bunkroom instead.

When we returned, we lit candles, made short work of the pie, and exchanged stories. We heard about Figaro and Blazer's return to Mount Shasta, and how the store wouldn't exchange the ill-fitting shoes.

Disgusted, Figaro threw his pair in the hiker box, then whipped out a credit card and got a different pair.

Blazer was subdued as he told his tale. She knew she should have thrown her shoes in the hiker box, too, and bought another pair. On the hike back into Mount Shasta with Figaro she had realized her shoes were causing her a lot of pain. But when the store wouldn't exchange them, that sealed the deal. It came down to money. She just couldn't afford a second new pair of shoes.

The next day, we all took a full zero and headed over to the Scott Valley Drugstore. No hiker's stay in Etna was complete without a visit to their old-fashioned soda fountain. Bounty, Frodo, and Not-a-Moose sat on green leather stools nursing big malts and a sundae. Big smiles lit up all three of their faces.

Before heading out the next morning, Blazer mentioned Marcello, a friend of her brother's she'd met in D.C. during those frantic days she spent preparing for her hike. Frodo's and my ears pricked up. Marcello, a schoolteacher, had the summer off and he'd asked Blazer if he could tag along with her in Oregon, maybe for as much as two weeks. He was flying out to meet her just across the Oregon border, near Ashland. Neither Frodo nor I heard anything special in Blazer's tone, or read anything into how she described him. But we both found ourselves hoping there'd be chemistry between the two, that Blazer would let down her guard and break her years-long dating prohibition.

At the trailhead, Figaro took a photo. In it, my white beard is longer than Blazer's hair. My arm is around Frodo, and Bounty's is around Blazer. Not-a-Moose, her hair freshly braided, stands in the middle with her arms crossed on her chest and a pair of birding binoculars hanging around her neck. Not-a-Moose had an eleven-pound base weight, but over a pound was devoted to birding; after piano it was her greatest passion. Blazer had her toothbrush out in one hand—we'd gone off in such a rush catching a ride from Etna to the trail—and she was still wearing her Crocs. Blazer was delaying putting on those ill-fitting shoes till the last moment. You can almost see the telltale glow in our eyes in that photo— we knew the Oregon border was close, only five days away.

Thru-hikers call Oregon a freeway. That's not because the trail is crowded, but because it flattens out, relatively speaking, at the same time that most thru-hikers reach their physical and mental peaks. They fly through the state, or at least it seems that way: after the 1692-mile California section of the PCT, Oregon is only 458 miles long. Even Frodo and I were looking forward to hiking our first 30-mile day.

After pushing so hard and so long, Not-a-Moose was happy to crank it down a notch and hike with us, especially Bounty. She really wanted to talk to him more about how he made a living. She wanted to talk to him about master's programs in piano accompaniment and to hear what schools he'd recommend. Maybe she'd even be able to hear him play someday.

Four miles later, I took another group photo, of the threesome sitting on a trailside log. Bounty was in the center with Figaro and Blazer both leaning toward him, smiling. Something told me the three of them wanted to be alone. Bounty had just told Figaro and Blazer, "I'm done. I'm leaving."

31

The Cave

SUNDAY, AUGUST 5, 2007

IT WASN'T UNTIL near the end of California that we said our first goodbye to a trail friend. Or at least we would have, if she had let us. Since
Big Bear City, Frodo and I had hiked on and off with Glacier, a twenty-
five-year Forest Service veteran. Fresh out of high school, her first real
job had been as a seasonal backcountry ranger in the Sierra Nevada—a
coveted position. Leapfrogging with her throughout the High Sierra
was like having our own personal guide. But nearly two months later,
Glacier was planning to bypass Etna. She was insistent: "No one says
goodbye." When I woke at midnight, I saw seven shooting stars in a
short span. It was August, and these were the Perseids. Upon rising
the next morning, Frodo and I insisted on giving hugs. Glacier placidly
accepted.

After parting, I heard Frodo wistfully say, "We may not see Glacier
again." She was aiming to finish on September 29 and Frodo's itinerary
had us finishing a few days later. Though a thousand miles away, those
target finish dates cascaded back down the trail, driving a spike through
trail friendships. Before this day, if someone disappeared around the
bend, the possibility of seeing them again was always there. But now, we
saw hikers surge ahead, or linger at a town stop, and my heart told me,
"We won't see them on trail again." We'd already seen hikers wish each
other goodbye, believing it to be permanent. Today, I felt a chill in the

breeze—was it a taste of fall or a moment's realization that this boundless journey would come to an end?

"I'M GOING TO catch him." Nadine still recited that mantra, even if Pacha ignored her. She had thought of Tony when, 800 miles north of Kennedy Meadows, her shoes blew out and, like Blazer and Figaro, she bought a new pair in Mount Shasta. This time Nadine switched out the orthotics right away. Nadine, too, had started to feel the change.

She journaled: "The days are getting shorter. I know it's still summer, but it's starting to feel like harvest time out here. There's that great fall smell in the air, and it makes me homesick for the vineyard."

I'm going to catch him. Nadine had been enjoying hiking alone. She was purposefully hiking in a bubble, keeping five miles or more between her and other hikers. But then she ran into a large group that, like an accordion or a Slinky, would bunch up and then spread out over 15 to 20 miles of trail, which made it hard to out-hike the ten of them. Although at one time Nadine may have enjoyed the intense group dynamic, she now found their shifting personal relationships more distracting than fun. She didn't want to be part of it, so she deliberately took a couple days off to let everyone else go forward.

One of them called her cell phone and left a message that she listened to days later. "Nadine, catch up! We're having so much fun! This morning I woke up, my tent was in splinters, and I don't know why, but Gaby's underwear is down the trail and so is his wallet!"

Nadine would hear these stories and laugh. *I love those guys, but I'm glad I'm not there.*

Nadine was close to a point—was it possible?—where she had hiked as many miles without Tony as she had with him. Her mantra had become rote recitation, the passion gone. *What if I do catch him, then what? What's Tony running away from? Is he running from us?* But she wanted to see him face-to-face again. *There must still be something there.*

By holding back and dropping behind the large group, she had set herself back even further. Tony was past Ashland and approaching Crater Lake, so he was well into Oregon—ten days from where she was, a day south of Etna. Tony, too, had been thinking of Nadine. He had arranged for his friend Chris—who had just hiked with him for a week—to drop off a box at the Mazama campground store at Crater Lake. Tony knew Nadine planned to stop there for her own box. His contained Nutella for Nadine along with Milk-Bones and dog treats for Pacha.

He remembered when the two of them had shared Nutella while sitting on her Therm-a-Rest, near the start of the trail. That had been springtime and this was late summer. Tony had walked 1700 miles since then. He carefully labeled the box so another hiker wouldn't accidentally take it. The box would wait for Nadine—with a note alongside her name.

WE GET SO self-involved, so engrossed in our hike, but life continues off the trail. Two weeks before we arrived at Etna, our younger daughter, Nicky, left for a fall semester abroad. She was in Russia with a host family eleven time zones from the PCT. When we got our first email from her, it shared how she'd settled in and about the classes she was taking at Moscow International University. "Dad, I tried to explain what you and Mom are doing to my host family here, but no one camps in Russia. There's not even a word for backpacking. I asked a professor and he said the only word that means 'walking for pleasure' also means 'goofing off.' My host family thinks you're goofing off for five months."

"GO AWAY!" BOUNTY'S eyes bulged as he spat those cruel words at Not-a-Moose, glaring. She had only tried to ask him to reconsider. Figaro was there, but Blazer, Frodo, and I had not yet reached the spot that would mark Bounty's high tide line on the PCT. "Can we talk about it?" stammered Not-a-Moose. "Not now." She crumbled. Never outgoing, Not-a-Moose wanted to crawl into a hole. This was the man who'd drawn her a map of how to leave her dead-end job. This was the man she'd chased for 1000 miles of trail. If Bounty had slugged her, it wouldn't have been worse.

Not-a-Moose thought she'd have many more days on the trail with Bounty. That's the main reason she'd allowed all of us to talk her into taking a full zero in Etna. Yesterday, she was the one who had been persuaded not to leave. Today, she just wanted a chance to do the same for Bounty.

For the first 1000 miles, Bounty had tapped a reservoir of enthusiasm, a wild energy that fostered such fun for Figaro and those around them, no matter the harsh environs. Blazer saw that attitude on full display on Mount Whitney. Bounty may have thrashed his feet in the desert and refused ibuprofen, but he'd pushed that into the background when hiking with Figaro or a fun hiker posse. Without them, however, his resolve let go, and he thought of the bills waiting at home, of his mortgage, of life passing him by, of what it would feel like to get off the treadmill of 20 miles a day. He didn't know it, but Bounty had made the decision to leave the trail before he set foot in Etna.

On the trail, angry words between hikers are exceedingly rare. In the entire time I was out there—even in harsh conditions that warranted swearing up a storm—I never heard one mean word exchanged. And I wasn't alone. Nicholas Kristof, a two-time Pulitzer Prize winner and *New York Times* columnist, earned his backpacking stripes by hiking one-third of Oregon on the PCT when he was sixteen. Now in his fifties, Kristof hikes on the PCT each summer and, in no less a forum than the *New York Times,* he captured in an op-ed the same phenomenon I'd noted: "In thousands of miles of backpacking over the decades, I don't know that I've ever heard one hiker be rude to another."

When I heard about Bounty's outburst, I added it to a short list that included only one other incident. It was at Kennedy Meadows. There was no cell service and the only way out was a single, unreliable pay phone. With forty hikers staging for the Sierra, that phone had a hugely long sign-up list. One woman hogged the phone for forty-five minutes talking to her boyfriend. A hiker told her in no uncertain terms he was upset. That's my sum total: two times.

NOT-A-MOOSE WALKED AWAY disconsolate, deflated like risen bread dough into which Bounty had plunged a fist. Moments after she walked off, Bounty realized what he'd done. He'd just wanted to talk to Figaro alone, but now he wished he could take back what he'd shouted. Before Bounty said his final goodbye, before leaving to return to Etna, he emphatically told all of us to do one thing for him: deliver a message to Not-a-Moose.

Thirty minutes after taking Bounty Hunter's last PCT photo, I caught up to Not-a-Moose. She sat hunched over by the side of the trail, only a mile and a half from where she had last seen Bounty. Her pack was still on her back, and her arms hugged her knees as if she was freezing. She tried to hide her eyes—she'd never concede she'd been crying—but I saw they were moist and red. She barely cocked her head up as Frodo and I neared. "Not-a-Moose, Bounty's so sorry. He said he was a jerk. He's sorry he barked at you." She expressed no surprise at hearing Bounty's final message. A short while later, Figaro and Blazer came up and told her the same thing.

Figaro missed his friend. "Bounty's alive, so why does it feel like he died?" Bandannas came out when each of us thought the others weren't looking. For Blazer, missing Bounty was hard, but there was something almost worse. Bounty's leaving had cracked open a door she'd didn't want to peek inside, a door marked "Quitting the Trail." Someone she was close to, someone she respected, had actually quit. *That's the hard decision*, Blazer thought. *Staying on is easy.*

Not-a-Moose found herself lost in thought that day. *It must have been so hard for Bounty to decide to leave. How does Figaro feel hiking on without his friend?* Seeing someone quit so suddenly reminded her that there really was an option. No one was making her stay out here. But in the same moment she thought, *I still really want to hike. Sure, there are mornings I don't want to get up, but that's just because it's cold. I'm still so curious to see what's around the next bend.*

MAN EATEN LAKE is a Northern California rarity, a lake near the trail. We were due to pass it on the same day that Bounty left, and we talked about the possibility of swimming there. We needed a counterweight, something to set on the scales against the loss of our friend. Even so, I'd seen the contour lines on the map; it would be a 400-foot downhill scramble. Two miles before we got there, I told Frodo I was going to go ahead. I wanted to get to the lake first and I planned to tell Blazer, Figaro, and Not-a-Moose, "It's a bridge too far, we need to hike on." I'd be the adult. "We can't afford a two-hour delay."

Sixteen miles into the day, I ground up switchbacks that split a hillside of Shasta red fir, white pine, and mountain hemlock, passing the other three. When I finally crested the saddle, the sight of the lake stopped me in my tracks. Set in a bowl of jagged dark granite with talus slopes ringing its shore, Man Eaten Lake looked like a Sierra lake that had escaped north. Had there been a good reason for us to pass it and move on? If so, I'd forgotten.

I dropped my pack along the trail and dashed off a quick note to Frodo as the other three walked up. I grabbed my skimpy towel and bounded down the steep slopes, and the other three followed my lead. It didn't matter that there was no trail. Stripping, I jumped in, and when my head surfaced, I sucked in a mighty breath from the cold shock. I shouted and heard the echo bounce off the walls. "This one's for Bounty!"

Not-a-Moose put her own coda on Bounty's departure. She went skinny-dipping for the first time. As her body hit the water, and was slammed by bracing cold, she thought, *Those must be someone else's clothes staying dry on the shore.* None of us started dinner till well after hiker midnight.

"HEY, SCOUT, HOW would you like a refrigerator experience?" That got my attention. Northern California had been hot and the voice on the phone promised a forty-five-degree chill in the middle of the day. This was Sleuth's opening gambit as she told me about a secret cave.

I'd met Sleuth on the trail only once, when she was tramping a section of the PCT way back in the foothills of the San Jacintos. We'd both sniffed out that the other was a lawyer within a hundred yards. On our zero day in Mount Shasta, she had telephoned. "Scout, it's north of Etna. The Skunk Hollow Cave is unmarked. It's not on the map and the opening is hidden and tricky. You crawl through a ground-level crack and the first step inside is a six-foot drop. That's how you'll know it." Like much of the trail, that first step would be a leap of faith. Sleuth proceeded to give me directions.

We arrived at the intersection with the Canyon Creek Trail the morning after Bounty left. Frodo and I set our packs down at the junction post, near an old, padlocked cabin. A Boy Scout troop was just leaving. "You have twenty minutes," Frodo said, restating our agreement. Find Sleuth's cave or move on. "We'd heard about a cave," one of the adult leaders told me. "We spent half of yesterday looking for it." They never found it.

We live in San Diego—a county that has one mapped rock cave. I had taken my Boy Scout troop spelunking there a few times. When I'd asked Frodo once if she wanted to join us on an outing, she replied, "And what makes you think that I would want to crawl on my belly between rocks in the dark?"

I knew from my caving training that I shouldn't go in alone, and that I would need three independent sources of light. But first I had to find it. Sleuth's directions narrowed things down, but even then, the possible openings at the base of the thirty-foot cliff spanned the length of a football field. Holding my camera in one hand like a divining rod, I dipped my arm into every hole and fissure. The flash burst into darkness. Solid walls. Dead ends. No six-foot drops.

I was under a low overhanging rock when my twenty minutes expired. I squirmed, nearly face down in the dirt, edging forward into another fissure, this one half-blocked by a deadfall tree. The camera flashed, and I read the portents in pixels—it showed space and rocks below. "It's here!"

It was just past 9:00 a.m. and aboveground it was eighty degrees. I went in alone—Frodo stayed topside—but I brought four sources of light: a tiny headlamp, my emergency LED light, my lighter, and my camera. I also brought my warm watch cap. Descending thirty feet under the earth, I found myself in a series of rooms the size of Winnebagos. It was freezing—my cap was pulled tight over my ears, and I could see my breath in my headlamp beam. "I'm fine," I hollered up. I must have been at least forty feet below Frodo, and Sleuth was right. I felt such a surge—I had actually found it, I was in a cave in the wilderness and I'd nearly completed all of the PCT in California.

Sitting outside in the sun, Frodo thought, *I hope he doesn't take too long.* We had come five miles already, planned to hike at least seven more by lunch, and, as it was, we would probably end up having to cook dinner in the dark. The bugaboo of making miles was never far away.

Miles to go. Twenty-five was that day's goal, so I wrapped up my journey to the center of the earth in less than a half hour. When I came back to the surface, both Frodo and I were surprised that Blazer, Figaro, and Not-a-Moose hadn't shown up yet. The "kids" generally broke camp well after us, but always caught up later.

As I started writing a note, I thought twice. Going down in a cave isn't trivial. But I trusted these three implicitly. I left the note under a rock and made a stick arrow with twigs. "Don't go in alone," I wrote. "Watch the first drop. It's six feet. Go in all together or not at all." I left them my headlamp.

FIGARO WOULD SOONER face down a mama bear defending her cubs than a crying woman. As for Not-a-Moose, too, the choice would be a hard one. Yet there they were, deep inside Skunk Hollow Cave, cold as the inside of a walk-in refrigerator. The three of them had flicked their headlamps off—Figaro couldn't see his own hand in front of his face. That's when he heard the first sob.

Sitting next to the other two, Blazer thanked god she wasn't walking. Those new shoes were a curse; she should have replaced them when she went back with Figaro. Walking any farther in them was untenable. That's all she could think about. With the lights out, feeling invisible, Blazer started to cry. "I have to get off. My feet never hurt this bad. These shoes are killing me." Figaro and Not-a-Moose stood silently and listened. In the stillness, Blazer knew how much she would miss them and the rest of us. *I don't want to leave this new family yet.*

Blazer's pained voice bored into Figaro and Not-a-Moose. They couldn't see the tears, but they could imagine the two warm streams that ran down her face in the chill. Figaro placed one hand lightly on her back and felt her rocking back and forth. Neither of them said a word. There, in the dark, he and Not-a-Moose gave Blazer exactly what she needed, the gift of listening.

Back aboveground, Blazer resorted to using her trekking poles as crutches, walking, stopping, and walking again. Short distances were all she could muster. Figaro and Not-a-Moose waited for her every time without a word.

"I hate that I'm holding you up," Blazer told them. "Go on without me." But neither did. Blazer was especially surprised that Not-a-Moose stayed, since she hadn't felt that the two of them had really clicked. *We're such different people. She says so little and I'm such a talker.*

Toward the end of the day, Figaro turned to the other two and said, "I'm going ahead to find a campsite." *Finally,* Blazer thought, *someone's going on.*

And then it was just Blazer and Not-a-Moose. Blazer knew how fast Not-a-Moose could hike, close to four miles an hour, easily. But she stayed just in front of Blazer, looking back often and matching her pace. With Blazer's beat-up feet they were barely making a mile an hour. She wasn't even aware she was whimpering.

That's when one of the quietest people Blazer had ever met started up a story. Not-a-Moose told her how she got her trail name. How her feet had hurt so much the first 700 miles, but the pain had gone away. Story after story to keep Blazer's spirits up. When Blazer would think, *Just cut off my feet. I can't stand it anymore*, Not-a-Moose would start another tale, carrying her along on a stretcher woven from a quiet voice.

All afternoon, Frodo and I had expected the other three to catch up. When they didn't we stopped two miles before we'd planned, after 23, not 25 miles. At 8:00 p.m. with dinner in our bellies, I'd decided if they didn't show up that night, I'd hike back up the trail the next morning. Finally, at 8:30 p.m., we heard the clicking of Figaro's hiking poles.

Just before Not-a-Moose and Blazer reached the campsite, they had to cross a stream in the dark. Not-a-Moose shined her headlamp on the water, then insisted on taking Blazer's pack across. *She's anticipating every need I have.* When the two finally arrived at the campsite, Blazer broke into tears at what she saw—Figaro, Frodo, and I had a spot for her sleeping bag ready, dinner was made, and we'd filtered water for her. Most of all, she couldn't believe that we'd waited instead of hiking on toward Seiad Valley.

After Blazer spread out her sleeping bag, Figaro started singing. When he finished, Frodo and I took over. We told the other three, "These are the same songs we sang to our kids at night when we tucked them in." With the weight off her feet and lullabies in her ears, Blazer fell asleep to the thought, *This is my family. How can I leave them?*

There was no question in my mind that we had to get Blazer out of those awful shoes. But first we would have to hike 14 miles to Seiad Valley, and then contend with Blazer's stubborn thru-hiker pride. And even if we could convince her to accept an offer of help, there was a small, practical problem. If Etna called itself "the last stop in civilization," then even more remote Seiad Valley was completely lost in the woods. Our only contact with the outside world was going to be one semi-reliable pay phone.

In the wee hours of the night I woke and watched the Perseids fire off meteors that faded into nothingness. Between the streaks of light, I schemed. How to get a pair of those New Balance shoes that Blazer liked, the ones that had worked for her before she got to Mount Shasta. How could we get them to Seiad Valley, where the "business district" consisted of a post office, camp store, and cafe, all housed in a building smaller than the footprint of our house? *Mother PCT*, I thought, *watch over us.*

BEFORE THE FIRST glow lit the horizon, Figaro and I set out. After days hovering between 6000 and 7000 feet in the Trinity Alps and Marble Mountains, we made a long, slow descent to 1400 feet, to the broad plain of the Klamath River valley. We paralleled Grider Creek as it rushed to the Klamath, heading downhill at a fast clip. I told Figaro both stories of my marriage to Frodo. It was becoming less and less uncomfortable to tell the second one out loud. I heard tales of his I was sure few others had been told. But we were no closer to solving Blazer's shoe problem. It was unspoken, but that's why we'd left more than an hour before the rest.

Seiad Valley is a blip on Highway 96. Even in isolated Northern California, it's hard to find a village more remote. I'd been focusing on what we'd need—someone on the outside with the time to drive for hours, someone willing to search shoe stores for Blazer's size and model, someone who'd take this to heart and make this problem their own. We needed the tenacity of a bulldog mixed with the altruism of a Saint Bernard. I had two phone calls I wanted to make. Between stories, I plotted what to say and how to couch it.

The fact that Figaro and I had left before the rest of our group was awake that morning had barely registered for Blazer. It was all she could do to focus on her own plans—get to Seiad Valley and collapse. She had decided that she would rest her feet for a week and see what happened. She'd have to tell Marcello, Ian's friend, that the trek was substantially delayed or maybe off entirely. *Please, please, just let me get off these feet.*

Seiad Valley's single pay phone was on the column of the portico near the cinder block wall marked "U.S. Post Office." Right below that was another sign stating with equal billing: "State of Jefferson."

In the late 1930s, this area, along with parts of southern Oregon, had wanted to secede and form their own state, Jefferson. They elected a "governor" and set the date for their big convention: December 4, 1941. Days later the Japanese struck Pearl Harbor. That punctured the movement, but signs, here in Seiad Valley and scattered throughout southern Oregon, remain. Ashland's public radio station even calls itself "Jefferson Public Radio."

Locals here know Highway 96 as the State of Jefferson Highway, but it's better known as the Bigfoot Scenic Highway. We had been hiking for days already in Bigfoot country—the vast trackless forests around here harbored the man-beast Sasquatch, or so the story goes.

I was really hoping to reach my brother. Charlie is as can-do as they come. Three years younger than I, he gets up at 5:00 a.m. and rows his single shell across San Diego's harbor every day. *I'll tell Charlie, "Money's no object." If he makes this his problem, he'll find a way to get it done.*

I punched in the numbers. First, the eleven-digit toll-free calling card number, then our ten-digit personal code, and, at last, Charlie's area code and phone number. It rang. *Pick up,* I projected down to the opposite end of the state. *Pick up.* Charlie didn't answer. I left a message, with Figaro listening at my side. My second phone call was to the Mount Shasta outfitter. I was hoping to reach the manager, whom I had gotten to know on our zero day, but I reached an employee instead. She was willing to make some calls, but I heard neither bulldog nor Saint Bernard in her voice.

I tried Charlie a second time. No luck. As I was thinking about my next move, Figaro made his own call. "Hello, Mom." He had called Jan. Next thing, I heard Figaro parrot my words, telling her how far away we were— four hours from her home in Chico, California—the model number of the New Balance shoes Blazer needed, and the sizes that were likely to fit. I couldn't hear her side of the conversation, but I saw Figaro nod his head. When he got off, he looked satisfied and a bit incredulous. This wasn't a small task. It might be impossible. The number of shoe stores within driving distance of Chico and Seiad Valley was small. Figaro then told me what his mother had said: "Don't worry. I'm on it."

Blazer walked 14 miles in her Crocs with her torture-instrument shoes tied to the side of her pack. She got in after everyone, after the cafe had closed for the day at 2:00 p.m. She knew she had missed her chance for town food.

But Frodo had been watching the clock, and ordered a milkshake just before 2:00 p.m. When Blazer arrived, Frodo offered it to her, extending also the broad blanket of her maternal care. Sure, she felt that way about almost any hiker in need, but for Blazer it now ran much deeper—it was beginning to feel permanent. As Blazer sipped through the straw, she thought, *I am so, so grateful.*

Right next to the post office in Seiad Valley was an RV park. Ten dollars would buy a thru-hiker a spot on the shaded grass lawn, access to a coin-operated shower, a laundromat, and a palm-frond-roofed, open-sided shack complete with a TV and a dirt floor covered in straw. We lounged on the grass between town chores—organizing food, washing laundry, taking showers, and making multiple trips to the small store.

Blazer glued herself to one spot as much as she could. She was trying to psyche herself up to call Marcello and tell him to change his plane ticket for ten days later. For her, that's what passed for optimism. She wasn't ready to face giving up on Canada. Just like Roswell, Blazer knew deep in her heart that what she needed was time to heal. In the meantime, she was trying to keep herself occupied, trying to put Bounty out of her mind. She didn't want to think about giving up the trail.

Meanwhile, the rest of us conspired. We knew if Blazer found out, she'd try to find some way to call Jan and tell her to turn around. As the afternoon wore on, with the five of us munching on store-bought goodies under the broad-leafed trees—we didn't hear anything more from Jan. Blazer bantered and carried on as though nothing was wrong.

Jan drove in at 7:00 p.m. straight up. Her dog bounded out of the car, followed shortly after by Jan carrying four shoeboxes in her arms. She'd called around to widely disparate shoe stores and found Blazer's model in four different sizes. *Is this possible?* Blazer thought. Her eyes struggled to hold back tears. She opened the boxes as if making up for every botched birthday in her past, feeling only slightly embarrassed as we all watched her. Her smile was little-girl huge when one pair of gray and yellow New Balance shoes lingered on her feet. "This one's just right."

WE'D BEEN WARNED that the hike out of Seiad Valley was brutal. The first eight miles climbed 4500 feet vertically, an elevation gain of nearly a mile. And our low elevation meant that conditions were just right for poison oak.

The four of us—Frodo and I, Figaro and Not-a-Moose—weren't going to say anything as we slowly leapfrogged up the hill, the broad bends of the Klamath River receding below us. There was an elephant in the room, and we didn't want to stare. It was as if the fifth hiker with us was made of crystal, and might break from a single look. Blazer had hiked out with us that morning wearing her new shoes. So far, she was keeping up a good pace.

We had lunch together at the top of the climb. "How are they doing?" Jan had driven dirt roads to meet us for lunch and she was the only one brave enough to ask the question. The moment before Blazer spoke seemed so long. I almost dreaded the answer. Then, chewing a bite of her lunch, Blazer said, "I think that my feet are doing okay." Manna delivered straight from heaven. Jan and Figaro beamed. So did I. That night the five us camped together 10 miles before the Oregon border and Blazer made pudding to share.

On the PCT, we all lived on such a slender thread. Sometimes it could be as slender as a pay phone in the State of Jefferson.

32

Superheroes

WHERE WERE THE fireworks? The trail looked the same, but we were at last in a new state: Oregon. The weathered sign proclaimed the miles we'd traveled: "Mexican Border 1706." It was near noon when I opened the rusty trail register box and saw the names of our friends—Ryley, Tony, and so many others. It felt like old home week.

This is where the country began to change. The skinny on the Oregon crest was that here the PCT made a devil's pact—selling its soul for soft tread and minimal ups and downs. The price? It gave up miles and miles of views. For certain, there's Crater Lake, plus a string of majestic volcanoes, from Mount Thielsen and the Three Sisters to Three Fingered Jack, and Mount Washington, Mount Jefferson, and Mount Hood. But there's also Mount McLoughlin, which you see from 20 miles ahead and then don't see again till 40 miles beyond—even though you walk right past it. In years past, Frodo and I had read about hikers doing 30-mile days. This was the place to take up that challenge—we talked about when.

THIS HAS TO *be a practical joke.* That was Blazer's first thought when she saw Frodo's face, just four hours north of the Oregon border. Next came disbelief and shock. Then quickly she said, "How can I help? What can I do? How bad does it hurt?" *This can't be happening.*

Only minutes before, I had been resting and journaling at the north end of a broad-swept bowl at the head of an open valley. I was waiting for Frodo who'd stopped to heed nature's call. Looking back, I could see the trail's lazy rise between stands of hemlock and fir, as well as Mount Shasta behind us, glaciers strewn over its brawny shoulders.

By Oregon, we were well used to how dirty we could get on the PCT. It took no time once we started hiking for a freshly laundered trail shirt to bear grime streaks and sweat stains. But as Frodo caught up to me, the dirt staining her shirt was every which way wrong. She tried to say something, but I couldn't make it out. That's when I saw her mouth. One front tooth was half gone, broken off, and the other was partly out of its socket. She pulled her tongue away from the damage, and I heard her say, "I fell."

Two rocks, like icebergs with barely protruding tips, extended just a half inch above the trail's surface. One had tripped her. The second she'd hit, the full force of her weight smashing front teeth against stone. One moment she'd been walking, the next she was facedown on the trail.

One tooth dangled loose in her mouth—instinctively, she shoved it partway back in its socket. Her first coherent thought after she realized the extent of the damage was: *At least we're near a town.* Her next was to look for the broken-off half of her tooth, but the pieces were scattered every-where, indistinguishable in the pea gravel. Then she cursed, castigating herself. She was so mad that she'd fallen.

The exposed, raw pulp on her broken tooth meant that every breath of air was a new shock. "Shit, shit, shit." She pressed her tongue over the tooth's stump to tamp down the pain.

We'd barely been aware that the trail was paralleling a faint dirt road a hundred yards up a steep bank. Now that dodgy jeep track loomed large. When I saw how badly she was injured, I became very focused. *We need an emergency room.* With no phone, I left a note on the trail weighted down by a rock: "Frodo broke two teeth. Hiking the road. Trying to get to Ashland hospital. 3:30 p.m."

Moments before seeing Frodo, I'd rechecked the guidebook map and the data book, thinking of Ashland and town food. *Less than a day,* I thought. Now, as we started hiking the road, I was hyperaware—Ashland was 23 miles away. "Let me take your pack." I was insistent. She moved her tongue off the stub and grunted. "It's my mouth that hurts. It doesn't affect my ability to hike." We hadn't walked ten minutes before another hiker, Red

Baron, came bounding up behind us. He'd seen our note. He offered us his cell phone, saying, "I've got good coverage. Take it. I'll get it back from you tomorrow somehow in Ashland."

As quick as he'd come, he left, and I was dialing Glacier. She was likely a day ahead of us, so I thought she must still be in Ashland. But as I was making the call, Figaro and Blazer, both out of breath, overtook us. Figaro said, "My mom is in Ashland. She's expecting to meet me tomorrow. I'll call her."

When he reached her, Jan was herself hiking, a mile from a trailhead outside Ashland. Figaro described Frodo's teeth, told Jan where we were, and described the hour-plus drive on the rattletrap dirt road. We were hoping his mom's Prius could negotiate it. Figaro hung up and reported, "Mom is jogging back to her car." Before the words left his mouth I knew exactly what was coming next: "My mom said, 'I'm on it.'"

I CALLED DR. Shaw, our home dentist, once we were in Jan's car. He told me, "There's an outside chance the teeth might be saved. But you have to find a dentist now. You have a three-hour window." He's a friend, too, and he didn't soft-pedal the rest. "Tomorrow morning," he said, "both teeth will be dead." Until that moment I had only incidentally been aware it was Sunday. That fact was now driven home with a vengeance.

At the emergency room, the doctor finished his examination and shook his head. Given the impact to her teeth, he was amazed that nothing else was seriously damaged. Then he laid out the facts. "There's a dentist on call but he won't come in. It's Sunday night. That's why they're dentists." Earlier, in the waiting room, Jan and I had already tried calling every Ashland dentist office. We repeatedly reached answering machines, each another dead end. After delivering his news, the doctor added in a wan voice, "Welcome to Oregon."

"Please call anyway," we asked him. He'd already given up. "Tell the dentist what we're doing. Tell him money is no object." I knew that sounded entitled and self-centered. The doctor went off and we waited. It was 7:30 p.m.; the three-hour mark had passed an hour ago. The sun was setting.

When the ER doctor returned, he had something else besides discharge papers in his hand—it was an address. When the doctor reached the dentist on call that night, he was at a family gathering with his three children and nine grandchildren. But David R. Layer, DMD, was also an ex-scoutmaster and still-avid hiker. We clutched the paper slip, a glimmer of hope. "David Layer says to meet him outside his office in twenty minutes."

He was such an affable man. First, after Frodo lay back in his dentist's chair, he took an X-ray. "The nerve isn't severed. It's still intact." The dangling tooth might be saved. He set to work, pressing me into service as his assistant. I held lights and gave second opinions on what color of high-density plastic matched Frodo's teeth. I watched as he tapped in the one tooth, resetting it, and then painstakingly over the next hour rebuilt her broken tooth and fashioned a temporary, three-tooth splint out of composite resin. I wanted to kiss this man's feet, but when I tried to abjectly thank him, he brushed it aside. "I know how unpleasant this is for you, but what I do all week is fillings, crowns, and root canals. This is creative. I'm having fun."

Two hours later, near 10:00 p.m., we walked out of his office. He told us frankly that Frodo's teeth might turn gray and die tomorrow, or they might last a week, month, or maybe years. But for right now they were repaired. We walked to the motel across the street and checked in. Then I went off to scrounge dinner. Something fat and fried for me and, for Frodo, a clear soup.

Months later, our home dentist examined Dr. Layer's work. Steel probe in hand, he adjusted the light shining on Frodo's mouth and he wagged his head from side to side—reminiscent of the emergency room doctor in Ashland—telegraphing that he had something unpleasant to say. "I wouldn't have done it that way." Yet there were Frodo's teeth, gleaming up at him. As the years continue to pass, with Frodo's teeth still intact, I sometimes think of Dr. Layer when she smiles.

ON HER FIRST day out of Ashland, Blazer swept past Pilot Rock, a gnarled pinnacle that towered 570 feet over the trail. Such a monument would have been visible for hours in Southern California, but Blazer barely saw it before thick forest cloaked the spire like a shy bride under a dark veil. The lush vegetation was no surprise, given Oregon's reputation for rain, but Blazer was surprised at the scarcity of drinking water. Her next source, dubbed by the data book a "very refreshing fenced-in spring," was no longer fenced and was instead overrun by range cattle and heaped with fresh cow pies.

Two miles later, the tantalizing "spring-fed tub" was a cistern with dead chipmunks. Blazer didn't even try to filter that water, choosing to hike through the unplanned 16-mile dry gap.

It wouldn't get better for some time. Later in Oregon, Frodo thought about the state's water issues. *The problem is our main water sources are shallow lakes with muddy shores. Unless there's a rock or log to stand on, it's hard to scoop up clean water without getting any muck.*

But what filled Blazer's mind that day, aside from relief about Frodo's teeth, was Marcello's arrival. She had been hiking alone since leaving Ashland. Now, their rendezvous was set for tomorrow, and it was the polar opposite of the Kennedy Meadows meetup with her brother. Where Ian's deadline had been immutable, Marcello's was soft. Blazer felt almost no pressure. The latest plan was that Marcello would hike south from a road crossing to meet her.

In her journal that night, Blazer wrote, "Feelings? I feel crazy. Glad to be by myself." Long dormant emotions were surfacing like the mushrooms dotting the Oregon forest floor. She'd met so many downright decent guys on the trail. There'd been Dalton and Bounty—getting close to them was no small step for her. All these experiences had chipped away at Blazer's prohibition on dating. She'd also told people that she was a physical therapist, and, except for that first twenty-four hours at Old Station, they weren't constantly clutching at her, just occasionally asking for advice. Her anger at men, specifically her anger at her dad, didn't feel so close to the surface. She felt strong. *Marcello is a handsome guy*, she thought. She remembered when he visited Ian last April during her frantic pre-hike preparation.

A schoolteacher by profession, Marcello was quite outdoorsy and prided himself on knowing his forest flora and fauna, particularly birds. So his ears had perked up the weekend he visited his friend when he heard that Ian's little sister was hiking the PCT. With summers off, he proposed hiking with Blazer for a week or more. She acquiesced, even though at that point she didn't know if she'd even make it to San Diego, much less last three months on the trail.

The next day, Marcello beamed a half-sleepy smile at Blazer when they met on the PCT. He'd hiked south from a trailhead till he met her, just like they'd agreed. Olive skinned and tanned, Marcello had a broad nose, black eyebrows so bushy they looked like caterpillars resting above his brown eyes, and a five-day-old beard. He was also playful, fun, and cute. After their first day together, Blazer thought, *He's a treat. He points out the sound of every bird. He knows every plant. He makes me wish I knew more.*

"Don't let me hold you up." Marcello had jumped in and started hiking 25-mile days, even though Blazer tried to dampen his ardor. "Let's ease into this," she said, but Marcello insisted. He didn't want to slow her down, nor did he want Blazer to lose contact with other hikers.

Their first night together, Blazer made a batch of pudding. Near the end of the next day, when it started to get chilly, Marcello stopped at a downed log on the trail and waited for Blazer. When she sat down, shivering, he reached out and put an arm around her waist. Blazer's first thought was, *Was I that naïve?* And her next was, *I feel so alive.*

NADINE ARRIVED AT Fish Lake on August 19, her fourth day in Oregon. Located two miles off trail, the pint-size marina and resort had a store and cafe not much larger than Seiad Valley's. Two days ahead was Crater Lake—at the rim of its ancient crater, Nadine would be nearly a third done with Oregon.

I wonder if he got it. Nadine had mailed a postcard from Etna to Crater Lake, addressed to Tony. *I wonder how far past Crater Lake he is now.*

Nadine had been bookin' it. Instead of the 20 miles she had averaged each day in California, now she was averaging more like 25 to 30 miles a day. Most thru-hikers were doing the same, but only half of their original number were still on trail. They'd fallen off in the deserts, in the High Sierra, and a few, like Bounty, had dropped out at the end of California. On the opposite end of the spectrum, a handful had closed in on the finish, and three hikers had even reached Canada already.

The first, Eric D, had reached the Canadian monument on July 29 and then turned around, storming back south. He was attempting a

PCT "yo-yo," traversing the entire length of the trail in both directions in the same year. Only one person had successfully completed a yo-yo, and that was Scott Williamson in 2004. Williamson was basketball tall and as recognizable in the hiking world as Michael Jordan is in basketball. An arborist in the winters, in the summers he hiked. He had failed five earlier yo-yo attempts, beginning in 1996, but on November 13, 2004, Williamson succeeded and then in 2006 he did it a second time, walking into a media circus at the Mexican border. Eric D was now flying under the radar, keeping his attempt largely to himself.

At Fish Lake, Nadine and Pacha ordered two hamburgers, one without a bun, for lunch. They both salivated—it was such a nice change from their typical trail lunches of tortillas, chips, cheese, peanut butter, tuna, dried fruit, salty nuts, or candy bars. Even a casual glance at Nadine made it clear that she had walked there—she was a distaff Grizzly Adams with a half-wild dog that had just dropped in on the cafe. Soon, a group of women surrounded Nadine, asking her all sorts of questions about the trail. As they devoured her stories, Nadine stood at the center and glowed. One offered, "Can I buy you lunch?" At this Nadine demurred, before prying herself away to find a quiet corner to eat.

She'd only been alone for a minute when a guy walked up and introduced himself. "I overheard you talking about the PCT. I'm a thru-hiker, too." He'd been sitting there the whole time, listening to her and the other women. "I just wanted to say hello. I'm Eric D." When it eventually came out what he was doing, Nadine grew red behind her freckles. As the two chatted, she couldn't help but think, *I feel like such an ass—he's the real deal. He's yo-yoing! He's who they should have been talking to, but they surrounded me like I was the celebrity. And there Eric D sat in the corner just being cool.*

BEING A THRU-HIKER sometimes feels like being a superhero. That's how Tony felt as he hiked through Oregon. *We're superstars, right? I see people climb out of their RVs to take pictures of Crater Lake and I hiked here. I walked here to see this.* But he was also a mite sheepish about it. *I know I feel more superior than I have any right to be, but you know, I'm feeling pretty good about life.*

The day before Frodo and I walked to Crater Lake, we chanced on a Sierra Club group out for a Sunday hike. Passing the seven hikers near

Devils Peak, we couldn't even get out a greeting before one exclaimed, "Frodo, how are your teeth?" They'd recognized her from our online journal. *We have a following*, I thought in wonder. When we walked away, one hollered, "You're gods and goddesses!" How could that not go to our heads?

Dalton would get laughs every time he told the story about being a "celebrity" in Tehachapi. We heard about it the day after: "I had four Starbucks employees surrounding me and listening to my stories. They were right to admire me. I mean, I am practically a superhero. A superhero that eats a ton, moves really slowly, and no longer cares about personal hygiene or farting in public."

Blazer was more ambivalent. *At times I feel like a celebrity, for sure. Sometimes I like to tell people, "I hiked from Mexico," just to see their response, but for the most part, I downplay it.*

IN SOUTHERN CALIFORNIA and the Sierra, hikers could decide on a whim that it was time to camp and soon enough they would find a good spot. Now miles could go by. Oregon's forests self-prune, dropping a dense thicket of twigs and branches, resulting in few open, flat spots. One evening, Frodo and I marched eight miles, looking for a campsite the whole way. At 9:00 p.m., we finally crossed an abandoned dirt road that would suffice. After that, we paid more attention to the campsites mentioned in the guidebook.

Another change was that, like lizards, we'd seek out the sun at every opportunity. In California, we'd sought shade. *Get me out of the heat.* But with a chill in the air and three days of rain around Crater Lake, we had grown increasingly interested in absorbing heat and drying out. We could almost feel the power of the sun grow weaker as the days progressed.

That change followed us indoors. Our motel rooms were now festooned with clothes hung from every possible protuberance, drying out. At Mazama, in Crater Lake National Park, we crammed five into a little cabin and draped the interior walls like a gypsy encampment, with tents, ground tarps, sleeping bags, packs, pack covers, jackets, and rain pants— I'd strung clotheslines with my emergency mountaineering cord. In the background was the constant noise of the hair dryer. No, we hadn't all become vain—jamming that nozzle into our shoes and gloves and running it on high was our only hope of drying them out.

After a day and a half of rain, only a few of these rooms were available at the Mazama campground. So, for once, Frodo and I were quintupling up. Frodo and I were in one bed and a retired navy captain, Disco Dan, was grateful for a spot on the floor. Blazer was on the other bed. We tried to give it as little attention as we could, but sharing Blazer's bed, with whom she'd now hiked for three days, was Marcello, this Jersey-accented guy who had already won over Frodo and me.

Since Etna, Blazer had been calling us her "trail parents." And now in this small cabin room she thought, *It feels awkward that I'm not even dating this guy and we're sleeping in a bed together in a room with my trail parents.*

Shoes dry, early the next day we hiked the four miles up to Crater Lake's rim. Most of the rim is a thousand feet above the lake's deep blue surface, but at the Sinnott Memorial Overlook the drop is "only" 900 feet. That's where Blazer and Marcello posed for a photo in front of the deepest lake in America. Behind them was a double dose of heavy cloud cover, one in the sky and the second reflected on the lake's surface. The forested cone of Wizard Island jutted into view just off Marcello's right shoulder. His left shoulder was hidden behind Blazer, who was pressed against him, her red rain jacket zipped tight. She'd raised her arm across her chest and grasped Marcello's hand in hers, their thumbs and fingers intertwined. It was cold that afternoon and even in this brief respite between rain squalls, they wore headbands like earmuffs—in the photo the headbands gently touch. It was here at Crater Lake, with the tread of the PCT subbing for a high school locker-lined hall, that Blazer released a smile she'd held tight for years.

NADINE WAS GREETED by a pleasant surprise when she arrived at the Mazama store to pick up her resupply box—a second box with her name. *And it's from Tony.* She tore it open. Her smile flashed to find the treats for Pacha and the Nutella for herself. Then she stared at the note on the outside. She rifled through the box one more time. Then she made a face. There was just that one short handwritten note that began, "Congratulations."

I have to make sure that it doesn't break, Tony had thought as he wrapped the Nutella. He'd bent Chris's ear with so many Nadine and Pacha stories.

"Nadine sat there eating some vegetarian whatever while feeding Pacha greasy hot dogs." "That woman was so fixated on watermelons." "I thought they were crazy insoles—they were orthotics!" After writing her name on the box, the next thing was to tuck a note inside. *But what can I write? Missing you? Thinking of you? That's not enough. Caring for you and Pacha and the good times we had?* None of it felt right.

Now Tony was nearing the Bridge of the Gods, where he would cross the mighty Columbia River and walk into Washington State. Over 200 miles separated him and Nadine. As conscious of his base weight as he was, Tony carried one scrap of extra weight in his pack. It was the postcard Nadine had mailed to him at Crater Lake. It had Pacha's footprint on it and read, "We miss you." Tony had added it to his pack, but he didn't slow down.

At the Mazama store, Nadine stood there perplexed. She wasn't sure how to make the pieces fit. How could she reconcile the jar of Nutella and all that it meant, with this handwritten note? The note read, "Congratulations on making it to Crater Lake! You are doing great." And it wasn't from Tony. It was from Chris, the friend who had joined him for a week at the start of Oregon.

Why didn't Tony write? Nadine mulled it over, like chewing trail jerky, before making a decision. *I don't care anymore. Tony's putting himself first, just like he did when he left. Just like when he walked off at Echo Lake. It's time for me to do the same.*

Only a few days later, Nadine decided on a whim to take an alternate route off the PCT. As she walked away from the junction, she was overcome by a flood of emotion. She felt so completely free. *It's just me. I get to make whatever decision I want. I don't have to choose the PCT just because everyone else does.* She felt lighthearted. *Right now if I want to go swim in a lake or stop and pick huckleberries, I can do that.* At that singular moment, alone in Oregon's wilderness, Nadine felt that everything was perfect.

If Nadine had been listening closely, she might have heard an echo—the squeals of laughter from a young, freckle-faced girl riding a bike around her neighborhood on the other side of the continent. Across a gap of nearly thirty years, Nadine had reconnected with her younger self, circling those tree-lined streets that spelled freedom—Harvard, Yale, and Princeton.

AFTER ASHLAND, FRODO and I hiked fourteen straight days without taking a zero. On one, we got in that 30-mile day. On another, we stepped over rocks in the trail that formed "2000"—we had hiked 2000 miles on the PCT. But we didn't see Blazer again until Timberline Lodge, only 48 miles from the Washington border.

MARCELLO HAD USED the word "pretty," and Blazer hadn't blanched. She usually shunted compliments aside, purging them from her memory or thinking, *They must not mean it anyway.* Pretty was what *he* had called her when she was fourteen. Bounty and Dalton must have paid her compliments, but Blazer had no recollection. A few days before, Marcello had brushed aside the hair hanging over her forehead and said, "You're pretty." Those words kept merging with her footsteps, softly keeping time.

The end of the trail for Marcello was at Santiam Pass, just six miles north of the 2000-mile mark. From there, the two had an easy time hitching to the eastern Oregon town of Sisters, and Marcello bought a ticket for the next morning's bus. That night in Oregon's high desert was their last chance to be together for a while, and Marcello splurged on a small cottage at a cute bed-and-breakfast. Blazer was so relieved to share a room with just him, instead of with a group of hikers.

Days earlier, on a night of cold, driving rain, Frodo and I had drifted off to sleep listening to singing and laughter issuing from their tent. What we couldn't see or hear was Marcello edging forward, or Blazer quietly saying, "I'm not ready." That same pattern repeated as the miles and days passed. Each time, Blazer thought the same thing afterward. *I know how much he wants to. Yet, he's so accepting when I say, "I'm not ready."* Each time she was surprised, as if she thought she deserved the worst. Each time it endeared him to her more.

In Sisters, the two were giggling again. This time, they giggled their way out of their clothes. Blazer couldn't believe how natural it felt. She'd expected to be self-conscious, hyperaware of each step. The laughter helped her overcome that. Their lovemaking was sweet, and fun. She wasn't ashamed.

33

Tazul

THE HIGHEST AND most popular peak in Oregon, 11,239-foot Mount Hood is nearly rivaled by a structure on its southern face: Timberline Lodge is a shrine to fine craftsmanship. Today it is as much a museum as it is a seventy-room hotel, with wood-carved animals adorning stair rails, a towering, ninety-foot fireplace, and a steep roof supported by beams more like tree trunks than lumber. The lodge's iron scrollwork, fine masonry, and handwoven carpets and drapes were all the product of hundreds of stonemasons, weavers, wood-carvers, and blacksmiths brought together by the Great Depression.

Just as the Works Progress Administration built Hoover Dam and New York's LaGuardia Airport, it swept up and deposited these craftsmen high on the slopes of Mount Hood to build Timberline Lodge. Franklin Delano Roosevelt dedicated it in 1937, and it was declared a National Historic Landmark in 1977. A few short years later, Stanley Kubrick would feature the lodge in *The Shining*. And the PCT runs just a few hundred feet north of the building.

None of this history is what draws thru-hikers inside. After 2000 miles, these town-food locusts come for Timberline's all-you-can-eat breakfast buffet. It's the stuff of legend. Buckeye, a 2005 thru-hiker, waxed rhapsodic, "I often dream of Timberline Lodge. I want to transport myself there RIGHT NOW. The breakfast buffet CANNOT be missed. Omelet bar, freshly cooked Belgian waffles with fresh berries, fresh-squeezed-right-before-your-eyes OJ. My heart aches as I miss this meal so much. And it is only $14."

The lodge rooms were pricy, but like Marcello in Sisters, Frodo and I splurged. We paid for two rooms—one for ourselves and one for our daughter, Jordie, our resupply queen, who'd hiked with us the previous two days. We knew that Blazer would arrive the next day while we took a zero, but we were sad to have missed Figaro—he'd left the lodge hours before we arrived. As for Not-a-Moose, our best guess was that she was four days behind. Two days north of Ashland she'd gone home for her sister's wedding. She was the maid of honor and hoped that her spaghetti-strap dress wouldn't hang too loose after all that hiking. But she'd fretted more about her prominent V-neck-shirt tan. The week before she flew home we saw her take every opportunity to tan her shoulders.

That afternoon, Frodo and I sat in the lodge's huge outdoor hot pool, feeling indolent and indulgent. In the rising mist, we almost passed as tourists. Another couple lounging in the pool started up a conversation. They were from Chicago; we talked about being from San Diego. They said, "We flew in yesterday. How did you get here?" Frodo and I exchanged looks. When I answered, we both tried to suppress a smile. "We walked." The other two leaned forward, "From where?" Ah, life is good. We both answered, "From Mexico."

Outside our window the next morning, Mother Nature delivered a clear warning. When the gray clouds and rain cleared, we saw that Mount Hood was covered in a dusting of snow.

"Wow," exclaimed an eighty-year-old Oklahoman gazing south from the porch of Timberline Lodge. "If this state was pounded flat, it would be bigger than Texas."

AT TIMBERLINE LODGE, Blazer was surprised to see Tazul—she hadn't seen him for weeks. "Blazer, my back still feels great," he told her. She glowed just to think of it—then shuddered, remembering how close she'd been to keeping her mouth shut. Now she would get to hike with Tazul on his final two days. "Those exercises were a miracle." Tazul still worshipped Blazer.

Though usually a slow hiker, Tazul had managed to keep up with the Oregon speedsters. And on the first day after Timberline Lodge, he set a new personal best, 27.7 miles. It was no slouch of a day—there were two dangerous crossings, one over the blown-out floodplain of the Sandy River and the second on a fallen log precariously perched fifteen feet above a stream.

Five of us hiked near each other for our last two days in Oregon: Blazer, Tazul, Frodo, myself, and a younger hiker, Odysseus, who, like Blazer, was in his twenties. We all took an alternate route for the last 14 miles down to Cascade Locks on the banks of the Columbia River, the border between Oregon and Washington. The Eagle Creek alternate was a mile longer, and was not the official PCT, but nine out of ten thru-hikers still took this route. The main draw was the waterfalls—it was as if all of Oregon's waterfalls had repaired to Eagle Creek for a convention. Squeezed between narrow canyon walls, we followed the trail around, over, and even behind one of them.

Six weeks had passed since Old Station, and both Tazul and Blazer had changed. At Old Station, Tazul had been bent, shoulders hunched, looking older than his seventy-one years. Now, with 750 miles added to his hiking odometer, Tazul stood erect, every aspect of his body radiating pride, from the glint in his eye to the actual spring in his step. As for Blazer, her hair had advanced to the next stage, tight, short dark curls, but what had really changed was harder to pinpoint.

How does a person look when they feel more at home in their skin? For me, it was a small thing that underlined the change. One evening near the end of Oregon, Blazer heard Frodo and me start up a small spat. As we each lobbed our opening salvo, preparing to dig into the other, we heard Blazer say, "Trail parents, you are making me uncomfortable." Pulled up short, we each stopped and took a deep breath. What we'd started to argue about was silly; we were simply both dog-tired. Blazer's statement allowed us to press reset, and we both smiled gratefully at her.

OUR LAST DAY in Oregon, the five of us bunched together on a midmorning break. Thimbleberries and huckleberries dotted the understory of a dense, mossy forest—Eagle Creek had yet to show off its real plumage. As we chewed on trail bars and Snickers, we chattered about town food, about fat slugs and berries, and about Tazul's last day. "Can I tell you a story?" he asked.

As if we'd say no. He began: "I flunked the fourth grade. They held me back. I worked so hard to keep it a secret. Not the flunking, but the fact that I couldn't read." It was the 1940s—terms like "dyslexia" and "learning disability" weren't in anyone's vocabulary, but kids in the schoolyard could dish out "moron" and "retard." Tazul continued, "I had all this trouble in grade school. I thought I was defective." His bright elfin eyes had dimmed. "But what it was is, I just couldn't figure out how to read."

That summer after he was held back, his mother started reading a book to him. World War II had just ended, and there was optimism in the air. The book was *Mickey Sees the USA*, featuring Mickey and Minnie Mouse as they towed an old-fashioned teardrop trailer all around the country. "I just loved that book. I'd always liked adventure stories." Tazul, his hands spread wide apart, recited from memory the spots they visited: "Yellowstone, the Golden Gate Bridge, and up the coast to the Columbia River," near where we sat. His eyes were open, but they might as well have been closed. It was as if, right before us, he was flipping through the pages, wrestling with those words once again.

"By the summer's end," Tazul said, "I'd mastered that book." Now he brought his hands together in his lap as if he'd just closed the book. "When I left Mickey and Minnie that summer, I knew I could read."

At lunchtime, he asked again, "Can I tell you a story?" We were at Four-Mile camp, close to the end of Eagle Creek, and had passed a waterfall potpourri that included Punch Bowl Falls, shooting from between high cliffs, and Tunnel Falls, where the trail passes through sheer rock *behind* a 130-foot wall of water. It was his last day with us, so he could be excused for growing wistful. "I was forty-five years old when I got divorced. My wife told me, 'It's all your fault.' I just didn't understand it."

When he decided to see a counselor, she asked him to start talking about himself. After about ten minutes, the counselor asked, "Are you an alcoholic?" Tazul said, "No." After talking a short while more she asked, "Was your dad an alcoholic?" Tazul denied it again. "No." But then she asked about his grandfather. And he answered, "Yes."

"Well, I knew he was. He was a 24/7 alcoholic. He was so serious about it that he'd carry a flask in his suit jacket and sip on it so he wouldn't lose his buzz." The therapist gave Tazul one homework assignment, to buy a book, *Adult Children of Alcoholics.* "I went home and that evening I turned to the first page. It had a list of ten characteristics of children whose parents were alcoholics. Nine of those ten items described me. It was literally my story and I couldn't believe it."

Tazul said the book also described his father, a successful insurance executive who every few weeks would be away for three or four days. "I realized he must have been going on binges." Tazul said he finally understood what he'd done to hurt his marriage. "From my dad, I'd learned to be irresponsible—I learned so many negative things. He wasn't a bad person.

"Years after reading the book, when he was near death, I said, 'Dad, I've got to talk to you. I feel like I missed out on a lot of my childhood and that you just weren't there.' Oh man, I didn't know what he was going to do when I said that. But what he finally said was, 'You know, Son, I did the best I could.' I didn't like that answer. I didn't say anything, but looking back on it, I realized, *Yes, I guess that's right. He was doing the best he could.* He did provide for us, but there's so many things I'd change. I never had a good dad. I had friends that did."

Sitting there, I knew that if Tazul ever had another relationship, he'd be a very different man. I also couldn't help but wonder, *What is Blazer thinking?* After all this talk about an alcoholic dad, what triggers were going off for her? Was she taking mental notes? In the rush to get to town, I simply forgot to ask.

I wouldn't get her impression of Tazul's story until years later. "What was that?" she asked. I read her Tazul's story, expecting recognition, but instead she said, "I don't recall it at all." Memory is so selective.

Tazul went home. We got ready to cross the Bridge of the Gods and enter our last state: Washington.

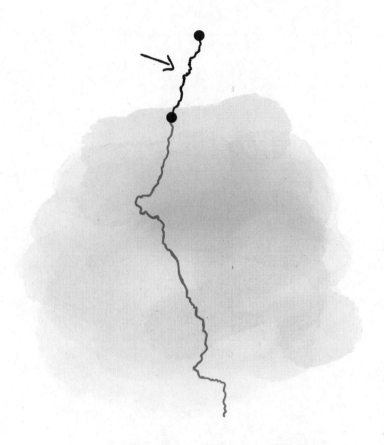

SNOW

Bridge of the Gods to Canada
500 miles

34

Shattered

THE BRIDGE RATTLED and shook. Through the soles of her feet, Blazer felt the 1800-foot span jerk as if there'd been an earthquake. She braced herself, pressing her back hard into the railing, and shut her eyes tight. The semitruck roared by, missing her by inches. Its *whoosh* sucked her and her pack sideways on the narrow roadbed. *How can they let them do that?*

The Bridge of the Gods. Even the name sounds like a rite of passage. Forty miles east of Portland, it spans the mighty Columbia River. Anyone walking across the bridge is acutely aware that the roadbed isn't asphalt, but an open metal grate. Those who dare to look down see the Columbia's roiling swells below their feet, barely obscured by a gossamer lattice of steel. It feels like walking on air.

The bridge is barely wide enough for two lanes, let alone a sidewalk or shoulder. Any ten-foot-wide load requires twenty-four-hour advance notice, a pilot car, and for traffic to be stopped. Hikers cross at their own risk, and pay fifty cents for the privilege.

Blazer was terrified. She clung to the outside rail, hating that open grid. Looking straight ahead the whole time, she repeated to herself, "This is temporary. People do this all the time."

Welcome to Washington. Only 500 miles to Canada.

IT WAS HARD, but finally Blazer broke down and called Ian. She'd stretched her dollars as much as she could—skipping overnight town stays, skimping on gear and town meals. Her friend Heidi's two-month budget had made it almost four, but the words still felt like sawdust in her mouth. "Ian, I'm nearly out of money."

The last time she'd seen Ian was when he boarded the bus in Yosemite. He must be all shaved and clean by now, but she doubted he smiled as much as he had in the High Sierra. Ian listened to Blazer describe her plight. As soon as it sunk in, he said, "You made it this far. You're not giving up now." He sent her five hundred dollars.

She was so grateful. Teetering on her financial tightrope felt worse than any thousand-foot climb under a late-summer sun. *I want a trail life like everyone else, with motel stays and town meals.* But deep down she knew five hundred dollars wasn't enough. She would manage to feed herself, and squeeze in with four hikers in a town room overnight, but her rain jacket needed replacing—her zipper was broken—and that wasn't going to happen. *I'm not asking Ian again.* She and Ian had made such a connection in the Sierra. *I'd sooner quit the trail than jeopardize that.*

ON TUESDAY, SEPTEMBER 11, Blazer wrote: "Today I saw Mount St. Helens and Mount Rainier. We hiked around Mount Adams. I'm stressing about returning to life, to bills and no money!" With nary a gap she went on, "Reunited with Dalton. I'm so glad to be here right now, even though I am sore and tired. About 20 days left."

They hadn't hiked together since Blazer left Dalton at Walker Pass, back on day forty-one. Now, ninety days later, both were excited to see the other. He couldn't get over her full mop of curly hair. She wanted to reach out and tug his bushy amber beard. Both found it hard to believe how long they'd hiked apart. But amid the joy, for Dalton, one aspect was bittersweet. He'd heard the trail scuttlebutt about Blazer and Marcello—it felt like visiting an ex-girlfriend happy with a new partner.

They filled their miles in southern Washington with stories—each had so many to tell. Dalton told her about a dinner at a rustic resort where he'd asked for a big mound of complimentary dinner rolls and the waiter brought him a "freaking mountain." They exchanged High Sierra tales, with Dalton groping to describe the grandeur: "The mountains were storybook. I half expected a unicorn to run across the scene." And his own story of Hike Naked Day dwarfed Blazer's naked swim. "It was fantastic. I hiked fifteen miles completely naked. Except for the American flag bandanna hanging off my hip."

Dalton also told Blazer about Walker Pass, how he'd stayed up most of the night. How he'd heard her sobbing. She'd tried so hard to be quiet, but Dalton was only ten feet away and they were both cowboy camping. *That is so like Dalton,* Blazer thought, *finding a way to be there for me, but not letting on.* Hearing him talk, Blazer felt like they'd never parted on the trail. Tale by tale their stories rebuilt the implicit trust they'd once had in each other.

There was one thing Blazer did not need to be told: why Dalton's guitar was gone. Like so many others, he had culled his last ounce of frivolous weight before crossing the border into Washington. At the same time, worried about snow, he beefed up his gear, making room for down mittens, a ski mask, and a second pair of long underwear. Washington was where the trail got serious again. It not only marked the return of big ups and downs, but parts of the trail were as remote as the High Sierra. As the guidebook said, Washington was "real wilderness, not wilderness in name only."

Around Blazer and Dalton, the change in leaf colors marked the changing seasons. The yellows of the larches and aspens screamed, "Hurry!" The reds of the vine maples and huckleberry bushes warned, "You'll have to stop soon." Daylight was pinched at both ends, the weather was deteriorating, and everyone's bodies were finally signaling, *This abuse must end.* It was like being squeezed in a vise.

Like Dalton, Frodo and I made some changes to our gear. We swapped out our two-pound Tarptent for our Big Agnes. We bought new rain pants and gloves, and Frodo bought a double-layered cap. Her hair was growing in frustratingly slowly—more slowly than mine—and it was hard to keep her head warm. We switched our alcohol stove for a canister stove. Odds and ends of gear were sent home. But Blazer had to work with what she was already carrying.

After a few days hiking together, Blazer and Dalton ran headlong into forty-eight straight hours of rain. This rain was of a different stripe than what they had previously experienced in Oregon or California, much colder and more penetrating. Worse, they had to camp on an exposed ridge—it was the only usable flat spot in four miles—and the wind howled. All night, Blazer tossed fitfully as rain pinged her Tarptent, gusts finding every crack. Shivering, her mind spiraled into overtime. *I'm going to die.* The next morning, she journaled: "The worst morning of my life!" Both her shoes and socks were frozen stiff. It took hours before she could feel her fingers.

BETWEEN THE WEATHER and the diminishing daylight, Frodo and I were frequently driven into our tent. With more time to spend writing our online journal, Frodo told me, "It's time for you to fess up—you need to write about your trail injuries. You wrote about mine." Strangers still greeted us on the trail with: "Frodo, how are your teeth?" But she wanted people to know that I, too, had suffered.

I cracked a rib at Man Eaten Lake. My bare feet slipped on a mossy rock and I crashed hard on my chest. Hiker pride meant I didn't tell anyone for two days. For two weeks that meant to cough, to breathe deep, or even to laugh, I had to press a hand hard against my chest to lessen the pain.

Two months earlier, just after Wrightwood, Frodo heard this *whump* behind her and turned to see me sprawled, embarrassed, on the ground. My shoe caught on a root and I fell, ripping my pants above the knee and opening a gash. If we'd been in the city, I might have gone for stitches.

Earlier still, in the Laguna, San Jacinto, and San Bernardino Mountains, a muscle knotted behind my right shoulder blade on cue every day at 1:00 p.m. It disappeared somewhere before the Sierra. Starting in Oregon, both my Achilles tendons had been so tight in the morning that I had to shorten my steps for at least the first forty-five minutes on trail. And I won't speak of all the blisters and lost toenails. Everyone had those. "So, Frodo, that's my list of trail woes. Now are you happy?"

UNDERSTAND PAIN AND you understand the trail. In southern Oregon, a young man jumped onto the trail, planning to "section hike" the entire state. After leapfrogging with us for a few days, he stopped by one morning at a quarter before six as Frodo and I were breaking camp. "Can I ask you a question?" We must have looked like trustworthy, parental types—from his tone we knew he was sharing something in confidence. "Sure, go ahead." He leaned in close. "So tell me, when does the pain stop?"

Frodo and I burst out laughing. He was so sincere, and with such hope. But what else was there to do? Pain was as much a part of this hike as the pines, the Douglas firs, and the thick-bark cedars. Because the truth is that the pain never stops, it merely ebbs and flows. Sometimes it's loud and angry. Sometimes it's quiescent. Sometimes it's eclipsed by the wonder of the people of the trail. Sometimes you break a rib. Sometimes you break a tooth.

That section hiker was lucky he hadn't asked Switch. Switch and her husband had hiked the Appalachian Trail seven years before. So when they hiked the PCT, they were the experts. During the first few weeks, someone asked her, "When do you stop hurting?" Switch looked at him, paused, and said in a deadpan, "Three months." She saw the wheels turning around in his head. The guy nodded, as if thinking, *I can handle that.* Then she gave the full answer. "Three months after you get off the trail."

To hike a long trail, you have to learn the truth about pain: There are two kinds—pain that can be tolerated and pain that must be dealt with. Failure to recognize the second puts you in peril.

When Frodo broke her teeth, she was still able to hike, but accidents can be so severe that they incapacitate a hiker—or worse. A small plaque on the final approach heading north over Forester Pass bears the name of eighteen-year-old Donald "Buck" Downs. Most hikers don't notice it.

The John Muir Trail surveyors thought that crest so daunting they hoped to avoid putting a trail there. But in the summer of 1930, the National Park Service sent in a six-man crew. They carried shovels, pry bars, and no small amount of dynamite. "Fire in the hole!" At every blast the six of them hid behind the largest boulder. Then one day those protective boulders rolled.

Young Donald fell, his arm caught, crushed between granite blocks. They had to use sledgehammers to break him free. One crew member glimpsed a hole in the middle of Donald's arm as two others carried him six hundred feet to their camp. They had no morphine and Donald's pain was excruciating.

It was three days until a doctor rode in on horseback—by then the limb was gangrenous. The doctor amputated the arm by lantern light. Donald Downs died, still in the backcountry, four days later.

BY THE TIME Blazer and Dalton had reunited, Tony was eight days ahead of them. He was focused on the finish line—Tarik's wedding was barely three weeks away. That particular morning, he was six miles north of Mount Adams, camping just before the third branch of Muddy Creek, the one with no bridge. He was only there because Allegheny, his current hiking partner, didn't like night hiking. That's how it came to pass that Tony camped for the first time with Ladybug and her hiking partner, 30-30.

Ladybug looked taller than her five feet five, and younger than her fifty years. Her bright brown eyes, straight nose, and well-proportioned face might have graced one of the marble statues atop the Acropolis— appropriate given her Greek lineage. She spoke with a Mason-Dixon accent and had the long arms and lithe waist of a competitive swimmer, which indeed she'd once been. On the PCT she found hitchhiking a snap.

A thousand miles south, Ladybug had taken a bad spill and broken her right hand in a nasty spiral fracture. The cast had to stay on for eight weeks. At the time, she'd been hiking casually with 30-30, a thirty-seven-year-old. Suddenly Ladybug couldn't even pack her gear. Staring at the prospect of a one-handed hike, she knew she needed help. "What do you think, 30-30?" He didn't think twice.

Even with assistance, the pain was staggering at times. It was hundreds of miles before it subsided and the bones knit back together. But Ladybug didn't consider quitting—she had made a promise. Her sister Cheryl had died from breast cancer nine years earlier. In her last months, she confided her biggest fear, "I'm worried no one will remember me." Ladybug made her sister a promise: "You will not be forgotten." She had dedicated her hike to her sister, and was raising money in Cheryl's name for hospice care for people with cancer. A broken hand would not drive her off the trail. By the time Ladybug reached Washington, the cast was gone and the pasty flesh on her arm had tanned.

Tony knew none of this when, at dusk, Ladybug and 30-30 pulled into camp. He and Allegheny had already turned in, and the four spoke only enough to establish that they had each previously hiked the Appalachian Trail. Ladybug and 30-30 were also in a pre-celebratory frame of mind. With only a chunk of Washington left, Ladybug knew she was going to finish.

The next morning it was time to cross the third branch of Muddy Creek. Allegheny left first and negotiated a narrow, slippery log over the stream. The Muddy was fast and deep, its milky-white glacier runoff obscuring a jumble of boulders jutting from the floor of the waist-deep flow. Fifteen feet long and three feet above the water, the log bowed under Allegheny's weight, but he was loathe to wade through the icy water on such a cold morning. He was well out of sight when 30-30 crossed, using the same route. Then came Ladybug.

This is no big deal, she thought. *I've done so many log crossings.* She put one foot in front of the other, as 30-30 watched. Then she felt the log bow. He saw her hesitate. *Should I be doing this? Should I turn back and wade across?* Her debate ended abruptly. *Whoosh.* The soles of her feet flew off the log. She dropped three feet, and her left leg slammed into a submerged rock. The blow shattered her tibia and fibula—in that moment, she knew that she'd broken her leg. Flailing her arms, she fought to keep her head above the rushing water as 30-30 hurled himself into the icy flow to reach her. When he pulled her head and shoulders out of the water, she shouted, "My hike's over!" He quickly shot back, "Don't say that."

When Tony arrived at the stream, Ladybug was still lying in the water. She refused to be moved or touched, but Tony and 30-30 were afraid that she'd go into shock. Once they'd helped her out of the stream, the two used a fireman's carry—their hands crossed and grasped beneath her rear end—to carry Ladybug as gingerly as possible back to where they had camped the night before. She screamed the whole way. Once there, they laid out a Therm-a-Rest pad and made a nest out of their three sleeping bags.

They were deep in the Mount Adams Wilderness of the Cascade Range—the closest civilization was the sparsely settled Yakama Indian Reservation. They had no cell coverage, nor any idea where the nearest ranger station was. Two miles ahead, barely warranting a number, was Forest Road 5603. "I'll go for help," Tony said. 30-30 would stay with Ladybug.

When he reached the road, Tony found Allegheny sitting on a rock. After he explained what had happened to Ladybug, the two pored over their maps. *What a crapshoot,* Tony thought. *Which way to go?* The guidebook maps covered such a narrow corridor. He took off, jogging east, because the maps indicated that at a crossroads three miles away there might be a ranger station. Allegheny would man the trailhead, ready to flag down any vehicle coming from the opposite direction.

Back at camp, 30-30 gave Ladybug ibuprofen, but it did nothing for the unbearable pain in her left leg. She could only lie there, alternately crying and whimpering, not knowing how soon Tony would bring help.

The sun was high in the sky when Tony reached the crossroads. When he saw what was left of the building, he was crestfallen—there was only a cracked concrete foundation. He caught his breath and then continued east. Finally, Tony saw a car belonging to an off-duty Yakama Reservation policeman. The officer had no radio service or way to contact the outside world, so they started driving back to Allegheny. On the way, they saw a logging truck and flagged it down—that driver also had no radio contact, but offered to drive to the nearest town. "I'll send medical help," he said, and then mentioned it was 30 miles away.

When the car reached the trailhead, Tony hurried back to the camp-site. He let 30-30 and Ladybug know how soon help might be there, then turned right around and went out again. He wanted to be there to lead in the rescue crew. By this point, Tony had walked, jogged, or run at least 10 miles. It felt like it had been hours since he had come upon Ladybug and 30-30 at the Muddy Creek crossing.

The weak sun had passed its zenith when a Yakama Tribal ambulance finally arrived. Two EMTs and four members of the Yakama Nation Foresters hiked back to where 30-30 was waiting with Ladybug. The EMTs then went to work stabilizing her leg. She pleaded for painkillers, and couldn't believe it when they answered, "We can't. We're not authorized."

Next, they loaded Ladybug onto a stretcher and headed back down the trail to the ambulance. Taking turns in teams of four, they inched ahead in two-hundred-yard increments. The trail was narrow and depressed, like a ditch, and the stretcher carriers fought to keep their balance as they continuously bumped against the sides. Even with the Therm-a-Rest and sleeping bags helping to cushion her, Ladybug continued to beg. "Please give me something." Worse, she was losing circulation to her left foot.

They were close, a quarter mile from the road, when two burly paramedics from the town of Yakima arrived in the heart of the afternoon. Finally, *finally*, painkillers. Finally, some measure of relief for Ladybug. Back at the road, they planned to transport her by ambulance. But they'd grown increasingly worried about the state of her foot.

This was the moment where Ladybug's story parted ways with that of eighteen-year-old Donald Downs. After Downs lost circulation to his limb, gangrene had set in. Blessedly, for Ladybug they called in an army helicopter.

At the Yakima hospital the next morning the doctor told her, "I can't count how many places your leg is broken. It looks like a bomb shatter." He minimally set and cast it so she could fly home. 30-30 was there— after Ladybug left in the helicopter, a sheriff had driven him over 50 rumbling miles of washboard and potholes to the hospital. Before he left to head back to the trail, he made a promise. "I'll hike with you next year. I'll help you finish." No matter how unlikely that seemed, given the state of her leg, she made him write it on her cast. "I'll hike with you next year. —30-30." A few days later, she flew back home to Ohio. Her husband, Bruce, had paid for a full row, all three seats. He sat just across the aisle. Ladybug stared at 30-30's promise as the plane took off.

Eighteen screws and two plates. That's the hardware it took to wire her bones together. One doctor said, "You'll never hike again."

Ladybug closed her ears to the naysayers. From her wheelchair in rehab, she stayed focused on a piece from her plaster cast. When the doctor cut off that first cast, Ladybug had insisted, "Make sure you give me this part." It held 30-30's promise to hike with her the next year. She was determined to hold him to it.

BY THE TIME the helicopter was airborne, Tony and Allegheny had already started hiking again. With miles still to cover, they headed north. Tony didn't begrudge a minute he had spent helping out; he didn't mind that it set him back a day. But another consequence of racing miles for help was shin splints that wouldn't quit. He started taking two thousand milligrams of ibuprofen a day to manage the pain. Four tabs, five times a day. You're not supposed to do that. When the pain got too bad, he would think, *If I wasn't so close to finishing, I would stop and leave the trail.*

35

Lost

SATURDAY, SEPTEMBER 22, 2007

INDIAN PASS WAS the crossroads, a point of no return. It was a place where hikers asked one another, "Are you taking the detour or the old PCT?"

The focal point of the old PCT's flood-ravaged 45 miles was the Suiattle River crossing. Swifter, deeper, and triple the width, the Suiattle made Muddy Creek look like a diminutive cousin. Had Ladybug fallen into the Suiattle, 30-30 would have had no chance to act before she'd been swept away. Even before setting foot on the trail, hikers spoke of the Suiattle River in hushed tones.

Twenty-five hundred miles later nothing had changed. Every year, boulders crashed loudly as they raced down the milky flow roaring off Glacier Peak, but for decades the lion had been tamed. The Suiattle bridge had been a wilderness wonder—miles from any road, 150 feet long, high off the water, a buttress of four-by-four timbers, six-inch logs, steel girders, and I-beams held together by inch-thick bolts. The US Cavalry could have thundered across it two abreast, but a single Cascades storm four years before had ripped the bridge from its moorings and deposited it in a twisted heap downstream. The guidebook and the Forest Service now advised taking an official but unmaintained 50-mile detour.

You'd have to spend a day and a half retracing your steps if you reached the Suiattle and it was impossible to cross. If someone got injured or worse, you were on your own, with no way to call for help. We'd heard the rumors, both good and bad. Of the good, "There's a log over the Suiattle near the old crossing," and "Last year, some late-season hikers took the old PCT." Considering the bad, "Landslides washed away the trail. It's crazy." And, "There are hundreds of blowdowns—trees fallen across the trail." Many of Washington's steep slopes are passable only because of deep-cut trail; it was hard to imagine traversing one with the trail obliterated. For us the decision loomed two days ahead. At its center was the Suiattle, a black hole, the big unknown.

IN THE ELEVEN days since they had reunited, Blazer and Dalton had taken no zeros. In fact, Blazer hadn't taken one in almost three weeks, not since Timberline Lodge. Now, a day before they reached Highway 2 at Stevens Pass, and still 205 miles from Canada, the first snowfall arrived. They woke to a winter wonderland and a thick layer of snow weighing down their tents. With it still snowing outside, Blazer slept in, delaying their start. Once they were finally up and moving, their "wonderland" glee melted. Snow and rain tag-teamed the pair for miles. All day, the overgrown, waterlogged brush soaked them. Their fingers and toes were numb. If they had stopped to eat, they would have frozen.

I felt the same initial glee on seeing the snow that morning. Frodo and I were a half day ahead of them, and we climbed Trap Pass in three inches of accumulating snow. "Slow down," I told Frodo. I had my camera out. I wanted to work the scene, to capture these shots. After all, this might be our only snowfall, and I wanted photographic proof that we had hiked in snow. The first deep drifts usually weren't till mid-October, so I knew Frodo and I were safe. We planned to finish two weeks before that.

No matter how harsh the conditions, the Cascades charmed us, ensuring the day wasn't an entire drudge. Every bend held the promise of a miracle. One day at noon, on a high pass above tree line, I was hunkered down in a drenching rain, answering nature's call in thirty-seven-degree weather. Suddenly I felt a large displacement of air around me. I looked up. Gliding slowly as if I didn't exist, a bald eagle passed over. Barely clearing the pass, its wings were stretched out to their full width—possibly as much as seven feet or more. It was so close I could have reached up and touched the feathers on its breast.

That first day it snowed, the thermometer on Blazer's pack never topped forty degrees. She and Dalton pushed through 27 teeth-chattering, tough miles without a break, finally arriving at Stevens Pass at 9:00 p.m. The two huddled under an outhouse awning, vainly punching cell phone numbers. No service.

They were trying to reach trail angels Andrea and Jerry Dinsmore. The Dinsmores were as famed in the north as the Saufleys were in the south. Blazer sat, fully spent, her back to the outhouse, as Dalton ran off to find a pay phone. Pressed against the rough siding, she drew her knees to her chest, trying to ward off the sleet.

Thirty minutes later, when Blazer saw Andrea Dinsmore's headlights pierce the rain, her weary spirits surged. She melted into the warm car seat before the three of them drove off, the windshield wipers thrumming. Blazer thought, *Just sitting here is a miracle.* When the two arrived at Andrea and Jerry's home, they found hot pizza waiting. Blazer could have cried.

TOWN STOPS WEREN'T the only thing that offset the misery of the rain. The countryside stunned the senses. The glaciers here are at 6000 and 7000 feet, not 10,000. Dark, razor-edge peaks marched rank upon rank, the rows split by plunging valleys with dangerous rushing streams. The views—when the weak sun deigned to spotlight them—could thrust even Muir's Sierra Nevada onto the back shelf. And it might snow any month of the year.

One northwest attraction was both a threat and a treat. Huckleberries. The scrumptious delights were nearly enough to derail a hike—something we learned just north of Timberline Lodge when we hit our first big patch. Blazer, Frodo, and I stopped so often we stained our tongues purple. "Look, there's more over here!" It was Frodo who saved us in the end. Stamping the trail with her high school teacher feet, she ordered, "Let's get hiking!" Even now, in late September, we ran into significant patches.

Anytime Blazer or Dalton started to wallow in rain- or cold-induced self-pity, they only had to think of hikers who were worse off. Once, when Blazer was joshing about how hard it was to leave her tent at night, a guy brought up his bout of stomach flu. To go puke in the rain, he first had to force himself into his half-frozen rain gear. And there was the Appalachian Trail veteran who confessed that this was the first time he'd ever cried from misery on any trail. At the Summit Inn at Snoqualmie Pass—Blazer had allowed herself a one-night stay—she watched a hiker walk into the lobby directly from the rainy trail and hyperventilate for minutes. It was the pure release of not having to hold it together anymore. Washington was serious country.

"COME ON, DALTON. Let's get going!" Blazer's voice rang out brightly, calling from inside her tent. It was September 24 and the sun was shining, giving them both a morale boost. There were only eight days and seven nights left. The detour decision wasn't till tomorrow. She'd woken early and eager, her body suffused with opened-eyed enthusiasm. They had camped by Lake Janus, a half-mile-long jewel set high in the Henry M. Jackson Wilderness. The spacious lakeside site was theirs alone, besieged and surrounded by a riot of colored flora—swaths of brilliant red huckleberry bushes, carpets of yellow sedges and fescues, and, on higher ground, stands of deep green conifers: Alaska cedars, firs, Engelmann spruce, and pines.

Bright as it was, the sun was a pale candle compared to the heat lamp of Southern California. Still, it was such a blessing, welcome after so much rain. Blazer shivered only a little as the pair set out from Lake Janus. She might have done well to remember her Roman mythology—the lake's namesake was a two-faced god.

Dalton suggested they have lunch at a campsite roughly 12 miles ahead. With Blazer's nod, he sped ahead toward their destination. Having found a groove, Blazer hiked more slowly and reveled in the beautiful day. She had her first view of Glacier Peak—the snowcapped volcano dominated this section, like Mount Shasta had in the south—and let her mind wander. At Pear Lake, eight miles along, there was a fork. Stuck on autopilot, she took the path down toward the lake.

Hiking on, Blazer climbed a terribly steep hill. *Man, it would stink to have to go back down that.* After two hours, she realized, *I'm seeing fewer footprints, and where's the campsite?* A good hour later she came to a sign. Trail signs are few and far between in Washington, and usually Blazer found it a relief to see one. This one, secured by thick lag screws to a tree, marked the wilderness boundary. If she'd walked into it and banged her head, the result wouldn't have been more sickening.

I shouldn't be here. She sat down, pulled out the map, and plotted where she was. When she realized she had walked six miles out of her way, Blazer was pissed. As she started backtracking, the consequences sunk in and she kicked herself harder. *Dalton will be worried. He won't know where I am.* She even tried running once, but that ended fast.

As the sun set, it became clearer that she wouldn't be able to make up the miles between her and Dalton tonight. Blazer stopped, her chest heaving, and threw her arms up. She screamed, "Why!"

THE SAME DAY that Blazer took that wrong turn by Pear Lake, over 140 miles farther north Tony was unerringly headed toward his objective— the northern monument was in his sights. He hadn't seen another hiker for 60 miles and three days, not since the PCT's last trail stop before Canada, the village of Stehekin.

Layered clouds roared in and just as quickly fled again, whirling from translucent white mist to polished gunmetal blue and then thick, puffy gray. As the sun set, they took on yellows, ripe shades of orange, and then deep pinks. Over and over Tony thought one word, *Breathtaking.* It never got old. Even when he woke to snow blanketing his tent, the sun would come out and turn the mountains golden. But amid all this wonder Tony felt he was on his last legs. At this point, he was practically shoveling ibuprofen into his body.

Only days before, Tony had left a phone message for Nadine, hoping it would catch her shortly after she crossed the border into Washington. He'd heard she was hiking solo. "Nadine, don't hike the Goat Rocks alone." That length of trail—called the Knife's Edge—was like a tightrope along the spine of the Cascades. Tony had been exhilarated—this was the adventure he'd craved and sorely missed on the Appalachian Trail— but he'd hiked near others for that high-wire act. Windswept and miles long, the narrow track had multiple points where the drops on both sides were more than five hundred feet. You needed the sure-footedness of the mountain goats for which the wilderness was named to safely traverse it.

In good weather, Goat Rocks required careful footsteps. In bad weather, it required extraordinary care. And in truly inclement weather, a transit of Goat Rocks might be life threatening. *Be careful, Nadine.* Tony was still thinking about her and Pacha as his hike came to a close—*There are people on this trail I know I'll be close to forever. That's what I want with Nadine. I'm just not sure if she'll allow it.*

I'D FOUGHT FOR one particular photo since the start. My point-and-shoot lived in the front cargo pocket of my pants so that, like a high-noon gunslinger, I could slap my hand down, whip out the camera, raise it, aim, and fire. Mostly I'd miss, but what I wanted to freeze-frame was a butterfly poised on a wildflower. In five months, I had succeeded four times.

The butterfly effect. An MIT meteorologist, Edward Lorenz, theorized that the flap of a butterfly's wings in the Amazon basin might set a cascade of events in motion that could end in an Atlantic hurricane. Even the smallest movement could have an outsized effect. So, was it on this day, while Blazer wandered lost, that it all started? Was it a few days before? Somewhere in the Bering Sea on an Aleutian Island, a butterfly launched from a wildflower. No one took its photo. It flapped its wings and there was a swirl that begat a zephyr, which spawned a depression that rose to become a storm and then a series of storms, each lined up to wallop the north end of the PCT.

THE PHONE MESSAGE Glacier left us was joyous. We'd parted eight weeks ago, only days before Frodo broke her teeth. "No goodbyes." Now Glacier had finished. I doubt she'd ever sounded that elated in her entire twenty-five-year Forest Service career. I'd never heard Glacier sing or even hum, but the rise and fall in her voice had hints of Beethoven's "Ode to Joy."

"Hello, Scout and Frodo! This is Glacier calling. I am here in Manning Park. I rolled in last night and I am pretty happy to have finished the Pacific Crest Trail! I wish you guys were here! I'm thinking of you. I sure hope and pray that the weather doesn't close in."

NADINE WASN'T AMUSED when she put down the phone. *I'm a strong hiker, what's he warning me for?* Tony's message about Goat Rocks had backfired. Not only did Nadine still plan to hike the section alone, but his voicemail left her both insulted and scared. "Staying close forever" might be his goal, but Tony hadn't done much for his chances.

Nadine walked smack into four days of freezing rain and then snow, which dusted the Goat Rocks. Just trying to stay warm had her and Pacha eating their food bag down to the dregs—for the final two days she gave Pacha her lunch. On the Knife's Edge the wind keened fiercely. Worried that Pacha might be knocked off her feet or blown off a ledge, Nadine roped the two of them together. More than once Nadine thought of Tony's warning. But despite the conditions, and despite missing the long-promised views, Nadine stayed optimistic, focused on the end. She'd reach White Pass in a few hours, where she'd connect with a friend.

Chris, an old boyfriend, was going to hike with her for the rest of Washington. Another friend, Rob, was driving him out, and they would have her resupply with them. Of primary importance, she knew they'd have town food.

But still it was a great surprise when they greeted her on trail six miles in from White Pass. Rob handed Nadine a quarter of a chicken; she snatched it from his hand. He then turned to Chris and asked, "So how does this work? Do we keep throwing food at her like at a petting zoo?" Nadine attacked all that they'd brought—chicken, pizza, and a whole blackberry pie. She would have warned them to watch their fingers, but her mouth was too full.

Nadine got lucky with Chris. Many hikers find that when friends or relatives hop on trail it can be a mixed bag. Thru-hikers wonder: *Will they keep up? Will I need to watch out for them?* But Chris proved the exception, remaining good company even as the weather continued its downward spiral. He was the first up in the morning, popping out of his tent before Nadine to get coffee ready for when she emerged. She journaled: "He jumped right into the thru-hiker routine without a hiccup. From day one we were hiking 20-mile days and he wasn't daunted at all by the Cascades' rough terrain." She continued, "Chris and I have about two weeks and 250 more miles to go. Then we'll celebrate in style at Manning Park Resort."

Somewhere far away, a pair of butterfly wings flapped.

PASSING THE BANKS of Pear Lake a second time, Blazer allowed herself a moment's relief. She was finally back on the PCT. But when she looked at her watch, she saw it was 6:30 p.m., nightfall, even though she'd been hiking hard. Instead of dinner, Blazer pulled out her last two Snickers bars and wolfed them down.

Frodo and I both saw the headlamp bobbing along the trail. I had just finished brushing my teeth at our makeshift campsite near Saddle Gap. We'd had a sunny day, no rain, and we were within 150 miles of Canada. Moments before, I'd done what I did every clear night—spotting the Big Dipper and tracing a finger to the North Star, I'd pictured myself at the monument. I saw those five fir pillars, and my hand signing the register. "I, Scout, have completed the Pacific Crest Trail."

During the last few weeks, I'd augmented that vision. My parents—Dad was eighty-three and Mom was seventy-seven—had decided to meet us at the end, Manning Park Resort. They'd fly from Los Angeles to Seattle and then make the four-hour drive. From the PCT monument, at the border between the two countries, I'd hike the final eight miles to Manning Park. There, I'd find my father and give him a big hug. After five months of persevering, hiking through a cracked rib, losing toenails, and always keeping that steel fist clenched inside, I'd hold tight to the man who had cheered me when I'd taken my first tentative step almost fifty-five years ago. I'd lean down and whisper in his ear, "Daddy, I'm done. I don't have to be strong anymore." Deep inside, for the first time in five months, the fist would unclench; I'd let myself relax.

Frodo had painted her own portrait of what the end would look like. She'd asked our stalwart resupply daughter, Jordie, to ship CDs and a player to Manning Park Resort. Frodo imagined soaking in a hot tub as part of a celebratory night at the lodge, then boarding the train in Vancouver for the two-day trip home to San Diego. And there on the train she'd put her feet up, move as little as absolutely possible, and

listen to Enya for hours on end—for her, the aural equivalent of comfort food.

It had been dark for two hours when we spotted the bobbing headlight.
"Hello, hiker, who goes there?" we called out. Puffing and out of breath,
Blazer stumbled into our camp. She started sobbing even before we had
her in our arms. "I lost Dalton." The story came out in fits and starts. "I
have to hike on. I have to find him." She'd covered 26 miles—rugged
Washington miles, not the Bonneville Flats miles of Oregon. "I have to
go on." She sloppily wiped her nose on her threadbare yellow bandanna.

Frodo looked at her, hazel eyes boring into Blazer's brown ones. "No,
child, you need sleep. Stop here. Dalton will be fine." Closer to the end
of her rope than she once thought possible, Blazer set up her tent as we
turned in to ours. When we heard her rustling stop, Frodo and I, from
inside our snug nylon home, began singing. It was a lullaby, one we'd
sung to her the night before Seiad Valley. Then we went on to the next.
Inside her tent, Blazer listened, and soon her red-rimmed eyes closed.

IN THE DIM early morning light, Dalton hiked alone until he saw a tilted
signpost emerge from a chill fog. He had reached Indian Pass. There
were two aged trail signs, one for the PCT and one for Indian Creek. On
the post the Forest Service had thumbtacked two notes. "Please take the
Detour," implored one. The "please" was underlined three times. The second described an ongoing search and rescue mission for a missing PCT
hiker not many miles before the Suiattle River. Standing alone in the wilderness, Dalton had to decide.

He hadn't planned to be here by himself. The night before he'd stayed
awake into the wee hours, hoping Blazer would arrive. That morning,
he'd drawn out his normal packing routine. He kept looking up, wishing
Blazer would catch up to him. But she hadn't, and he'd pressed on. *I only
hope she's hiking with others.*

He had been stressing about this section for weeks. While he knew
there were trail washouts and intimidating river crossings and hundreds
of blowdowns, Dalton fought his urge to prove that he was strong, capable, and worth a damn. That was both a strength and a weakness on the

PCT. He had heard that a few hikers had successfully navigated the old PCT route, and, after so many miles, the drive to stay on the official trail ran strong. But the deciding factor for him was his need to prove to himself, "I am a courageous person."

North on the PCT or east along Indian Creek? As the fog changed to drizzle, Dalton headed out north, bound for the Suiattle.

Four hours later, Frodo, Blazer, and I reached the same spot. The fog had lifted and was now hovering a hundred feet above our heads. We saw the warning notes—"Please, take the Detour." We did the opposite. After 2500 miles, we made our own decisions.

The Forest Service hadn't officially closed the trail, and at Stevens Pass we'd spoken to someone who'd hiked the old route southbound. So our decision wasn't totally foolhardy. But the magnitude of the choice to head north on an unmaintained trail started sinking in as we began tallying the blowdowns. Step-overs didn't count—a blowdown had to significantly interfere with our pace. Often we veered yards left or right, scrambled through broken limbs and brush, or passed our packs over a tree trunk, rock, or other obstacle. It chewed up time, tried our patience, and sometimes led to taking a dicey shortcut. As dusk approached, Blazer looked up one gorge and spied a twenty-foot log bridge wedged sideways between bus-size rocks. "Why's a bridge up there?" Then she realized—upslope we'd recently forded a stream—that bridge had spanned the stream before the 2003 flood.

At nightfall when we made camp, the blowdown tally had reached sixty-two. Our group of three had expanded to eight. Of the newcomers, Blazer was especially happy to see Not-a-Moose. They'd last parted in Ashland, six weeks ago. As for the other four, three were close to Blazer's age—Chigger, Miso, and Mr. Pink, Miso's boyfriend from the trail. Miso would answer to Tofu, or for that matter, any soy product. The eighth and last was Lotto, who was new to us.

We counted the hundredth blowdown the next morning—leaving a trail note to designate it as such—but it wasn't the most memorable blowdown. Neither was number two hundred or three hundred. Nor was the blowdown that dwarfed Frodo, an ancient western red cedar with a twenty-five-foot circumference. What a sound that forest giant must have made when it crashed!

The most memorable blowdown wasn't nearly that large. The trail had been crabwalking sideways across a steep-angled slope, and this blow-down was a ten-foot-long, chest-high broken stub lying across the trail, its rotted top hanging out over a cliff like a slide to oblivion. *One slip and you're airborne, launched off the mountainside,* I thought. With chilled fingers I clawed into slimy, partially rotted wood as I clambered over first, and then reached back to help Chigger. Blazer came next, but she waved me off. "You've got this, Blazer," I said as I started to turn. She placed one foot on the top. As she lifted her other foot off the ground, her foot on the log slipped. Her body hit the slick wood and her feet shot over the edge as my hand flew out to grab her—my fist quickly closing around her wrist. Blazer's weight hit me with a jerk, and my arm tensed like a steel rod. Chigger's chin dropped as she watched me start to slide toward Blazer. I dug in my feet and leaned back, my heels searching for traction. My other arm flailed behind me for something to hold onto, but found only air. The quick intake of our breaths was drowned by the roar, far below, of a Cascade river tumbling boulders like a child's marbles. Then I regained my balance. And my grip held. Blazer's legs hovered over air as we looked at one another.

When she was finally able to walk again her knees trembled. *I nearly went over,* she thought. *I could have been just like No Way Ray.*

The second day after Indian Pass we reached the Suiattle. Once a channel, the streambed was now a wide, rock-strewn floodplain. Trail ducks, a trail marker of three rocks stacked one atop the other, led us to the log. Two feet thick and six feet above the water, the trunk spanned forty-foot-wide rapids. I went first, unbuckling my hip belt to lower my center of gravity, and to make sure I could wiggle the pack off my back if I fell in. I walked across upright, but just past halfway, I thought, *This is really stupid.*

Nevertheless, I pressed on, heart in my throat. Next, Chigger scooted slowly along the length of the log, lifting her rear and inching forward time and time again. Frodo followed. It took sixty to seventy scoots to cross. Then Lotto stepped out. He looked like he might walk across, but after three steps he retreated—then scooted across too.

Blazer hadn't seen any of this. Over the roar, we hollered out, "Scoot across," and pantomimed the motion. She nodded an acknowledgment, but then stepped confidently out onto the log. We held our collective breath as she moved, her hiking poles marking time in front of her. I'd never seen her concentrate more fiercely. The exhale of breath was palpable when she reached the other side.

Four hundred and twenty-six blowdowns. That was the final tally when the detour track rejoined the PCT, seven miles past the Suiattle. We were so pleased to be back on the maintained official trail we could have kissed the ground. Twenty miles of tread now lay between us and Stehekin. For most, it was the final resupply stop before the end. With 100 miles and five hiking days left, we were on track to meet Frodo's itinerary end date of October 2.

36

Before the Storm

AS OJ DESCENDED the final miles through dense forest to the northern monument, she wasn't sure what to expect. The closer she got, the more she started hurrying. Then she saw the line of missing trees. *It's as though someone waxed a thirty-foot-wide strip of the forest as far as the eye could see.* OJ veritably skipped down the last switchbacks and then she heard familiar voices. Her mom and dad were there, having hiked in the last eight miles to meet her. Just as they'd planned. And there was the monument. And there was Canada.

Her parents asked, "What do you feel?" OJ answered, "Relief, excitement, and disbelief." But what she actually felt was surprise. She had started the hike with hundreds of other people, including superathlete types and Appalachian Trail veterans. She thought so many of them had been better prepared than she was, with better gear, better physiques, better brains, better senses of humor. Now, at the border, she thought, *I'm an occasional jogger, an excessively poor organizer, and a perfectly ordinary person. Who would have imagined I would make it? How crazy is that? That I could walk from Mexico to Canada? It blows my mind.*

TUESDAY, SEPTEMBER 25, 2007

WHAT? I STILL *have eight miles to hike? But I just finished!* Tony stood alone in the darkness by the PCT's northern monument—he hadn't seen another hiker since he left Stehekin. He'd known the border monument marked the end of the PCT, not the start of civilization, but it was only now sinking in—he still had one more night to sleep on the trail.

Tony took two dark, grainy photos and then found the trail register. Not everyone does, as it isn't actually on the PCT monument. The slender volume was secreted inside the official border marker, Monument 78, a neck-high brass obelisk a few feet away. To open it, you had to yank off the heavy metal top like you're ripping it in half. It almost felt like you were destroying government property.

Tony's handwriting hadn't changed from his May entry in the Campo register. He still printed all the letters with his *f*'s and *y*'s dropping well below the line, but the man was much changed. He'd climbed Mount Whitney, he'd experienced real adventure, and his time with Nadine left him hopeful for the future, even if he never saw her again. "7:20 pm— Seems weird to be 'finished' and still have 8 miles to go. Wish I hadn't missed that last campsite . . . Oh, well, seems somehow appropriate to night hike my last day on the trail. Big congrats to all of us!! Manning Park, here I come. Tony."

WITH 419 MILES left, Roswell was nearly played out. After Frodo and I witnessed her helicopter rescue, she had taken two weeks off to recover from giardiasis. Then she'd hiked like a hard-charging steed through Northern California and Oregon. But crossing into Washington, Roswell hit the wall. It wasn't just the rigors of the hike or the gut-wrenching illness that wore her down—it was also her lack of money. Roswell had saved so little before she left for the trail, starting with only two thousand dollars. Twice she'd exchanged work to get a bed in a trail town. On Father's Day she'd raked pine needles—it was the only way to earn calling card minutes to phone her dad.

Now Roswell was in Trout Lake, only 83 miles north of the Bridge of the Gods. She'd just taken four zero days here, hoping the time would recharge her flagging spirits. But all that rest in the hole-in-the-wall trail town with fresh huckleberry shakes didn't dim the hard reality she faced. As Roswell got back on the trail she thought, *I'm the last of the 2007 thru-hikers.* The closest hiker she knew of was three days ahead.

For a while back in Oregon, she had been hopeful. *Maybe I can make Canada. The snow just needs to be a little late.* At Trout Lake, Roswell, now too thin and with her stomach acting up again, did the hardest thing for a thru-hiker to do. She let Canada go. *I won't make it to the border or to Manning Park.* This 67-mile stretch from Trout Lake to White Pass would be her last.

WEDNESDAY, SEPTEMBER 26, 2007

TONY ARRIVED AT Manning Park Resort early in the morning after hiking those last eight non-PCT miles. There he celebrated, feeling a rush of gratitude and relief—particularly for the hot shower. The next morning, he took the once-a-day bus west to Vancouver, where he stayed with Ryley. The guy who had once peppered Tony with raw-beginner questions had finished ten days before him. While he was there, Tony saw Ryley's new tattoo—the PCT trail symbol large as life on his calf.

There was no tattoo in Tony's future, but the trail had inked him just as indelibly. He was staggered at the toll it had taken on his body, and he was near dead broke. But at the moment none of that mattered. *I have walked from Mexico to Canada through some of the most incredible country.* All his adult life Tony had felt passed by, as he'd watched others make their mark. All he'd done was get married and become a landscaper. Yet only a few hundred had set out on the PCT, and he was one of the fraction who made it the entire way. *I've proved myself to the world.* But his most important audience had been himself.

THURSDAY, SEPTEMBER 27, 2007

TWO DAYS AND almost forty miles past Trout Lake, Roswell snuggled in her tent, dry and at peace. *Tomorrow I'll be in Goat Rocks. I'll walk the Knife's Edge.* She'd seen photos of it on a clear day, Mount Rainier in the background. Glorious. It would also be her last night on the trail. She was so ready. Pulling her sleeping bag tight, she asked Mother PCT for a final boon. *Good weather, please.*

FRIDAY, SEPTEMBER 28, 2007

NADINE WAS HIKING out of the Summit Inn at Snoqualmie Pass—253 miles to go. *Chris and I are on target for an October 11 finish*—nine days after Frodo and I were set to finish. This country felt familiar to Nadine. She had hiked just north of here during her first PCT attempt in 1998—that stretch remained some of the most challenging backpacking she'd ever done. At one point she'd had to self-arrest with her ice axe. When she looked down, both hands firm on the dug-in axe, she saw the steep, icy slope continue until it was out of sight. Now, she was thinking, *I have been looking forward to getting here all summer. I want to hike strong and fierce through this wilderness that once scared the bejesus out of me.*

ONE MAGAZINE CALLED it "the most remote community in the Lower 48 states," but for PCT hikers, Stehekin is their last connection to civilization along the trail. Home to eighty souls, this hamlet is the last ferry stop on 51-mile-long Lake Chelan. Pressed into the mountain walls rimming the lake, Stehekin can't be reached by roads. You get here by floatplane, boat, horse, or foot.

To hikers, Stehekin is renowned for one thing: The Stehekin Pastry Company. Its to-die-for pies, cakes, pastries, pizzas, and hot-pocket sandwiches alone would have made it the most talked-about eatery on the trail. But its cinnamon rolls—sticky, gooey, and usually hot from the oven—give the gods' ambrosia a run for its money.

Frodo, Blazer, Chigger, Not-a-Moose, Lotto, and I emerged from the trail at the High Bridge Ranger Station, 10 miles north of Stehekin. Here, we waited for an old yellow school bus, the shuttle that drove between here and Stehekin Landing—the waterfront center of town—three times a day. When the bus arrived, we piled into the back with our bags. On the way to town, the bus stopped at The Stehekin Pastry Company—that's when we realized we would be last off a bus full of tourists who had been sightseeing in the valley. Frodo, a mischievous glint in her eye, pointed at the rear emergency exit, through which our packs had been loaded. She opened it and we scrambled out and into the bakery.

During their four days apart, Blazer had worried about Dalton like a parent over an absent child. The moment she stepped off the bus at Stehekin Landing, she blurted out, "Dalton, where's Dalton?" At the same time, when Dalton heard the midday bus arrive, he raced outside calling, "Blazer! Blazer!" She was achy and stiff, but Blazer tried to run to him. When they came together, Blazer lifted Dalton off his feet, she was so happy to see him. Soon, they were jabbering at each other, catching up on missed adventures. "I wasn't sure if you were ahead or behind." "Dalton, I got so lost. I was so angry at myself." "I'm so glad to see you."

There were more reunions. Figaro had been a day ahead of us since Crater Lake in southern Oregon and it was in Stehekin that we at last caught up with him. This tall man was even thinner—I could feel his bones when I hugged him. It rang true when he told us that while visiting an urgent care center for a foot infection the nurse sternly asked him after he stepped off the scale—six foot four and 145 pounds—"Do we need to have a talk about anorexia?" With icing from a cinnamon roll on his lips, all we could do was laugh.

We all had stories. That night we swapped tales around a long table at the ferry landing's sole restaurant—Blazer, Dalton, Figaro, Not-a-Moose, Chigger, Guts, and Chuckwagon together with Frodo and me. With a groaning board of rich food in front of us, we reverently spoke of the full moon two nights before. It was our sixth since starting, our very last on the trail. We spoke of conquering the Suiattle and laughed about counting blowdowns. We grew silent when one person spoke of seeing three numbers spelled out in rocks alongside the trail. In our mind's eye, we all traced out the number one hundred—100 miles left. Blazer had felt a rush when she'd seen it. She swore to herself, "This close to the end, I'll crawl to Canada if I have to."

That night we could hear the water lapping at the docks from our rooms at the North Cascades Lodge. I knew tomorrow we'd hike through an arm of North Cascades National Park—a place so wild that it's part of an official "Grizzly Bear Recovery Zone." I had heard rumors of grizzly sightings, and while we'd eaten dinner, the park's cavernous visitor center next door had featured a talk about bears. The title was "How to Avoid Becoming Dinner."

As I brushed my teeth I thought of the Big Dipper outside. I thought of those five wooden pillars only 82 trail miles ahead, and I thought of Manning Park, of hugging my dad and resting my head on his shoulder. A few doors down, Blazer was in her room with Dalton and two others. She wasn't thinking of the monument. Since taking her first steps away from the Mexican border she'd never pictured it again. What she'd begun to think about more and more was the hot pool she'd heard about at Manning Park Resort.

Outside, the near-full moon reflected off the lake. Mountain sentinels rose above its north end, brooding guards in shadow, but it wasn't their steepness or height that was scary. It was their snow line—how close it was. The next storm was already closing in.

37

The Knife's Edge

ROSWELL DIDN'T GET her wish. Silent as a cougar stalking prey, the first snow crept from the sky as she slept. There was no breeze as a telltale, only the gentle sag of her tent. Roswell woke to an inch of snow. All morning she couldn't shake a sense of foreboding, and as she climbed above tree line, conditions grew worse and the snow grew deeper.

At midmorning, she left the first in a series of notes. She might be alone, but Roswell was going to do everything she could to look out for herself. In a ziplock bag on the signpost for the junction with the Walupt Lake Trail, she left her name, her mother's phone number, where she was heading—the information that rescuers would need—and "Snowing, weather worsening. I'm happy, staying warm."

When the snow let up for a moment, the only time that day, Roswell paused to admire the frosted scenery. Experiencing nature in the raw was why she'd started her hike. *It's so beautiful. I'm so nervous.* Her pace slowed as she struggled up 6500-foot Cispus Pass. When she reached it at noon, the snow was inching up her leg. The note she left there had the same information as the first, but this time she added, "Not exactly happy anymore."

ABOUT 130 MILES ahead of Roswell, Nadine, Chris, and Pacha were climbing 2000 feet, heading north as the first storm raged on. They trusted their gear and themselves as Pacha bounded through an inch, then three inches, and then five inches of snow. Nadine was thinking, *I'm so glad this isn't freezing rain*, but she also knew that at the top of their climb they'd reach the Kendall Katwalk. In good weather, the Katwalk was an airy ledge, a testament to what dynamite could blast from a sheer rock face. To traverse it in these winter conditions was to court disaster.

BACK AT TROUT LAKE, Roswell had purchased a silver-faced thermal emergency blanket. But when she hiked out, she regretted it. *I have 67 miles left, I didn't need to cram one more thing in my pack.* Now she'd started wondering, *How do you use that thing?*

With her black pack cover, black rain jacket, and black pants, Roswell was a gaunt snow ninja, a single figure tossed in a sea of white. A few rock outcroppings still formed islands visible above the snow, but they were disappearing fast, swallowed by drifts. Roswell had cinched her jacket hood as tight as it would go. Her eyes barely showed, her nose and cheeks were chapped, bright red from the cold.

Near 4:00 p.m., Roswell passed the remnants of the Dana May Yelverton Shelter. At one time the twelve-by-twelve-foot shelter had rock walls on three sides supporting a wood-shingled roof. But now the walls were ruins, the roof rotted; all invisible under the snow. She stopped and told herself, *This is where I need to decide. Camp now or try to push past the high point.* In more than a foot of snow, the trail had been playing a vicious game of hide-and-seek. In front of her lay the west shoulder of Old Snowy Mountain—after that she would have to negotiate the two-mile-long Knife's Edge. But then the trail would drop quickly, the snow would thin, and in five miles she'd be 2000 feet lower and could camp safely. Freezing, with her core temperature dropping, Roswell made her decision. *I have to get out of this. I'm pushing on.* She didn't leave a note.

SATURDAY, AUGUST 4, 1962

DANA YELVERTON HAD almond eyes, delicate freckles, and oh-so-pale skin. So said Chris, a fellow teen hiker with a serious crush on her. She was out on a church-sponsored weeklong trek through Goat Rocks with her best friend, Margie. Both were high school students from Bellevue, Washington, with plans to go to Whitworth College together and become missionaries.

Lured forward by the prospect of the lower trail ahead, the church group hiked in a driving rain uphill toward Old Snowy Mountain. Dana's and Margie's cotton clothes soaked through as rain changed to sleet, and then into a freakish blizzard. *It's a whiteout,* Margie thought as their group of twenty-six struggled to stay together. As they broke into ever-smaller clusters, Dana was left exposed, wet, and freezing. Her prospective boyfriend got frostbite, but he barely mentioned that when recalling the experience, "I was with Dana at the end, holding her to keep her as warm as I could. We were waiting for more people and a sleeping bag to use as a litter. At the moment I could see the group coming up the mountain, she passed. Her pulse stopped."

Much later, Margie named her own daughter Dana. Margie says that they built that shelter to remember Dana, and they built it with the hope that it would offer protection for others caught in whiteout conditions. For many years it did.

ROSWELL NEVER EVEN saw the loose pile of rocks. She had no idea the Yelverton Shelter had ever existed. She did see a rock cairn, however, and was so grateful. Then up above and ahead she spotted a second. The rock cairns led straight for the top of Old Snowy. Roswell hadn't eaten for hours and she hadn't bothered to drink. At times, she couldn't see more than five or six feet ahead. Farther up the hill, she took a misstep between two cairns and pulled up short—she'd almost walked into an abyss. She trudged from cairn to cairn, higher and higher, the snow knee-deep and then thigh-high. One drift reached her shoulders. Then the cairns disappeared. No hint of the trail in any direction—she was no longer on the PCT.

Roswell had never camped in the snow, but instinctively she dug with her feet, poles, and gloves until she had cleared a two-foot-deep flat spot. Then she painstakingly set up her tent, piling snow high up each side. She'd gotten it into her head to make her shelter a virtual snow cave.

Exhausted, and at last in her sleeping bag, Roswell fumbled with numb fingers as she put on every piece of clothing she had. She pulled on extra hats. She pulled a sports bra on her head. She puzzled much too long over the emergency blanket. *Shiny side in? Shiny side out?* Nothing had cut the cold. Roswell began to feel drowsy—she still hadn't eaten anything. In her haze, she felt an impulse. *Write.*

She reached for her journal and her fingers fumbled to open a page. Shaking, she tightly clenched a pen in her hand as she tried to think what to say. Syllables jumbled in her head, thoughts blurred, and the lines wouldn't stay still. Roswell began making peace with a thought—*I might die right here.*

NO ONE HAD any inkling of where she was. But what Roswell didn't know was that another woman thru-hiker was holed up in her tent nearby. Like Roswell, Sandals had been hiking by herself for some time, and she too thought she was the last of the pack. Less than two hours after Roswell had started following those rock cairns up Old Snowy, Sandals arrived at that same spot. But in that difficult moment, Sandals made the opposite choice. *I'm stopping right here. I know I'm still on the trail.* All day, Sandals had been seeing one set of footprints. She'd watched as they made ever-deeper impressions in the snow. But she hadn't seen Roswell's notes—the blowing snow had obscured them.

Sandals had set her tent up quickly. *I better work fast if I don't want frostbite.* She piled the biggest rocks she could lift on top of her tent stakes. She was so envious of the hiker in front of her. *Whoever it is must be past Old Snowy and the Knife's Edge and hoofing it to the safety of White Pass.* Sandals chewed on a cold energy bar—her dinner—and listened to the wind howl. In all her life the only experience she'd had that came close was sailing in a North Atlantic gale. But that was rain. This was a deadly blanket of snow.

It was strange that Roswell and Sandals hadn't met. Five months earlier, they had started in Campo only two days apart. Sandals was twenty years older than Roswell, and had a husband in Texas. She liked to tell others, "I've completed life's requirements—home, career, and children—and now I've moved to electives." Now Sandals and Roswell were only a half mile apart; it may as well have been a hundred.

IN A NEAR whiteout, pushing the envelope, Nadine, Chris, and Pacha safely reached the other side of the Katwalk. With the snow continuing to fall and dusk approaching, the trio holed up where they could, hunkering down near Ridge Lake in their respective tents. *I wish I was in the desert,* Nadine thought. *The PCT is supposed to be beautiful, sunny days and cowboy camping outside. Not scary traverses.*

With the snow creeping up the side of their tent, Pacha whimpered and curled up next to her, shaking. Nadine tried to banish the one thought she simply couldn't bear—*What if we have to hike back across the Katwalk?*

ONE MOMENT, ROSWELL was staring at the blank page, the next she jerked as if someone had struck her. *No! No, I'm going to tell this story in person.* Realizing she'd been about to write a "final" note, she dropped the pen like it burned. Roswell grabbed her food bag and started stuffing everything in her mouth. Frozen granola bars felt like chewing sawdust and swallowing dirt.

With some food and water in her belly, Roswell managed a bit of fitful sleep. When morning broke, the sky momentarily cleared. Both Roswell and Sandals woke to the same internal debate. *Move or stay put? Go forward or back?* Roswell acted first. Still shaken to the core, she made that hardest of thru-hiker decisions. *I have to head back.* Sandals meanwhile took a break from poring over the guidebook maps to grit her teeth as she made a short call-of-nature foray outside. Then she was back in her tent reviewing options once more.

Packed up, Roswell descended, picking her way carefully, backtracking along the mounds she hoped were those rock cairns. She reached a spot that seemed familiar. But she couldn't make out the trail and she saw no evidence of foot traffic. *Am I back on the PCT?*

Then Roswell saw the indentations. *Fresh footprints!* Roswell hollered, "Halloo! Halloo!" She was astonished to hear someone shout back. Within moments, the two women were outside, hugging in the snow. They soon

crammed into Sandals's tent and an earnest powwow ensued. First, they
made a pact to stay together. But then it took ninety long minutes before
they agreed to backtrack—for Sandals, the prospect of turning back was
absolutely heartbreaking.

While in her tent, Sandals had gleaned every bit of information she
could from the guidebook and map: two miles south was a junction with
Trail 86, which would lead in three miles to a dirt road. *Which must lead
to a paved road eventually,* she thought. Breaking trail in the drifts was like
plowing through knee-high pine duff. After an hour they had traveled
less than a mile, but there were two of them now and by 3:30 p.m. the sign
for Trail 86 rose out of the snow.

There's another hiker! Jim was well into a long section of the PCT, but
when he heard about the conditions ahead, he decided to turn around,
too. Consulting his comprehensive Forest Service map, the trio saw that
once they hit the dirt road, it was only six miles to paved Road 21, then a
14-mile hitch to Packwood. As they hiked, the snow thinned, then cleared,
and when they reached the Road 21 trailhead after dark, two day hikers
agreed to cram the three of them into the rear seat of a Honda Civic.

The faux-chalet Packwood Inn felt like four-star accommodations, with
knotty pine walls, a phone to order takeout, and hot showers. The owner,
George, did their laundry for them. Sandals called her husband. "Hello,
Pete," she said, "The good news is I'm alive." Roswell thought to herself,
I was so cold only a short while ago. Soon there was a knock on the door—
gleefully, the two women chowed down on fried chicken.

38

Cutthroat Pass

IT WAS HARD for all of us to believe that we were leaving our last PCT trail town. When we'd stood at the Mexican border this moment had seemed impossibly far away. At the time, Stehekin and its cinnamon rolls had seemed like a mythical land where angels and giants roam. And now we had trod its paths and eaten of its bounty.

The snow line from the first storm was 3000 feet above us—we wouldn't climb that high until early the next day. With only 82 miles left, it was easy to be optimistic in the weak morning sun. With Stehekin behind her and a one-pound cinnamon roll in her pack, Blazer sallied forth. "Five months! Only three nights to the border and Manning Park!" It didn't crimp her smile that the roll was from the day-old bin. Not today. But after the many times she'd watched others replace gear while she nursed the broken zipper on her jacket, all that scrimping had grown tiresome. Two nights before the Suiattle River, she'd lost a glove—now she had to make do with one. Still, it was her 150th day on the trail and she didn't have a sliver of doubt. *I have this in the bag.* She saw herself in that hot tub at Manning Park Resort, cavorting in rising steam and jacuzzi jets.

As Dalton climbed steadily from Stehekin's 1600-foot elevation back onto the ridges of the North Cascades, he felt resigned. *It's not going to happen.* He wasn't referring to Canada. Having hiked the Suiattle portion alone, he believed the hardest part of the PCT was behind him. Now he was hiking on cruise control. The blown opportunity Dalton was regretting was one he'd joshed about with Blazer for months—even before Walker Pass. "Blazer, I want you to teach me how to give a good massage." It was part of her suite of physical therapist skills.

He had only himself to blame. When he said it, Dalton knew he sounded only half-serious. And he was so cautious about the two of them touching. With all his proximity to Blazer, others had pressured him that the two of them should be a couple. But Dalton had taken to heart what Blazer had said in Big Bear City. "You're like a brother to me, Dalton." He would not do anything to jeopardize that.

Even though it was their third-to-last day on the PCT, Dalton and Blazer weren't hiking together. At the trailhead that morning, Blazer discovered she'd left her wallet in town. It took an hour to retrieve it and get back on the trail again. That night, Blazer camped with Frodo and me at Rainy Pass, 21 miles from Stehekin, 61 miles from the border, on the last highway we'd cross before Canada. Dalton was camped two miles ahead with Chigger, Figaro, Guts, and Chuckwagon.

ONE FLAKE WAS how it began. The first flurries started in the middle of the night, and they were as soft and harmless as photographs in a winter calendar. There was enough to catch on a tongue, and then enough to stick. Not enough yet for me to get out my camera. White splotches marked the ground, evergreen boughs frosted white. It was so beautiful you could pinch yourself—if you watched from inside a window. But as the night wore on, the snow began to build and pile up, and to grow increasingly heavy. Our nylon tents, pitched in a deserted gravel parking lot off Highway 20 at Rainy Pass, started to sag.

The first time I got out to knock snow off our tent was 2:00 a.m. Blazer didn't hear me as I brushed the snow off her tent as well—she'd been restless and groggy when she went to bed. Her Tarptent had a single pole located right next to her head. Aside from that, the structure relied on tent stakes and tension to stay upright. Under the ever-thickening winter blanket, the tension started losing as the snow began winning.

Blazer woke in the wee hours to find her tent collapsing. First, she felt it on her feet and curled them up, and then it began to press on her knees. She didn't want to get out of her warm sleeping bag. When the tent had bowed so much that she felt it pressing against her side, she tried to knock the snow off from the inside, but her efforts were futile.

In the morning Blazer's sleeping bag was wet in places—not a good sign—and she ate breakfast inside our tent. Afterward she dragged her gear to a nearby outhouse and tried to warm up as she packed. Frodo and I were talking, looking at options and maps—we could hitch 35 miles east to Winthrop to dry out and let the storm blow through before returning. Blazer listened with increasing impatience. *Cut it out*, she thought. *Stop weighing pros and cons. It's snowing harder. Let's get going. We have to get over the pass before we can't see the trail.*

We started the five-mile climb to Cutthroat Pass in four inches of snow. We were hunkered down, focused, even as snow seeped into our running shoes. Then the four inches became six, and the six became eight, rising into drifts, climbing up our calves. Visibility faded in and out as we walked through whiteouts. Blazer was sobered by how fast the snow obscured the trail. Working hard to put her feet in our footsteps, she stifled the thought, *We need to turn back.* She'd been cold when she started and even the exertion of the trail wasn't warming her up—now she alternated between jamming her ungloved hand in her armpit and down her pants.

Near the top of the 2000-foot climb, we reached a series of exposed, sharp switchbacks. Blazer rounded one and exclaimed, "Dalton!" White crystals hung from his beard as he emerged from the fog. But Blazer's elation turned to puzzlement when she saw that he was with Chigger, Figaro, Guts, and Chuckwagon. *What gives? Why are they walking toward us?* That's when we realized the five of them were headed back.

I have hiked in snow. I have taught snow backpacking. I wanted to head on, so I started to talk it out. Chuckwagon told us, "It's crazy up there and it's only getting worse." Listening to me, Blazer oscillated between her strong impulse to proceed north and her gut's directive to get out of the cold. And while I was puffing words into the fast-falling flakes, Frodo was staring at Blazer's bare hand and her flimsy, broken jacket. In a moment's lull, Blazer softly announced—her gut feeling be damned—"If Scout and Frodo go on, I'm going too." That left the others quiet—neither agreement nor dissent. As I began talking again, Blazer pressed her numb fingers hard into her armpit.

It took me ten minutes to talk myself out, to agree that it was time to turn and head back down the trail. I lifted a foot and took a step. Something cracked inside, stopping me dead in my tracks. *South. I can't do south.* For five months I had followed the prime directive, "Hike north." Mom and Dad were going to meet me at Manning Park. I opened my mouth and started talking again.

Frodo and I had a tacit agreement—if one of us felt strongly about an issue, we had the right to exercise a veto. This wasn't just for the trail, but for all aspects of our lives. In thirty years, neither of us had ever taken that nuclear-option step. But now, in the increasingly heavy snow, Frodo looked up and said, "That's it. I'm exercising my veto." My next sentence hung waiting in my mouth. Then I turned, lifted a foot, and started downhill, walking south.

During our retreat down to Highway 20, we added Lotto. At the trailhead six of us quickly got a ride in a crammed van, but Blazer, Frodo, and I waited a half hour with our thumbs stuck out—only two cars passed, going the opposite direction. Then a truck stopped, disgorging a fellow hiker we hadn't seen since Crater Lake. It was Disco Dan, the retired navy captain who'd been glad to sleep on the floor of our room. Looking into the white gloom, Disco decided to retreat to Winthrop with us, and we all climbed in the truck for the 35-mile ride east.

AT FIRST, BLAZER found Winthrop to be a blur of fake-western storefronts. But behind the kitsch façade lurked a town of four hundred with a beating, caring heart. We all needed it. Like storm-tossed flotsam, we washed up at the quirky Duck Brand Hotel and Cantina.

Dalton was first in the door—he disappeared to converse with Joe, the sixtyish, large-bodied, garrulous owner. We leaned our dripping packs in a line by the bar that doubled as the hotel check-in counter. Dalton soon returned, saying, "Hey, guys, I got us four large rooms for one hundred dollars." That was ten dollars a head, a quarter the regular rate. Joe and Dalton were our new heroes. Blazer was so relieved—she had no money in her budget for an unplanned town night.

We quickly reconnoitered and found Winthrop Mountain Sports across the street. This small-town outfitter had a big-city selection of gear. The owner, Rita, was diminutive, spirited, and took an immediate interest in our plight, becoming our biggest Winthrop booster. She got us the latest forecast—after a slender break tomorrow, two more major storms were going to lash the Cascades. The first and largest was going to roar in two days hence, on Tuesday, October 2, Frodo's birthday.

Rita recommended we take two additional sets of maps, not just the guidebook's small, squint-inducing pages. We bought a set of large-format Green Trails Maps and US Geologic Survey topographic maps. To keep them safe from the elements, Rita pointed Frodo toward a waterproof plastic map case. That was just the first piece of gear we purchased there. Everyone made the pilgrimage across the street to Winthrop Mountain Sports—everyone, that is, except Blazer.

What are thru-hiker snow boots? Running shoes with two pairs of socks. What are thru-hiker insulated snow boots? Running shoes, two pairs of socks, and a plastic bread bag layered in between.

Like most, Dalton had heard Frodo and me rave about our Sealskinz waterproof socks. They were so much better than a plastic bread bag. The thin outer shell was like a diver's neoprene wetsuit. The inner lining functioned like a lightweight sock. So, for fifty dollars, Dalton added a pair to his rain pants purchase. He thought it was the greatest piece of gear he bought on the trail.

At the Duck Brand, Blazer was sharing a two-bed room with Dalton, Figaro, and Chigger. She saw Dalton burst in the door and lay out his purchases. When he tore the Sealskinz socks out of their packaging and tried them on, Blazer turned away—one more thing she couldn't buy.

FRODO WAS ON a hunt, prowling Winthrop's two-block-long main street. She knew what she wanted, but what were the chances of finding ribbon by the yard? Since arriving, she'd been on a constant adrenaline rush. There was so much to do before heading back out. She kept reassuring herself that it wasn't irresponsible to hike back up Cutthroat Pass.

Frodo was pleased when she found a clutch of rolled ribbon spools in the Winthrop Emporium basement. She bought forty yards, choosing the brightest, most garish shade: hot pink. Back in our room, she cut out one hundred equal lengths. These were insurance. We would tie them to trees—if we had to backtrack through the snow, they would guide us. We hoped the ribbons would serve us better than Hansel and Gretel's bread-crumbs. With a look of weary satisfaction, Frodo set the cluster of ribbons aside. She had a much harder chore to tackle.

BLAZER WAS HOLED up in her room two doors down from ours. She was subdued, still feeling shell-shocked. When she'd arrived, the first thing she did was trim and clean her nails. Habit runs deep, and she'd give her hands what care she could, even if she couldn't protect them from the cold. Next up was a blessedly warm shower, but it wasn't the usual comforting balm. Soaping up, she couldn't shake an unsettled feeling. Suddenly thrust from extreme cold to civilized luxury, she knew she might be thrust right back again. The unease penetrated her bones, just like the bone-deep cold on Cutthroat Pass. Blazer could feel it—everyone was gearing up to hike out tomorrow.

She answered a sharp rap on her door. Frodo was there—short, stern, and intimidating. "Come on. You're coming with me." The conversation was crisp. "Where are we going?" "Across the street," Frodo said. "What are we doing?" "I'm buying you a jacket, gloves, and waterproof socks."

Blazer stammered, "No." She resisted, rooted to her spot inside the doorframe. *I'm a burden again*, she thought. *I've been bailed out too many times. No more. Not this close to the end.* Frodo looked up at the tall young woman and crossed her arms. "I don't want to hear an argument. You're coming." What was Blazer to do? Her Trail Mom had spoken. "Yes, ma'am."

At Winthrop Mountain Sports, Blazer steered them toward the least expensive jackets. "No, try this one," said Frodo. "What color do you want?" That's what broke Blazer's shield. *I get to pick the color. I'm getting something new.* Inside her still was the five-year-old girl who'd stared up at her mother paying with food stamps. She burst out with a smile. Soon after, Blazer walked out of Rita's clutching her new clothes in a bag.

That night we devoured pizza at a long table at the Riverside Grill. Our number had increased from ten to eleven—the two of us a couple, one pair of friends, and seven, like Blazer and Dalton, who'd largely hiked on their own. For 2600 miles we'd made our own decisions. Dalton said it best. "We've all become fiercely independent."

We'd also absorbed the latest information—Rita's weather forecast was bleak. We couldn't wait it out. It also wouldn't help to rail against the unheard-of-early snowstorms. We had a short window now to try to finish the PCT, or no chance at all. From Rainy Pass, we had 61 miles to Canada and 8 more to Manning Park—three days and two nights. That's all. Our last bailout point was halfway, at Harts Pass. There, the PCT crossed a dirt road that led 18 miles out to civilization. And just a few miles after Harts Pass there was a yurt near the PCT. We could stay there the second night. That is, if we could reach it.

All of this begged the question, would we—die-hard iconoclasts all—work as a group? We laid down parameters. "We stay together. We have a designated front and rear, who always stay in sight of each other." But what about peeing and pooping? Chigger popped off an answer, "I expect everyone to find something interesting and look the other way."

We talked on. The best navigator was Disco Dan—he'd stay right near the front, next to Frodo and the maps. We spoke of what can happen in the cold—not eating or drinking enough, hiding that you're hurting. From my Scouting experience I offered: "We should have an old-fashioned buddy system. Each person keeps a close eye on the other. If they're not peeing, make them drink. If they're not eating, get out an energy bar. Watch closely; you need to know if the other is in pain."

When was the moment? When did we cast in our lot? There never was a vote. Blazer sat there and just tried to absorb it all. This was completely outside her skill set, but she did sense, her ears perking up, the moment the group coalesced. It was Chigger who said, "Let's hear it for Team Snowplow." We had a name. We'd hike as one.

One of the last things I did that night was phone my parents. "Mom and Dad, we're going to be a day late. We got snowed out and we're going back again. Don't worry." Dad told me their travel plans, but I knew I'd unsettled him. I was fifty-five, but I felt like I was seventeen, describing an overly ambitious, dicey plan. Dad wished us luck, told me to give Frodo a hug, and mentioned something about a lower elevation alternate route. He'd read about it in a PCT coffee-table book, one he'd checked out from the library long ago.

39

Harts Pass

THE LAST THING Nadine had expected was to spend forty hours in her tent with a wet dog. But that first storm thwarted their efforts to continue north during that initial push. Running low on food, and having covered only the first 7 of the 76 miles, they retraced their steps back across the Katwalk to the Summit Inn, where they waited out the second storm.

Nadine was disheartened. She'd already crossed the Kendall Katwalk twice. But she and Chris planned to head out the next morning, so long as there was a chance to get through. The weather prediction was for a day of clear weather followed by a third storm overnight—with another eight to ten inches of snow. Their shared hotel room looked like a bargain basement sale at REI, with gear hung out to dry on every surface. In the back of her mind, Nadine had started psychologically readying herself for the possibility that she might not finish the PCT, but she was far from ready to throw in the towel. She kept coming back to one thought: *I can't imagine not finishing.*

At the hotel, Chris was subjected once again to a now-familiar phenomenon. "Hello, Nadine!" Everyone knew her. "Pacha!" Everyone not only knew Pacha, but treated her like royalty. No one called out, "Hey, Chris." He was a temporary sidekick, a role he good-naturedly accepted, even calling himself by the whimsical trail name Also-Ran. But other hikers included him within their ranks. Chris just got used to the fact that no one called his name.

IN LESS THAN eight hours, the time we'd been in Winthrop, our group of eleven had become the town's cause célèbre. There were whispers around us in the Riverside Grill that night.

"They're going to head back out tomorrow." "Don't they know about the storms?" "What are their chances?" "The Forest Service should stop them."

Rita at the outfitter had one request—we were to call her first thing when we reached Canada.

MONDAY, OCTOBER 1, 2007

THE NEXT MORNING, Nadine and Chris got an updated forecast at the Summit Inn. A third storm was on the way and was going to be followed by a fourth. Nadine thought, *We have to go now or never.*

They began their second attempt in a short spate of sunshine, but it turned nasty quickly—so much for their day of clear weather. Reconquering the Katwalk, this time in fog and snow, they hiked nine more miles over the top of Needle Point Gap before cresting Chikamin Pass. The snow was more and more unstable, and keeping to any pace was sheer misery. Once when Nadine took her eyes off the trail, she gave herself a shock. *I see the drop-off, but I can't see where it ends.*

They had finished the day in one piece. With a warm dinner in their bellies, and dry sleeping bags and gear, they felt cautiously optimistic. They were also confident in their plan, one cornerstone of which was alternating tents. The first night they'd sleep in his and the next in hers, maximizing the prospect of having reasonably dry shelter. The schedule they'd mapped out called for traversing the high points during the day and camping low at night, and to increase their safety margin, they were carrying an extra two days' worth of food. Finally, they both took comfort in knowing that they had company just behind them. As they were making camp they had seen five hikers pop their heads one by one over

Chikamin Pass—the group must have been following their tracks all day. Nadine and Chris were relieved to see that they looked strong and seemed to be hiking fast. *They should catch us tomorrow.*

TEAM SNOWPLOW LEFT early Monday morning for Rainy Pass to begin our second attempt to reach the northern terminus. And just like Nadine and Chris, we had a plan. The first day we would push 22 miles to reach Glacier Pass. The second day's weather was projected to be worse, but we still planned to cover at least 20 miles, a forced march to get beyond the rock shoulder of Devil's Backbone. For the third day, the plan was exquisitely simple: Canada! Blazer had memorized the national anthem—"O Canada"—and she couldn't wait to sing it.

We had alternate plans for that second day. First, we could camp in a yurt near the trail after 15 miles. Second, we could jump down to a lower, 3000-foot-elevation route for a dozen miles and then rejoin the PCT. And finally—the option none of us wanted to consider—at Harts Pass, only 31 miles from the border, we could hike out with our tails between our legs on the only dirt road between us and Canada. We'd face 18 sad and wretched road-walking miles south to Highway 20.

That first day was an intense blur. At the crest of Cutthroat Pass, not five miles in, one member of our group quit. That eleventh hiker we'd picked up in Winthrop decided, "It's unsafe. I'm turning back." Two miles later, busting our way through the lip of a new cornice, Frodo sank, her legs disappearing as she waded through thigh-deep snow. As for the pink ribbons, we used a quarter of them. Throughout the day someone would call, "Hey, look over there." Nine pairs of eyeballs snapped away while one of us squatted, dropping four layers of clothes to their knees. We practically welcomed the fog when it swirled in—it hid the sheer drops. It became harder and harder to break trail through the trackless snow. We traded off the lead, no more than thirty minutes each. During her turn, Blazer couldn't believe how long that half hour took to pass. We took only one twenty-minute break to eat.

Monday's most telling moment occurred near the end. Through a break in the dense clouds, a helicopter buzzed us, swooping low over the valley that led to Glacier Pass. It was late afternoon, near dusk. Blazer craned her neck, looking skyward. *They can't be looking for us, can they?*

TUESDAY, OCTOBER 2, 2007

THE THIRD STORM blew in overnight. Nadine and Chris kept to their plan. For this day, in particular, they'd set a modest goal—leave late and hike seven miles, plunging 1700 feet near the end, then set up camp. As they packed up, they saw no one and assumed their compatriots had passed them earlier in the day, while they were still in Chris's tent. As they hiked, the thick snow changed to pinging sleet, sheeting rain, and then back to snow again. They kept looking for evidence of the five. *Why aren't there any footprints?*

But Nadine and Chris's main focus was coping—staying on trail was an increasing challenge. The drifts piled up, reaching Nadine's thighs. Worse, she was still wearing trail runners. *If I could have one wish*, she thought, *I'd wish for snowshoes.* To protect her feet from the elements she had encased them in a double layer of socks with a plastic bread bag sandwiched between them. Pacha had to hop from one foot hole to the next to make forward progress. The second night, the three of them crammed into Nadine's tent. From here on out, the tents would be damp, if not wet.

Nadine still hoped the five others were miles ahead, the spindrift and snowfall masking their tracks. She knew they were strong hikers; what she didn't know was that Chikamin Pass had been their swansong, the farthest reach of their Pacific Crest Trail hike. Just before the pass, the five had watched an avalanche break free and thunder down near them, raising a cloud of spindrift. It could have been them in its path. When they rose the next morning, conditions still disintegrating, it drove them to one conclusion—*we have to turn back.* This was underscored by the fact that one of them had frostbitten feet. Five more were done, off the trail.

EIGHT MEMBERS OF Team Snowplow were packed, set, and ready to move by 6:30 a.m. Hoods were pulled tight over cold-weather beanies—Blazer had been living in her black watch cap. It was now more appendage than accessory.

Would we make it to Canada? Blazer knew that today would yield the answer, but waking to eight inches of new snow hadn't been a hopeful sign. Guts and Chuckwagon were still packing. Even with the Sealskinz socks, Blazer's toes were numb; standing still was a killer. She began stomping a path in the snow, cutting a figure eight and then another on top of that. Chigger joined her. Then Dalton and Figaro and Frodo and me. In the predawn gloom, made thicker by the falling snow, Disco Dan and Lotto watched.

As dim light penetrated the pine and spruce thicket, Blazer brightened. She piped up, "Happy Birthday, Frodo." Frodo and I were taken aback—October 2!—we had both forgotten. The hiker stomping out the cold behind Frodo almost bumped into her. Blazer asked, "What do you want for your birthday?" Frodo didn't hesitate, her breath starkly visible. "I want to finish the day alive." Guts and Chuckwagon finally joined us, just as someone muttered a postscript. "If this was my birthday, I think I'd shoot myself."

Right off we had to zigzag 1200 feet up to a pass that the guidebook called an "alpine garden." New snow soon piled on top of Blazer's pack. With numb toes and freezing hands, she thought, *Everything's getting wetter and wetter and we just keep climbing higher into deeper snow.*

We began changing the lead every fifteen minutes. Blazer insisted on her turn—when she took the lead, that was when she really understood. It had begun to feel mindless to follow somebody else's footsteps. But breaking trail through new snow, she felt the responsibility. *I'm leading all of us into this. We could be totally off-trail right now.* Blazer hadn't believed that staying hydrated and fueled up would be such a problem, but that morning she saw that none of us were eating or drinking because of the effort it took to remove a glove.

At every saddle and every pass, we lost the trail. Each time two or three members of Team Snowplow set off in different directions and then, once they returned, we'd strike out on our best guess. The smallest clues brought great relief. A log cut by human hands. An exposed rock face marked by a dynamite blast. When the fog lifted for a moment we could see the canyon bottom 3000 feet below—there was no line where the snow stopped. Dropping down to the lower route would make no difference at all.

Dalton took the lead. The buddy system had been working; we knew a few of us were really hurting—one knee, one ankle, and more. Disco Dan called out, "Fifteen minutes," but Dalton wouldn't relinquish the lead. The nine of us behind him were ever so grateful. "Thirty minutes." Disco Dan didn't say anything at the forty-five-minute mark or the hour mark.

Everybody was trying to be brave for everybody else. We were projecting our best selves, as we quietly wrestled with our own demons inside. By 11:00 a.m., the snow was falling even faster. We'd somehow managed to cover six miles, but we all knew that we were no longer hiking even a mile an hour.

At last, we came to a large wooden PCT sign—"Rainy Pass 29 Miles, Harts Pass 2 Miles." The base of the sign should have been waist-high, but now it barely cleared the snow. Blazer posed for a photo first, then Lotto and Disco Dan. Dalton posed next, then Guts and Chuckwagon. Irrepressible Chigger mugged for the camera. Blazer took the shots of Frodo and me standing on opposite sides of the sign, framing the weathered boards.

Blazer knew what the sign really said. As did I. As did Frodo and all the rest. There'd been no meeting of Team Snowplow; there hadn't been any group discussion. Over pizza in Winthrop we'd each made a pledge: No one will lose a finger or toe, no one will get seriously hurt or worse. We will not put others at risk because we need to be rescued. There was only one way now to honor that pledge. We were going to leave the PCT at Harts Pass, 31 miles from the border.

We trudged the two miles downhill to the pass and turned right onto snow-covered Forest Road 5400. No tire tracks broke the white. Chuckwagon now limped, favoring his knee, and Figaro winced with each step. We hiked a mile, then two, and then four, the snow turned to slush and then mud, white flakes becoming pellets, sleet, and then rain. Blazer had thought she couldn't shiver worse than she had the night she waited at Stevens Pass. All her layers were now wet. At 2:00 p.m. we hit our fifth road mile of loose gravel and mud. It looked more and more like we'd be walking the 18 miles to Mazama, a small community off Highway 20. Supposedly there was a store.

Blazer, Dalton, Frodo, and I had dropped two hundred yards behind the rest when we heard a noise over the rain pinging our jacket hoods—tires crunching on gravel behind us. I was ready to plead as we flagged down the Forest Service truck. *Please, please.* With a numb hand I motioned for the driver to roll down the window and looked to see how much space was in the crew cab. I thought of the six others ahead of us, of how Figaro and Chuckwagon were struggling. *Can I keep up this trudge?* Grimly I thought, *Yes.* I assessed the bedraggled figures next to me—Frodo, Blazer, and Dalton. *They can do it, too.* I quickly outlined our plight to the civilian government contractor behind the wheel, Dustin, as warm air flew from the driver's window and rain swept inside. He'd been surprised to see anyone out here—all of his crew but him had been helicoptered out the day before. *So that was the helicopter we saw.*

Our friends were out of sight around a bend as I made my pitch to Dustin: "Can you pick up the six down the road?" Dustin nodded, and threw the gear back into low. The tires crunched again and, as the sound receded, the four of us bent our heads downward, soldiering on.

We were still making forward progress ten minutes later when I saw the truck slowly backing up toward us. *What's wrong? Is the road blocked?* Dustin stuck out his head as he pulled to a stop—the rest of Team Snowplow were jammed tighter than sardines in the crew cab. "Jump in back," he hollered. "They won't go on without you." The four of us climbed over the sides, twisting our bodies between the tools in the pickup bed. This had to be totally against regulations.

Dustin stopped every few minutes to climb out and push away the boulders the storm had rolled onto the road. In the back of the truck, Dalton pulled his wind-whipped poncho over Blazer, pinning its edges to keep her warm. The gesture at least was dear. The only thing that sustained Frodo was the thought, *This is finite. Some time, eventually, I'll be warm again.*

40

Trail's End

BLAZER FOUND HERSELF back in her room at the Duck Brand Hotel, a place she had never wanted to be again. Her ratty bandanna was in her hand, but she was so dehydrated, she couldn't summon tears. Taking a scalding hot shower, she reflected on what had happened. *I just got within 31 miles of Canada. And now I'm done? Now I'm leaving? It feels like it was all for nothing. What am I going to say, "I hiked all of it except the last 31 miles"?* Her flight out of Seattle was in two days.

The air in the room felt like a funeral home. She'd had this goal in her head for five months, and now it was gone. Blazer felt she was mourning a death. Once more, she thought of herself and Dalton posing by that final PCT sign. *Why didn't I do it right then?* In her room on the bed, Blazer started humming. It was a dirge—"O Canada."

NOT THREE HOURS before, still dripping water from the pickup bed, Dalton saw Frodo rummaging through the Mazama Country Store's Green Trails Maps—he was incredulous. Watching her pick three to buy at the cash register, he was more than dismissive. *That's completely nuts.* Barely out of the snow and still reeling from our failed brush with Canada, he focused on a white mug of tea and its warmth in his hands.

SINCE THEY'D TAKEN showers, Dalton, Blazer, Figaro, and Chigger had been intensely talking in their room, the exact same room that these four had occupied two days ago—with one big difference. This time, their tents, clothes, and sleeping bags weren't hung up. No one was drying gear. No one expected to head out again. Figaro's mom was going to backtrack from where she'd planned to meet her son at the end of his hike. She would drive from Manning Park to Winthrop, arriving the next day to take a car full of hikers to Seattle.

Figaro had been in such pain since he'd packed his tent that morning in the snow. The road walk on irregular gravel from Harts Pass was excruciating. He could barely hobble—one heel had shooting pains with each step while the other foot could hardly bear any weight at all.

And Dalton, though not injured, was spent, his motivation gone. *I've shown I'm tough,* he thought as Figaro ran down the reasons he was leaving. *I've done something huge. I crossed the Suiattle by myself. I broke trail for a full hour in the snow.* Dalton felt Figaro's need for solidarity, and told him, "I'm going to hop on your ride. I'm heading home."

As Blazer listened to Figaro, she couldn't have felt more defeated. Grasping at the thinnest of straws, she proposed to Dalton, "Why don't we just stay at the Duck Brand until the snow melts?" It was a fairy tale. Dalton didn't respond; instead, both of them listened to Figaro. "What do I have to prove? I've made it this far. What difference does it make if I push on a few more miles? What is Canada anyway?"

That's when Frodo and I entered their room, and spread the Green Trails maps on a bed. "Here's what we are going to do. There's no pressure. Just tell us if you want to come along." Frodo had been the one to look for these alternate route maps, but when I saw her I knew exactly what she was thinking. We both remembered what my dad had said about a lower route.

Dalton, Blazer, Figaro, and Chigger followed Frodo's finger as she traced the low route on the map. "We're going to start here," Frodo pointed, "at Rainy Pass." Four sets of eyeballs rolled back in their sockets. *Back to Rainy Pass a third time?* "And from there we're going to road walk 20 miles west. It's downhill, we'll drop from 4000 to 1600 feet, and then we'll reach Ross Lake. There's a trail along the lake. It's so low there should be no chance of snow. Then in 31 miles we cross the border into Canada."

Chigger didn't wrestle with obstacles or doubts. "Count me in." Figaro seemed dead set on going home. Dalton, too. Blazer's eyes had briefly lit up, but neither Frodo nor I knew what to make of it. The two of us left and made the trip to the other room, laying out the maps in front of Guts, Chuckwagon, Lotto, and Disco Dan. Our plan tore at all their hearts. Team Snowplow was being ripped asunder.

Later that day, we started hearing back from the others. Guts and Chuckwagon were in. Lotto and Disco Dan were out. We found two other thru-hikers at the Duck Brand, Patrick and Clara, who had also retreated from Rainy Pass. They were young and not long married; turning back had crushed them. Clara asked, "When does Canada, a country, become an obsession?" They had given up jobs, their home, and comfort to pursue a dream that had fallen apart before their eyes. Patrick and Clara decided to throw in their lot with us on the lower elevation route.

But between Figaro, Dalton, and Blazer, the debate raged on. Blazer thought Figaro made solid points, especially when he said emphatically, "What do I have to prove?" Then Figaro threw out, "I'll just come back and do it again. It's no big deal." Figaro lived in Northern California, within driving distance of the North Cascades, but that wasn't true for Dalton. He lived in Colorado. It was even less true for Blazer. She knew she'd never be back. Living on the East Coast, she may as well be on the opposite side of the world.

Blazer wrung her hands and pressed them tightly together. The faintest part of her still thought, even while listing the pros and cons, *I'm finishing, no matter what it takes. Why are we having this discussion?* Blazer paid homage to that trail-hardened woman who only days before had sworn, "I'll crawl to Canada if I have to." Then she remembered the one impediment. Money. There was no getting past that. She was flying out of Seattle in two days. Changing her ticket this late would be horribly expensive, impossible. She shook her head. Then she heard Dalton announce that Frodo and I hadn't swayed him. "Blazer, I'm going home."

Blazer called her brother Ian. Someone in her family should know where she was. Someone should know what she was doing. After all, he was going to see her in two days—her flight was from Seattle to

Washington, D.C. She'd stay with her brother. She'd sleep on his couch again. She'd try to find work.

"IAN, WE RAN into high snow. It was really bad. I'm coming home."

This wasn't the call Ian had been expecting. He'd been certain Blazer would call him next from Manning Park. Just as he'd been confident that she'd reach Kennedy Meadows on time, Ian knew she'd make Canada. His little sister didn't quit. The last time they'd talked, Ian heard that Blazer was surrounded by strong hikers. And she was so close to the end—snow wouldn't stop them. Ian had planned how he was going to celebrate her feat. She'd call him up and then he'd tell her, "Blazer, I'm upgrading your plane ticket. You are going to fly first class." Ian didn't care how hard Blazer tried not to accept. He was going to insist. "You deserve it."

Ian had to pry the story out of Blazer. Slowly, she told him what had happened. How awful and scary it had been. She sounded so deflated and depressed. As she was talking, Ian moved to his computer. He pulled up her flight information on the screen. Blazer told her brother that a few of the others were going to go on to Canada by an alternate route. It would take three more days. "But my ticket is in two days. I can't change it. It will be really good to see you again."

Ian made the decision Blazer wouldn't make for herself. "I've changed your ticket," he said. "I've built in a buffer, too. You don't fly out of Seattle for six days." He then added, and for the first time she heard emotion in his voice, "You go for it." With Blazer still on the phone, essentially speechless, Ian thought he heard a hushed thank you, and then he hung up the phone. After spending those weeks around thru-hikers, Ian knew. He knew exactly what finishing meant. Canada: That was the gift he gave his sister.

WITH BLAZER IN, we were up to a count of eight for the alternate route. Blazer's abrupt change hadn't altered Figaro's or Dalton's plans. They were going home, as were Lotto and Disco Dan.

"Dalton, will you talk with me, please?" Blazer pulled Dalton aside in their room. Before she could get the words out, she'd already begun crying in dry sobs, her shoulders shaking. "I'd always envisioned the two of us finishing together. We're best buds. It's not right. I've thought we would, for so long." She wondered as she finished, *Does he feel the same way?*

Dalton knew he wasn't great about letting others know when he cared about them, and here Blazer was laying it out. Dalton ran over Figaro's reasons—*What's Canada, I have nothing to prove*—and he thought of his own—*A third time is nuts, I'm spent, I crossed the Suiattle by myself.* But in front of him was the woman who'd answered his cry at Scissors Crossing— "Blazer, I need you." Who'd treated his foot in Tehachapi. Who'd been so happy to see him in Stehekin she'd lifted him off the ground. It wasn't Canada that mattered, Blazer did.

"Sure, let's do it." Dalton would worry about his plane ticket later. Right now, right this minute, there was nothing more valuable than showing Blazer that she had a true friend.

In their room after dinner, Dalton had a question for Blazer. He had thought the time to ask her had long passed, but Blazer responded by reaching down next to the bed and pulling up a small plastic bottle from her food bag. It was a vial of olive oil. Blazer motioned for Dalton to take his shirt off. She started to give him a massage, talking as she went along. Step by step, she told him what she was doing. Figaro and Chigger were in the room, but it was as if they weren't there.

When Blazer finished, she pulled her own shirt off and lay on the bed facedown. Dalton had never been that relaxed with a woman. It didn't feel romantic; it felt incredibly close. *We're so open with another*, he thought. *I wish we hadn't been so afraid of touching each other. A hug, a cuddle would have been nice.* But now he realized just how important it was for Blazer to keep their relationship clear. As the two of them slept on separate beds that night, they were closer than all those times they'd shared one in Southern California.

WEDNESDAY, OCTOBER 3, 2007

THE RECONSTITUTED TEAM Snowplow was nine strong. We all chuckled the next morning when Chigger showed up, her two pigtail braids tied with lengths of Frodo's neon pink ribbons. And as we left the Duck Brand

Hotel—this had to be the last time—Joe, the colorful proprietor, gave us a send-off: "You folks don't give up. You're all crazy, but if there's ever a World War III, I want you on my side."

During the ride out to Rainy Pass, our driver told us how we'd become the talk of the town. *Wouldn't you know it*, Blazer thought, *I get my fifteen minutes of fame and it's in Winthrop, Washington.*

The alternate started with a 20-mile road walk, a slight, steady, monotonous downgrade. Not a single uphill. From everything we had hiked north of the Bridge of the Gods, we would never have believed so much gentle grade existed in Washington. With the rain starting and stopping, we passed the time telling trail stories. Patrick and Clara had a slew of new ones for us. One of the best was from near the start of their hike, in mid-April. A half day out of Warner Springs, they were caught in a late-season snowstorm. After quickly setting up their tent, they looked at their dinner—mashed potato flakes—and at the only liquid they had—a liter of Gatorade. So, they boiled the Gatorade and mixed in the mashed potato flakes with some dried veggies. Pink mashed potatoes.

Despite how hard it was to accept the turn of events over the last few days, we perked up when a Prius honked at us around noon. It was Figaro's mom, Jan, and she stopped to give out a round of hugs. She was heading into Winthrop to pick up Figaro, Lotto, and Disco Dan, and also the backpacks the nine of us had left at the Duck Brand Hotel. She was going to drop them off at the motel nearest to the Ross Lake trailhead. Thanks to Jan, today the nine of us were slackpacking. But that was only half of the plan we'd concocted.

My parents were the other half. Mom and Dad were driving their rented van from Manning Park down to the Ross Lake trailhead. At the end of the day, they'd pick us up and take us to the motel. Then they'd drive us back to the trailhead the next morning. A little more than a day and 31 miles later, we would cross into Canada. While we hiked, Mom, Dad, and a thru-hiker friend of Chigger's would drive back into Canada and negotiate a 25-mile dirt road to meet us. Then we would all head to Seattle.

AS WE EXPECTED, two hours later Jan passed us going the other way. This time her car was full of our three compatriots—Figaro, Disco, and

Lotto—and all of our packs. At 3:30 p.m. we had only six miles left for the day when a van pulled over with its lights flashing. It was Mom and Dad. They had brought Subway sandwiches, milk, and cookies.

Everything changed as I hugged both of them. Leaning down, my mouth next to Dad's ear, I whispered, "Daddy, I'm done." I felt it deep inside—in a short while, I wouldn't have to be strong anymore. The steel fist would uncurl. I would hike the last miles because my hiker pride wanted to say, "I walked to Canada," but having received Mom's and Dad's hugs, my journey north was over in many ways.

Our motel that night was the Buffalo Run Inn, located in a hamlet called Marblemount on Highway 20. As we registered we were told, "Your rooms have been paid in full." Jan had not only reserved our rooms, but the grand lady had also paid for all of them. Blazer was floored and so relieved. I was amazed. One last time, Trail Mom Jan had wrapped us in her maternal blanket. As Frodo and I entered our room, I thought of what Jan had said so many times. *I'm on it.*

THURSDAY, OCTOBER 4, 2007

AT SNOQUALMIE PASS, Kim was worried about Nadine. Late on Tuesday, from behind the front desk at the Summit Inn, she'd seen five hikers return from their second attempt to head north, bedraggled, beaten, and whipped by the snow. Word of avalanches and frostbite had circulated. She saw them agonize, give up on Canada, and then disperse. A couple, Gesh and Junkfood, had also retreated, telling Kim similarly harrowing tales. "It's not like walking through a snow-filled meadow. Climbing some of these passes, one slip and you're dead," said Gesh. "You're hugging rock walls on narrow ledges with a thousand-foot drop-off."

Like Bounty Hunter hundreds of miles earlier, Gesh wrestled with the most difficult decision of all: "The hardest steps I'll take on this hike could be in walking away. All I know is that conditions have deteriorated and we're three days into a forecast calling for two straight weeks of rain and snow," he wrote in his online journal.

Late that morning Kim answered the phone. It was Recline—the same hiker who had helped Roswell back in Northern California. He'd traveled the same 76 miles that Nadine, Chris, and Pacha were trying to cover, emerging at Stevens Pass on Monday, the day before the worst of the storms. He'd had such a rough time on his last day in what he described as "ungodly, a horrible mess of blowdowns, endless deep puddles, and deep sucking mud" that he abandoned the PCT for a lower route. Now he was holed up at the Dinsmores'.

On Tuesday and Wednesday, Recline had witnessed a rash of activity around him. The Dinsmores' house felt like a wartime communication bunker with hikers, friends, and relatives calling and emailing to see if so-and-so was okay. By Thursday morning, they had a clearer idea of where the remaining hikers were. That's why Recline had called Kim. The four of them—Recline, the Dinsmores, and Kim—had all come to the same conclusion: all thru-hikers within a 100-mile radius were accounted for. All except Nadine, Pacha, and Chris.

It was Kim who made the call to the King County Sheriff's Office. She had no idea what it would unleash. Within two hours, sixty search and rescue personnel were packing, dogs were loaded into cars, and two helicopters had been assigned to the search. A sheriff's unit arrived at the Dinsmores'. "What route are they on? What alternates might they take? How are they equipped?" Rumors circulated. "The woman is hiking in shorts."

Sheriffs accessed Nadine's bank account and studied her records. That evening, a uniformed policeman showed up in Davis, California, at the home of Lori, Nadine's resupplier. "Have you heard from her? She's missing." By that time, many search and rescue units and their trained dogs were struggling in the high country, making their way up into the snow.

They pulled out all the stops, but it wasn't just because of Nadine. Only a few days earlier, a woman was found after she'd been missing for over a week. She had rolled her car off the road and lay hidden in a ravine. The authorities had brushed off her husband's missing person calls. "She's an adult. She can go where she wants. She does not have to tell you a thing." There was a public furor when she was found barely alive, trapped for eight days without food or water. That was still fresh on everyone's mind as they searched for Nadine.

Stacie Chandler and her forty-pound rescue dog, Sage, were part of the sixty. By midday Thursday she was carefully loading her pack—with winter in the air, she knew they were going out for the long haul. She reached the trailhead at 4:00 p.m. Along with her partner, Conrad, they were to approach the PCT from a side trail and hike the last 14 PCT miles north to Stevens Pass. Stacie, Sage, and Conrad didn't bed down till midnight, still some distance from their assigned PCT segment. She had a sleepless night.

AT THE BUFFALO Run Inn that morning, I wanted the world to know Team Snowplow hadn't been thwarted—we were still hiking. On a paper plate from breakfast I wrote: "Still Walking to Canada!!" Under that bold proclamation were all nine of our names. We thumbtacked the plate to the Ross Lake trailhead sign.

Ross Lake is a long, narrow body of water framed by snowcapped mountains. It was hard to connect the stunning beauty around us with the danger and cold we'd so recently endured—the distant white on the mountains might just as well have been cake frosting instead of frosty ice. Green moss hung in thick clumps off rocks and rotting logs while red vine maples made the avalanche chutes look like fiery gashes. The low elevation had brought a profusion of deciduous trees—alders, bigleaf maples—the likes of which we hadn't seen since the Columbia River. All those weeks ago they were so green, but now they were orange, umber, Indian summer yellow, and scarlet. And the colors were thinning; many leaves were spent splotches on the ground.

Near dark, Chigger stopped and stared at a trail sign. "Oh my god, it shows kilometers. We must be close to Canada!" All day we had passed campsites with such pleasant-sounding names, Rainbow Point, Lodgepole, and Deer Lick, but happenstance dictated that our last campsite on our thru-hike was Nightmare Camp.

When dinner was nearly done, Blazer turned to Frodo and said, "I've made you a belated birthday dessert." Frodo and I dipped our spoons into the offered pot. A shared meal, a final act of love between trail parents and trail daughter. The chocolate pudding was bittersweet.

FRIDAY, OCTOBER 5, 2007

5:00 A.M. BREAKING News, Seattle King 5 TV: "Three Pacific Crest Trail hikers are reported missing between Snoqualmie and Stevens Pass. A search is under way."

5:30 a.m. News Update: "Woman, man, and dog missing on Pacific Crest Trail. Search and Rescue teams from three counties mobilized."

6:00 a.m. News Update: "Nadine, a Pacific Crest Trail hiker, her dog Pacha, and a male companion are the subject of an intense Pacific Crest Trail rescue effort." The reporter described Nadine's "incredible Mexico to Canada journey." The television screen flashed photos, showing Nadine and Pacha in much warmer times. However, there were no photos of Chris, and they never mentioned his name. "Now with only two hundred miles left to go, Nadine and Pacha are missing."

Hours before the news report, a search and rescue team found two abandoned tents on Deception Creek. The tents were on a side trail near the PCT.

AT FIRST LIGHT, Sage was ready to go. Following her dog's lead, Stacie radioed back to base to confirm her assignment. She learned that weather had grounded the helicopters. Her partner Conrad wasn't traveling with a dog, so his pack was much lighter. Stacie told him, "Go on ahead." She attempted to take a picture of Sage in the accumulating snow, but she couldn't—her camera battery was dead from the cold.

Stacie and Sage reached the PCT and the start of their 14-mile segment. Ascending the crest shortly after Conrad, she heard him say, "Look, there's something over there." Conrad was pointing 150 yards away. Stacie traced the path with her eyes and immediately hollered out.

UNLIKE OTHERS, NADINE'S trek through the stacked-up storms had proceeded according to plan. It was hard, harder than anything she had ever experienced, but she and Chris were making miles, hitting the highest passes during the day, and camping low at night. They had camped in each of their tents twice. It had rained and snowed on them the entire time—everything was soaked through. Regardless, they had plenty of food and plenty of fuel and the hard hiking kept them warm.

They were lucky—the trail was cut deep, leaving a depression they could follow, and both of them knew how to read a map. This was the fourth morning since they'd departed the Summit Inn for the second time. They had only 14 miles left to Stevens Pass and the trailhead at Highway 2.

Nadine left camp early. She was usually the first one out. Then Chris would catch up, following her deep tracks. This morning she stopped twenty minutes up the trail, and waited for Chris. She was still there a half hour later, cold and annoyed in equal order, but then worry took over. Soon after she'd left camp, she'd seen fresh bear prints gouged deep in the snow. Sixty minutes after she'd left Chris, Nadine started to head back.

NOT LONG AFTER Nadine left, Chris had begun his daily push-ups. Snow wouldn't deter him. Long-distance hikers may have legs and calves strong enough to absorb sledgehammer blows, but they are notorious for having weak upper bodies. Chris was determined to keep his upper body strong during these weeks with Nadine. Working up a sweat, he was breathing loud and heavy in the small clearing when a woman's voice boomed out god-like from the wilderness. "ARE YOU CHRIS?"

Chris startled and thought, *Who knows my name? It's always Nadine, not me.* He shouted back, "Yes! Who wants to know?"

"ARE YOU NADINE'S CHRIS?" Ah, there it was, situation normal, they really wanted Nadine. And so, while doing push-ups in the snow, Chris found out they were being rescued.

"YOU ARE NOT going to believe this!" From afar Chris yelled to Nadine. "They've been searching for us!" When all four of them were finally standing together, Nadine learned from Stacie and Conrad that they had been "found." Now, she, Chris, and Pacha would be escorted to the nearest trailhead. It was ironic that, as they hiked along, Nadine and Chris often had to stop and wait for Stacie and Conrad and those heavy-weight packs. In the afternoon, when they finally reached the Stevens

Pass trailhead, the trio walked headlong into a media frenzy, complete with camera crews, rescue crews, emails, and phone messages. Later that day, an internet search pulled up wild news reports on how Nadine and Chris were found hypothermic, that they were wearing shorts, that they'd been buried by an avalanche and had to be dug out by thirty mountaineers.

That night Nadine began her online blog with: "Fifteen minutes of fame I wish I never had." She next shared the most important fact: "Chris, Pacha, and I are OK." Then Nadine gave her take on the rescue. "The hikers, rescuers, and everyone involved showed incredible selflessness and diligence. I'm awed by the power of community. Maybe there is hope for us after all."

Then Nadine jumped in the ring with that question so many of us had faced:

> *What now? Do I quit? But the window for us has closed. I want to think about this from every angle. Maybe the ultimate lesson I was supposed to learn out here is that the hike is bigger than me and whether or not I tag the border. For nine years I struggled with this. How do I let it go?*
>
> *It's hard to say goodbye. Hard to say goodbye to the summer evenings camping under an open sky, to the wonderful people I met, the ultimate freedom, being fit and strong and being able to eat as much ice cream as I can. I guess now is as good a time as any to admit that I'm not ready to rejoin the world. For now, I'll spend a little time visiting friends in Oregon, learning how to make goat cheese, and secretly planning my next long thru-hike.*
>
> *Thanks all, for an amazing experience this summer. Unforgettable. I'll be home by Halloween.*
>
> *Nadine*

WE CROSSED THE border into Canada at 10:05 a.m. Dead leaves were thick around the base of the metal sign: "International Boundary." After everything we'd been through, the actual border at the north end of Ross

Lake had no hope of meeting our expectations. We formed a line and all stepped into Canada at the same time.

Chigger couldn't wipe a silly grin off her face. My parents drove up with champagne while Blazer pulled out a shot bottle of Jägermeister she'd kept hidden in her pack. She captured a video of herself and Dalton. "We made it to Canada!" Blazer took the first drink and then passed it to her friend, exclaiming, "Here's me and my hiking partner!" Dalton lifted the bottle and polished it off. Blazer set her camera aside as she burst out singing. "O Canada! Our home and native land . . ."

THERE WAS NO one to meet Blazer at the end. Long past expecting it, she almost didn't notice the loss. We all left in a rush—Frodo, my parents, and I had to fly out of Seattle that night at 6:30 p.m. Blazer and Dalton hopped in with us, while Chigger and her friend took the rest. Speeding in a vehicle on the freeway felt like a cruel form of immersion therapy. Frodo didn't even look at the Enya CDs our daughter had sent. The train ride home was a vanished will-o'-the-wisp. None of the four of us were ready to reenter off-trail life, but we were barreling toward it.

When my parents pulled up to the airport curb, Frodo and I popped open the side door and jumped out. We were tight on time. The moment my feet hit the cement curb, I rushed to the tailgate and pulled out our packs. Blazer and Dalton were in the third row of the van. Cars were waiting. I thought, *Say goodbye!* But how do you say a quick goodbye after all we'd been through? Nothing excuses what we did next. Hoisting our bags, we turned our backs, and Mom and Dad pulled away.

"Did that just happen?" Blazer said, turning to Dalton. *Did my trail parents just walk away?* Frodo and I had rushed off without saying goodbye. She felt as though she had been hit by a ton of bricks.

BLAZER'S FRIEND HEIDI had arranged for her and Dalton to stay with Grace, a woman who opened her house to battered and abused women. But Blazer had no idea what to expect when the taxi dropped the two of them off. Grace greeted them at the door. They were the only ones there. Blazer was staying two nights, but Dalton's flight was quite early the next morning, and he soon repaired to his room.

"Can I run you a bath?" Blazer couldn't believe how lovely it felt to settle into lavender-scented water. When she came out, Grace had a warm robe, fresh out of the dryer. "What is your favorite food?" Blazer was so tired she gave a straight-up answer. "Homemade tomato soup." She had no idea when she'd last had a bowl. Not much later, Grace emerged from her kitchen with a freshly made bowl of tomato soup, snipped basil floating on top. Blazer was tongue-tied, savoring the dish.

All the while Grace was also asking her questions. "What was it like? How did it feel when you finished today?" Blazer started slowly, and then she found the stories gushing out. It felt like there was nothing more important to Grace than listening to Blazer's stories. Talking helped Blazer realize what she'd accomplished. *I just finished something so challenging. I hiked from Mexico to Canada.* Grace celebrated with her, hanging on every word.

There was a moment, when Blazer was nearly talked out, that her feelings started to jell—looking back on why she'd shaved her head, why she'd stopped dating, why she'd set off on this hike, they all merged into what she'd just proven to herself. She felt something so pure that she knew would never vanish. Blazer had wanted someone to meet her at the end of her hike. She'd watched Chigger and her friend, she knew Jan had come for Figaro. She'd witnessed me with my parents. Now here she was. She could not have asked to be met by anyone more wonderful than Grace.

On her first night off the trail, Blazer drifted off to thoughts of Ian, to snippets of "O Canada," and, for the briefest moment, to the picture of herself, five months before, on the plane flying from Washington, D.C., to San Diego. That's when she'd written in her journal for the first time. The hand-bound spine was now torn, and it bore the stains of 2650 miles, but if someone had asked, she could still recite the opening lines:

> *I've always been envious of people, well, fictional characters like Frodo from* The Lord of the Rings. *How amazing it would be to live so primal, having only to worry about the bare necessities: eating, drinking, sleeping, and navigating. And then there'd be the camaraderie, the*

experience of sharing a community without the business of the world getting in the way.

BLAZER SLEPT THAT night sure in the knowledge that she had done exactly that. She'd found the community she'd always wanted and never knew existed. She had nothing to be envious of anymore. For five months, Blazer had lived the life she'd wished for and even more.

Epilogue

"HELLO, DR. MANN." Not even seventy-two hours after reaching Canada, Frodo faced a high school classroom full of students. She dove headlong into the off-trail world, but I was a mess, in denial and in mourning. I wouldn't shave my three-inch beard. I still used a baggie as a wallet. It took me thirty days. Then I, too, went back to work.

Fifty-six thru-hikers were behind us when the blizzards hit. The storms flung them off the trail like bowling pins. Frodo and I got sad phone calls or texts: "We heard you found a lower route. Tell us the way." A dozen persevered. They followed our footsteps and signed the paper plate over four days—"Still Walking to Canada!!" Cloudspotter signed—she'd helped Blazer just before Kennedy Meadows. Stomp, who had shared a cabin with Blazer and Dalton way back in Idyllwild, signed on October 8.

Clockwise from top left: Blazer in the Sierra Nevada (photo courtesy of Blazer); Nadine and Pacha at Crater Lake; Pacha in the North Cascades (both photos courtesy of Nadine); Tony at Kennedy Meadows; Scout and Frodo below the crest of Muir Pass; Dalton celebrates reaching 500 miles

But one hiker was still walking. Recline started at Stevens Pass, the same place Nadine left the trail, walking along roads for 160 miles—a brutal ordeal. On October 23, he reached the trailhead at Ross Lake—by then, he hated road walking, rain, and the whole state of Washington, in no particular order. Worst of all, he hated being alone.

At the trailhead, Recline spotted the weather-worn paper plate. He grew weak in the knees as he read it. *Here are my hiker buddies.* He recognized so many names, recalled where he'd met each one. It transported him back to the hiker world he'd watched crumble and disappear in the storms. He no longer felt so alone. *I am a part of this group. I'm one of the ones who didn't quit.* Recline signed his name right above mine and stared at it a moment longer. Then he pulled out the three tacks and gently put it in his pocket. *This paper plate is going be my most prized souvenir of this entire trip.* Then he started to cry.

Over two thousand miles away in New Orleans, Tony had kept his pledge. He was on time to Tarik's wedding, checking into his posh quarters at the Ritz-Carlton on the same day Nadine was "rescued." Tony's suit was emblematic of how he felt—uncomfortable—too big on his whittled-down torso, too tight on trail-muscled legs. When he split the room tab with another guest, his share eclipsed the entire amount he'd spent on PCT motels. And as Tony stood for his best man's speech, he felt a jolt of panic. It had been five months since he'd faced two hundred people in one place.

Tony eventually moved west and settled south of Portland, Oregon. He lives a twenty-minute drive from Nadine. Tony is still part of Nadine's pack. Today he says he knows the two best days of his life—the days his two children, Nora and Sam, were born. Every day, Tony chooses life over death—he remains clean and sober.

Five years after ending her thru-hike, in November 2012 Nadine hiked the 490-mile Camino de Santiago in Spain, becoming one of the thousands every year who follow the centuries-old pilgrimage route. This time her companion was Jon. The hike wasn't about him, and it wasn't about her—it was about the two of them. They were married at the walk's end at Cape Finisterre. *Finis terrae* is Latin for land's end. Pacha stayed at home.

Today, Nadine manages a vineyard, which she converted to organic—no surprise there. The sound of free-range chickens and pigs can be heard not far from her front door.

After our abrupt departure at the airport, I didn't set eyes on Blazer for four months, and I could have walked right past her. It wasn't the town clothes; it was her hair. The length had doubled, the frizz had become fat ringlets that ran down her neck. We were in a hotel lobby in Washington, D.C., but Blazer had a handkerchief out, and was sobbing loudly.

All I'd done was ask, "How's work?" I remembered how she talked about her traveling physical therapy job, and I wanted to hear about it. "Scout, I never got my license. I am damn good, but I'm not licensed." She told me about the test and failing it three times. "They let me do physical therapy work now, but I also mop the floors and empty the trash." She was making twelve dollars an hour. "You're the first hiker I've told." I recalled all the times on the trail I'd heard Blazer tell others, "Three weeks before starting I told my family and friends, 'I'm shaving my head and hiking the Pacific Crest Trail.'" Each time we all laughed. So I sat there, put an arm around Blazer, and cringed for all of us.

In June, Blazer took the test for the fourth time. This time there was no code. No "champagne." No "whiskey." The envelope wasn't mailed to Blazer's mom's house; it went straight to Blazer's residence in Bethesda, Maryland. She was working as a rehab aide, cleaning the floors still part of her responsibilities, but her boss had started checking the licensing website daily. Then one afternoon Blazer was called into her office. The next thing Blazer knew, her boss was screaming and jumping. The other therapists dropped what they were doing and ran in. They all enveloped Blazer. *It's like I just kicked the winning soccer goal. I passed!*

In 2008, Ladybug proved the naysayers wrong. 30-30 kept his pledge and the two hiked north from the Oregon-Washington border. "When I saw the monument, I had a meltdown, because so much went into this hike." Since then, Ladybug's china cabinet has held not only her fancy wedding china—but also an index-card-sized piece of knit plaster cast.

After the PCT, Not-a-Moose went back to school. In 2014, she graduated from Michigan State University with a master's in music. She is making a living as a piano accompanist.

Bounty Hunter is a Bay Area accompanist in high demand. He is married now with a young son. Bounty still ponders that moment when he hiked north alone as Blazer and Figaro headed back to Mount Shasta. He wonders, *Would I have kept hiking if I'd walked back with them?*

The number of PCT hikers the summer after ours increased. In 2008, some 350 started out, 80 more than in 2007. More than 120 of them stayed with us in our house before starting their journey.

In September 2011, two trail crews vigorously cutting new trail finally met. After eight years, the closed section of trail in Glacier Peak Wilderness reopened. A new 275-foot bridge spans the Suiattle River. It was built two miles downstream, making the PCT 5.5 miles longer. All 426 blowdowns had been cleared.

Right after the PCT, with my beard still full, two facts stared me in the face: It is a wonder that in the twenty-first century a wilderness trail exists between Mexico and Canada. And I had a skill set not shared by many thru-hikers. Lawyers actually are useful for some things, so I got involved in the Pacific Crest Trail Association (PCTA), the nonprofit group that protects the entire trail.

The PCTA published a letter from a finishing thru-hiker in their 1991 newsletter that read, "I feel a quiet sense of rage at . . . the incredible erosion, the lack of maintenance, the clear-cutting right through the trail, the piles of blowdowns." He was right. The PCTA hired its first employee two years later. By the time I was elected to the PCTA board in April 2008, the PCTA had fifteen employees, and over 1500 volunteers who put in 75,000 trail maintenance hours that year. Finishing thru-hikers often crowed about the state of the trail. I served nine years on the PCTA board, including three as board chair—in that time, our donations doubled, staff increased to twenty-five, and trail maintenance hours exceeded 100,000 a year. I have since served as board president of the Continental Divide Trail Coalition, and was recently elected president of the Partnership for the National Trails System, the umbrella group for all thirty National Scenic and Historic Trails, a 55,000-mile network.

In 2015, I thru-hiked the Continental Divide Trail (CDT). The CDT runs over 3000 miles from Mexico to Canada along the spine of the Rocky Mountains. I finished on Frodo's birthday, October 2, 2015—no snow this time. Frodo never planned to thru-hike the CDT, but she did hike 600 miles of it and was out there for the whole five months, driving a borrowed camper van providing support not just for me, but for many others.

Two years later, in 2017, I thru-hiked the Appalachian Trail, making me a "Triple Crowner." More people have flown in outer space than have completed all three long trails.

Six weeks into my CDT hike, there was an event so important that I left the trail for four full days. It was a wedding. On the summer solstice, two time zones west of the CDT, imbued with the full power of the sovereign State of Alaska, Frodo and I joined a couple in marriage in front of the Tlingit Clan House outside Ketchikan, Alaska. In front of us stood Blazer and her groom, CJ.

Half a head taller than Blazer, CJ wore sandals, a black suit, and a wide tie. His short-cropped hair and trim mustache perfectly matched the color of Blazer's long hair. CJ was a geologist, a kayak instructor, and half-Korean. When Frodo and I finished, the two planned to retreat inside the Tlingit Clan House for a short, full-dress Korean wedding ceremony.

"Dear family and friends . . ." Dalton was among those who attended. He and Blazer had not seen each other since the day he flew out of Seattle in 2007. Since then, Dalton had earned his PhD in physics and secured a rare tenure-track professorship teaching shiny-eyed students at Allegheny College in Pennsylvania.

"I now pronounce you husband and wife . . ." I have lived to see Blazer married. And I have now lived to hold Blazer's first-born son in my arms.

Since I left the PCT's southern monument in April 2007, how have I changed? Warm water from a tap remains a miracle. People, for some reason, smile at me more. And more than seven thousand aspiring thru-hikers have slept at our house the night before they start their own PCT journey.

The Future of the Trail

YEARS AGO, MY father could find only five books that mentioned the PCT. Nowadays, you'll find an information explosion. There are multiple books on day hikes alone, and online resources have skyrocketed—just like the number of hikers. Whether you're considering a picnic, day hike, overnight, week, or five months on the trail, the **Pacific Crest Trail Association** website, **pcta.org**, is a great source to start with, as are local hiking clubs. Long-distance hikers should also consult *Yogi's Pacific Crest Trail Handbook.*

Double-check all information with local land managers when possible. Nature's one constant is change. Whether for the PCT or any other trail, route, regulations, gear, permits, trailheads, trail closures, trail towns, and trail angels are always in flux.

The PCT is one of thirty congressionally designated National Scenic and Historic Trails, forming a network of over 55,000 miles. One nonprofit works on behalf of them all: **The Partnership for the National Trails System**. You can support their work at **pnts.org**, and find opportunities to volunteer for trail maintenance or become a financial supporter of the PCT on the Pacific Crest Trail Association's website.

One final piece of advice. Frodo hiked only a fraction of my last two long trails, but her last words at each trailhead when she dropped me off were not "I love you." She said to me what she'd say to all of you: "Make wise decisions."

Acknowledgments

I KNOW THAT to complete a thru-hike I got lucky. I respect anyone who sets aside five months for a hike in the twenty-first century—whether they make it 20 miles, 400, to the California-Oregon border, or the end. I respect those who stay out for a week, a long weekend, or whose dose of the outdoors comes in day hikes. I respect those who dream of sleeping under the stars, smelling campfire smoke, and feeling the wind rippling through pines and firs. My hope is that, for a moment, *Journeys North* took you there.

So many helped with *Journeys North*. I am indebted to early readers: New Zealand journalist and Triple Crowner John "Rolling Thunder" Henzell, who responded to emails from nine time zones away; PCT section hiker Jan Hawkins, who was fiercely unafraid to share her thoughts; *New York Times* columnist Nicholas Kristof, a great hiking companion who more than once nudged me to stay true to the story; *Backpacker* magazine editor in chief Dennis Lewon, who exhorted, "I can't wait to see it in print"; and Oregon journalist Mark Larabee, who urged me along and whose quote I look at every day: "Write like the wind, amigo."

New York editor and writer Lauren LeBlanc taught me to pare, to trust the story and my narrative voice—we might argue over who mentors whom.

For their guidance in the later stages, my gratitude goes to writers and publishing professionals: Megan Michelson, Roslyn Bullas, William Gray, Susan Leon, and Jim Muschett.

To Blazer, Dalton, Tony, and Nadine, I can never say enough. It was your stories that inspired me to begin the book. To everyone included in *Journeys North*, thank you for trusting me; it is my fervent hope I have done justice to your stories. I am grateful for each member of our PCT class of 2007, whether we met or not—what a year we had!

The Mountaineers Books team warmed my heart with their enthusiasm, skill, and support—heaped on my book in generous quantities. You are all wonderful, but in particular I thank my editor Emily White, Kate Rogers, Katie DeCramer (and her husband Mike), Ellen Wheat, Laura Shauger, and Laura Lancaster. You might not be reading this book but for the efforts of the Mountaineers Books promotion team: Darryl Booker, Tess Day, and all the rest; and the efforts of my publicist Kim Dower to share news of *Journeys North* from the mountaintops.

Living in proximity to a writer is not always easy. For their support, understanding, and *patience*, I thank my brother Charlie and sister Shelley, and I can't say enough thanks to three bright lights in my life, Frodo's and my children Sean, Jordie, and Nicky.

To Linda Cheney for her forty-year abiding faith in my writing, and for her abiding faith during the time Sandy and I were apart—that the two of us would remarry.

To Mr. Massie, Mr. Quinn, and Mr. Metcalf—my Boy Scout leaders. I smile every time I say their names.

To a reader I do not yet know, who will fulfill my forty-year dream—that someday I will walk through an airport and see someone reading my book.

First and last, there is my Frodo, my wife Sandy. You are always the first I want to read my work. You are who I most want to thrill, make laugh and cry, or be gripped with suspense. In the time you've spent on this book—edits, comments, propping me up—you could have hiked a thousand miles. So, a thousand times, thank you. When you read this paragraph at long last, I hope you'll reach for me with a hug. We are now forty-two years married, and I still notice each touch.

About the Author

BARNEY SCOUT MANN is the author of *The Continental Divide Trail: Exploring America's Ridgeline Trail* and co-author of *The Pacific Crest Trail: Exploring America's Wilderness Trail*. Scout's articles have appeared in *Backpacker*, *The Oregonian*, and the *New York Times* online. He is a Triple Crowner, having thru-hiked the Pacific Crest, Continental Divide, and Appalachian Trails. He is the board president of the Partnership for the National Trails System and previously served as the board chair of the Pacific Crest Trail Association and president of the Continental Divide Trail Coalition.

Scout lives in San Diego with his wife, Sandy, who still wears "the one ring." Visit him at barneyscoutmann.com.

MOUNTAINEERS BOOKS is a leading publisher of mountaineering literature and guides—including our flagship title, Mountaineering: The Freedom of the Hills—as well as adventure narratives, natural history, and general outdoor recreation. Through our two imprints, Skipstone and Braided River, we also publish titles on sustainability and conservation. We are committed to supporting the environmental and educational goals of our organization by providing expert information on human-powered adventure, sustainable practices at home and on the trail, and preservation of wilderness.

The Mountaineers, founded in 1906, is a 501(c)(3) nonprofit outdoor recreation and conservation organization whose mission is to enrich lives and communities by helping people "explore, conserve, learn about, and enjoy the lands and waters of the Pacific Northwest and beyond." One of the largest such organizations in the United States, it sponsors classes and year-round outdoor activities throughout the Pacific Northwest, including climbing, hiking, backcountry skiing, snowshoeing, camping, kayaking, sailing, and more. The Mountaineers also supports its mission through its publishing division, Mountaineers Books, and promotes environmental education and citizen engagement. For more information, visit The Mountaineers Program Center, 7700 Sand Point Way NE, Seattle, WA 98115-3996; phone 206-521-6001; www.mountaineers.org; or email info@mountaineers.org.

Our publications are made possible through the generosity of donors and through sales of 700 titles on outdoor recreation, sustainable lifestyle, and conservation. To donate, purchase books, or learn more, visit us online:

MOUNTAINEERS BOOKS

1001 SW Klickitat Way, Suite 201 • Seattle, WA 98134

800-553-4453 • mbooks@mountaineersbooks.org • www.mountaineersbooks.org

An independent nonprofit publisher since 1960

OTHER TITLES YOU MIGHT ENJOY FROM MOUNTAINEERS BOOKS

Thirst
Heather "Anish"
Anderson

A memoir by the
first woman to hike
the Triple Crown in
a calendar year

Campfire Stories
Edited by Dave
and Ilyssa Kyu

Wide-ranging tales
about a half dozen
national parks

Hiker Trash
Sarah Kaizar

A curated collage representing
backpacking culture on the AT

**I Promise
Not to Suffer**
Gail Storey

Lighthearted
memoir about one
couple's adventures
on the PCT

**A Blistered
Kind of Love**
Angela and
Duffy Ballard

In alternating
chapters, a couple
describes their PCT
thru-hike.

The Pacific Crest Trailside Readers
Edited by Rees Hughes and Corey Lewis

Excerpts from classic works about
the PCT

Hiking the PCT
Full-color guides to
the PCT by expert
backpackers, focused
on section hiking and
four-to-ten-day trips

www.mountaineersbooks.org